Bob Wylie has a long association with t...
Scotland which started as a union rep in...
worker with Glasgow City Council. However, he is probably
best known for his 14 years as a news correspondent with BBC
Scotland. After the BBC he worked in media communications in
local government and with one of Scotland's biggest charities. For
two years until May 2017, he was the chief of staff and senior advisor to the Leader of Glasgow City Council. Thereafter he worked
with Unite Scotland and is now a media consultant with GMB
Scotland. In 1991 he co-wrote *Downfall: the Ceauşescus and the
Romanian Revolution* and in 2016 he ghosted the autobiography
of Mohammad Sarwar MP, *My Remarkable Journey*.

BANDIT
CAPITALISM

Carillion

AND THE CORRUPTION OF
THE BRITISH STATE

BOB WYLIE

BIRLINN

First published in 2020 by Birlinn Ltd
West Newington House
10 Newington Road
Edinburgh
EH9 1QS

www.birlinn.co.uk

ISBN: 978 1 78027 596 3

British Library Cataloguing in Publication Data
A catalogue record for this book is available from the British Library

Papers used by Birlinn are from well-managed forests
and other responsible sources

Printed and bound by Clays Ltd, Elcograf S.p.A.

For Lida
and all those fighting for a better deal

Contents

Acknowledgements

I need to start with an apology. That is to my family, who have all had to deal with my preoccupation, sometimes obsession and mood-swings related to the writing of this book. They have worn it well, to paraphrase a line. Everlasting thanks are due to Lida, Kathryn, Susan, David, Jennifer and Rory.

For the actual gaining of a commission from Birlinn to write the book there is an identifiable group of people to whom I am indebted. First of all, there is Gary Smith from GMB Scotland, who in a matter of days managed to get agreement from the GMB national union to sponsor the book. He also kept me going when times were tough. When the arrival of Covid-19 jeopardised the entire project, the GMB's Acting General Secretary, John Phillips, did not flinch in his support. In the same way, Rachel Reeves MP and Chris Stephens MP were enormously helpful with time and advice, which enabled me to write a proposal on Carillion from the wealth of knowledge they had gathered from the House of Commons Carillion inquiry. In like fashion, on the editorial side, Hugh Andrew, Tom Johnstone and Andrew Simmons at Birlinn were marvellous advisors.

When we get to the actual writing of the story, there are four people without whom the book would never have been delivered. They are those who formed the research and writing team – Hugh Bell, Graeme Jolly, Laurie Russell and Gary Westwater. Their intellect, tirelessness and writing skills have sustained the entire project, as well as their ability, from time to time, to insist on the consumption of copious quantities of red wine. I am indebted to them, as the book quite simply would have proved too big a task for me on my own. We did it together. Make no mistake about it.

I also need to thank another group who have given valuable

assurance, assistance and advice in getting the thing done. They are Ian Fraser, Andy Kerr, Philip Long, Peter McGinley and Prem Sikka. Those at the GMB union who have unstintingly given their time include Gary Smith, already mentioned, Wendy Bartlam and Justin Bowden, who deserve special mention. Jude Brimble, Lisa Johnstone, John Phillips, Barbara Plant, Peter Welsh, Rhea Wolfson and Alan Wylie also deserve my thanks. The media staff at the House of Commons Work and Pensions Committee gave invaluable advice regarding detailed information on the Joint Inquiry with the Business, Energy and Industrial Strategy (BEIS) Committee and its report on Carillion. The staff at Apple Buchanan Street, Glasgow, must also be mentioned in dispatches, as their technical advice on MacBook, including the retrieving of 3,000 lost words at one point, proved to be genuinely inspirational.

There are also a host of people who have given interviews, many of them more than one. They include the MPs Ian Blackford, Stephen McPartland, Rachel Reeves, John Spellar and Chris Stephens. Beyond the House of Commons, the time Steve and Steph Paul gave me, with all the personal pain that involved for them, is enduringly appreciated. As are the interviews and advice given by Grace Blakeley, John Guidi, Deborah Hargreaves, Rudi Klein, Gary Lemmon and Anthony Stansfeld.

There are a number of former Carillion employees who do not wish to be named but who know who they are, and who have given priceless insights and advice. Those among you who got the Italian Fiano will know how invaluable our collaboration has been for me.

I completed the book whilst for more than a year suffering from serious health issues concerning severe osteoarthritis in my hip which eventually culminated in a total hip replacement. At Hampden Sports Clinic, Louise Mitchell, Alan Scott and Evelyn Thomson were unbelievably supportive; at my GP surgery, Dr Colin Wilson and Dr Brendan Cunning looked after me for so long; and finally at the Queen Elizabeth University Hospital in Glasgow, Drummond Mansbridge, who carried out my hip replacement, Susan Robertson and all the staff there deserve my thanks. So does Tracey Naddell at ChiroCare Scotland, who, from time to time, helped to keep me fit enough to write the book.

Lastly, there is a roll-call of those who knew we would see it through. They are John Boothman, Ingrid Guidi, Brian McAlinden, Eddie McCusker and Dean Smith.

Prologue

'Let me tell you about the very rich. They are different from you and me.'

F. Scott Fitzgerald, *The Rich Boy*

According to Bloomberg, the American business TV channel, Vladimir Potanin is number 57 on their world billionaires list. His current worth is $29.3 billion. The Bloomberg Billionaires Index declares that his wealth was 'self-made'. Not quite. In the mid-1990s the Russian economy was in free-fall, inflation was 215% annually, and the budget deficit was on an Everest scale of billions of dollars. Following the collapse of communism many ordinary Russians had been reduced to the near penury of selling off their grandmothers' fur coats at flea markets – a state of economic perdition which threatened the political future of Boris Yeltsin, then the Russian president. Perestroika had become Catastroika.

And Yeltsin had an election to win in 1996. If he failed then the return of the old Communist Party apparatchik, Gennady Zyuganov, as President seemed certain. The 'new Russia' would then have a Communist Party president to match the then communist-dominated Russian parliament. History's stakes were looming large. The first Russian wave of privatisation – 1992–1994 – had faltered badly. Voucher capitalism, whereby every Russian citizen was given vouchers to invest in the great industries of the country, had not created the share-owning democracy that was planned by the Russian government. It was based on a relatively successful scheme for the privatisation of the Czech economy. However, most Russian citizens were not well versed in the workings of share ownership and flogged their vouchers.

In time, the former nomenklatura of the Russian economy – the former communist bureaucrats who headed up the great state-owned industries – bought up almost all the vouchers and emerged as the new class of 'red directors'. Although more than 15,000 Russian enterprises changed hands in this way, fundamentally the voucher revolution only changed titles. It was like a man moving from one train compartment to another. At the start of the journey he was a communist bureaucrat. Then towards the destination he – they were all 'he' – became a majority shareholder and owner of the same enterprise. The title on his office door might have changed but little else did. He was still travelling on the same train. Any genuine development of a market economy remained a long way off.

However, under Yeltsin, a group of young reformers all had an eye for the main chance. During the voucher privatisation they emerged as shrewd investors, took over the old Soviet banking system, among other job lots, and got rich. Banking offered the first post-Soviet bonanza and the young reformers grabbed it with both hands. They, and not the old-style red directors, would prove to be crucial to what happened next. Enter thirty-something Vladimir Potanin. He was the brains behind what would eventually become known as the 'loans for shares deal'. It is a complicated piece of economic history, which had many political twists and turns, but Potanin's own story might help to simplify it.

At the start of 1995 Potanin's pitch to Anatoly Chubais, then one of the key figures in the Yeltsin administration, was that he had a scheme which could kill two birds with one stone for Chubais – the 'loans for shares' scheme. In effect, Potanin and his band of zealous reformers offered to lend the Russian government 9.1 trillion roubles or $1.8 billion. In return the government would favour any bid Potanin and his backers made for shares in Russia's leading companies – mainly in oil, gas and minerals. The loans would reduce the fiscal deficit and there would be enough to create a TV station for the Yeltsin election campaign. In essence Potanin was offering to become a pawnbroker for the state. He announced the proposal to the Russian cabinet in March 1995. We get the shares, you get the loans, he must have told them. Then he offered the assurance that they should not be worried that they were selling Russia's 'crown jewels'. He explained that, in effect, the government was only pawning them for a while due to serious short-term problems. The crown jewels could be bought back for Russia by redeeming the loans later on when the economy was in better shape.

In August that year Yeltsin signed the decree for the scheme. On the afternoon of 17 November 1995 Potanin became the most successful pawnbroker in world history. He had always had his eye on the gem of Norilsk Nickel – the world's biggest producers of nickel, platinum and other precious minerals – in the far north of Siberia. Using his own Onexim Bank's assets and borrowings, Potanin bought a controlling 38% share in Norilsk Nickel for $170.1 million.[1] Then its annual sales were $2.5 billion. Now they are touching $10 billion. It was the sale of the century. A few weeks later Potanin bought a 51% controlling interest in Sidanko – a Siberian oil company – for just over $130 million. Two years after this BP paid Potanin and Co. more than $500 million for a 10% share. On 7 December Mikhail Khodorkovsky – one of Potanin's fellow travellers – purchased a 78% share in Yukos, Russia's biggest oil producer for $310 million. For the record, Yeltsin got the NTV station for the propaganda campaign he desperately needed to support his nationwide election crusade, and his victory stopped the march of Zyuganov's neo-communists. However, the crown jewels were never redeemed because the Russian state could never find the cash to repay the loans.

To Potanin and Mikhail Khodorkovsky add Boris Berezovsky, Mikhail Freidman, Vladimir Gusinsky, Alexander Smolensky, Pytor Aven, Vladimir Vinogradov and Vitaly Malkin. These men were the collective advance guard of what became known across the world as the Russian oligarchs. Some fell foul later of Putin, but many like Potanin are here today to tell the tale. There are now another hundred or so who have followed in those footsteps to become oligarchs with assets in the hundreds of millions of dollars. All of them stand united by one undeniable fact – they got rich by looting the state. In doing so they guaranteed that Russia's reform would create a Mafia-style capitalism from which there could be no return. Even now, decades after the history of Russia's sale of the century is known, analysed and explained, you still can't help shaking your head and asking the question 'How did they get away with it?'

However, this book actually isn't about them. They feature by way of an introduction to our real subject matter, the distant relatives of the Russians – the British oligarchs. Of course, given that they are not plundering the gigantic natural resources that became the launch-pad for the creation of the Russian plutocracy, the British oligarchy might seem a lesser power. That is only a matter of scale. By British standards the fully paid-up members of this plutocratic club are unimaginably rich, increasingly un-accountable and, it seems, untouchable. They are the top 1% in the UK and they live in a parallel country to most of us. The sum-mer of 2018 in the annals of the Royal Mail provides 'telephone number' evidence for accusations of looting the state. In 2010, Moya Greene, the former head of Canada Post, was recruited as chief executive of Royal Mail. Three years later, in October 2013, she masterminded the privatisation of the state-owned company. The plaudits for this 'exceptional executive' have been lavish ever since. Yet the day after the Royal Mail sale the share price rose by 40%. Did this mean the share offer devised by Moya Greene was hugely undervalued or was this another sale of the century?

An estimate of Moya Greene's total earnings from Royal Mail, in her eight years there, takes us to a figure touching £13 million. This is a Euro-millions jackpot where you don't need to buy the £2 ticket. According to media reports, on top of this astronomical sum Moya got a golden goodbye when she left – a cash bonus of £774,000 and 12 months' salary of £547,000. That's £1.32 million to you and me.[2] Mind you, there obviously has to be a reward for her persuading the Royal Mail's 110,000 workers – whose average top-line salary is £22,500 a year – to accept a cut in their final pension scheme to save the company hundreds of millions. But, as with all such attempts to justify them, the rewards seem to be extraordinary in scale when compared to the achieve-ments delivered. Ms Greene has been replaced as chief executive by Rico Back, who is German, lives in Zurich and commutes to work in London. Back was the chief executive of GLS, the Royal Mail's totally owned European subsidiary. The Royal Mail 2017 annual report and accounts notes he got a £6.6 million payment 'as consideration for termination of his contract with GLS . . .' The chair of Royal Mail, Peter Long, praised 'Rico's dynamic and astute leadership at GLS' when speaking to the *Guardian* about the new wunderkind at the helm. The same article noted that Rico has been offered an annual package of '£2.7 million if he hits his bonus targets'. Rico Back's 'dynamic and astute leadership' at GLS didn't transfer to Royal Mail. By May 2020 the company shares had fallen to their lowest level since privatisation in 2013. On 15 May, Black's departure was announced 'with immediate effect'. *The Guardian* reported that in lieu of notice, Back would be paid £480,000 and an additional £75,000 for legal fees and other support. That was on top of three months' salary which, according to the 2019 accounts, would amount to around £215,000. How did we get to this commonplace excess?

How did we get to the point, two years before Back's departure, when BT's sacking of its chief executive Gavin Patterson meant he received such a huge pay-off that it provoked an unprecedented shareholder revolt? With BT shares languishing at a six-year low, Patterson left with a golden goodbye topping £2.3 million. How did it get to the point where 100 or so managers at Persimmon, the housebuilder, can cash £400 million plus in bonuses – including a final £75 million for the chief executive? [3] This after the British taxpayer funded the government's 'Help to Buy' scheme for first-time home buyers, which was responsible for the sudden gargantuan profits at Persimmon and other housebuilders. How did we get to the point where the UK has a worse inequality index than Africa's Burkina Faso?

Finally, to get to the heart of this story we can ask the predominant question of these economic times – how did we get to the scandalous downfall of Carillion? Its last accounts were for 2016. The totals there mean that between 2009 and 2016 Carillion paid out £554 million in dividends to its shareholders. For the same period income was £594 million.[4] These figures don't account for the looting of Carillion by its executives. In the same period

Richard Howson, the chief executive, took £7.2 million out of the business in salary and pension.[5] These figures suggest Carillion was tobogganing to disaster. So it turned out. It's timely for the whole Carillion story to be told, because it is the embodiment of the state we are in.

CHAPTER 1

The Paul Daniels of Profit

'... the board has increased the dividend in each of the 16 years since the formation of the Company in 1999.'

Carillion plc Annual Report and
Accounts 2016/1 March 2017, p. 43

'In the five years to 2016, the directors recommended paying £357 million of dividends to shareholders, despite generating just £159 million of cash from operations. Over the same period, the bonuses for the two top executives climbed from nothing to more than £1 million a year in 2016.'

Jonathan Ford, *Financial Times*, 28 January 2018

Berkhamsted is prime commuter-belt territory, some 35 miles up the M1 out of central London. Off Shootersway in Berkhamsted there's a millionaires' row – Blegberry Gardens. On 1 March 2017, Richard Adam, the former financial director of Carillion, was probably in his six-bedroom mansion there waiting for the call. He'd left his post in Carillion the previous December. He'd just turned 59 the month before, and had told the Carillion board that he wanted to spend more time with his family. 1 March 2017 was when the Carillion 2016 Annual Report and Accounts was published. It was the first day Adam could cash in his first tranche of Carillion shares. He was satisfied that he was entitled to the return after all he had done for the company, and wasn't about to miss his chance. The call from the Carillion brokers came through. The first disposal of shares made Richard Adam £534,000 better off; not bad on top of the £1.1 million final salary and bonuses package he'd been paid by the company on his departure. That included £460,000 in base salary, £140,000 in bonuses, £278,000 in previous share awards and £163,000 straight into his pension pot.[1] Contrary to normal company protocols, the bonus figure was paid in cash. The usual practice was part cash, part share options.

Come the 8th of May, Adam's second disposal of long-term incentive shares – share bonuses to encourage top executives to stay loyally with their company – had been vested. That means the 8th was the next day he could cash in again. He did so – for £242,000 this time. That made his share bonus worth more than three-quarters of a million pounds – £776,000 to be exact. Thus Richard Adam went off to spend more time with his family with a golden goodbye from Carillion touching £2 million. Adam said that when he left Carillion it was 'healthy' and 'was operating in challenging markets but was managing those markets satisfactorily'.[2] Eight months later the company went bust.

Carillion folded with only £29 million in the bank and debts and other liabilities adding up to a staggering £7 billion. Within the total liabilities it was established that banks were owed £1.3 billion in loans and that there was a hole in the pension fund of £2.6 billion. In Adam's time as finance director bank debts grew from £242 million in 2009 to the £1.3 billion figure in January 2018.[3] If this is 'managing in challenging markets satisfactorily' as Adam suggested, then one wonders what failure looks like in Richard Adam's eyes. Following his own share 'sale of the century', Adam says he no longer holds shares of any substance in any company. When asked about any shareholdings he said: 'I do not take that type of risk.'

This chapter focuses mainly on Richard Adam because if we follow him we can follow the money. In that context it may be worth commenting on some of the issues concerning Carillion's pension funds. Whilst Richard Adam may insist that Carillion's downfall was nothing to do with him because allegedly he left the company in rude health, he simply can't offer the same mitigation as regards the pension fund's deficits.

Under the 2004 Pensions Act, company directors have legal obligations to ensure appropriate assets and funding are available for them to meet their liabilities in providing for employee pensions. As a result, independent valuations have to be carried out every three years to assess the state of funds, to determine whether the legal funding objectives are being met. If not, then the trustee of the employees' fund and the company concerned are duty bound to agree a recovery plan to return to the full funding, which will include deficit recovery payments to be made by the sponsor company. Where deficits emerge the recovery plans must be agreed within a 15-month period. On all counts Richard Adam and the Carillion directors abrogated their responsibilities and failed their employees. By the statutes of the 2004 Act this was gross negligence. In 2008, when the trouble with Carillion pension funds was growing, Richard Adam had been in post as the finance director for more than a year. In the next 10 years Adam would emerge as a Janus-like figure, able to resist claims for restitution of pension deficits determinedly because he argued that the company could not afford it, due to serious cash-flow problems, while facing the other way to the stock market, delivering optimistic forecasts and bumper dividends. In Adam's statement to the 2015 Carillion Annual Report and Accounts he noted: 'In 2015 the group delivered strong revenue growth with profits and earnings in line with expectations.' The report was published on 3 March 2016. By the end of that year, as Richard Adam was bidding goodbye, the pension deficit had reached £990 million.[4]

In his ten-year tenure as finance director, pension deficit recovery payments increased by 1% and dividends increased by 199%. The verdicts of leading agencies with knowledge of his management of the funds are unequivocal. Gazelle Corporate Finance, advisors to the trustees, declared 'Richard Adam had an aversion to pension scheme deficit repairing funding'. The chair of the trustees, Richard Ellison, said he believed that Richard Adam viewed funding pension schemes as 'a waste of money'.[5] Adam has always strenuously denied that this last statement represented his views or, indeed, that such a statement had ever been made by him. In an email of 15 May 2018, to the Business and Work and

Pensions Joint Parliamentary Committees, he demanded that the reference be removed from the report, arguing that 'There is no objective evidence that supports the contention that I have ever held or expressed these views.' The Joint Committees refused to delete the reference.

Richard Adam studied mathematics at Reading University. In 1976, when he was 19, Abba were chart-topping with 'Money, Money, Money'. After graduating from Reading, Adam studied for an accountancy qualification. On 1 January 1983 he joined the Institute of Chartered Accountants of England and Wales, serving his time with the audit giant KPMG. That would be his first introduction to the ties that would bind. By the time he left Carillion in 2016, he had made it to Abba's 'rich man's world' as a grade-A, fully paid-up British oligarch.

It seems that after qualifying he stayed with KPMG until 1993, when he joined International Family Entertainment (IFE) – an American cable network. Its origins were in the televangelism of Pat Robertson, the right-wing American preacher who once stood in the US primaries to be the Republican nomination for president. The UK arm of IFE, where Adam was finance director between 1993 and 1996, became the Family Channel, which specialised in game-shows, having left the bibles behind in America. It was formed through a buy-out of a former ITV franchisee, Southern Television, for $68 million. In turn the Family Channel was taken over by a British cable concern, Flextech. It had major holdings in a host of cable companies and in Scottish Television. It would go on to set up a partnership with the BBC for a series of new BBC channels. It could be reasonably speculated that this period as finance chief was Richard Adam's introduction to the world of big-time wheeling and dealing.

In 1996 he left game-shows behind and went into books with the publishing company Hodder Headline. At that time Hodder Headline had some 800 staff and an annual turnover of just over £100 million. Three years later he was in the major league as the finance director of Associated British Ports (ABP). Twenty-one ports were in the portfolio and there were more than 2,500 employees responsible for shifting more than 100 million tonnes of cargo every year, as well as 2 million ferry passengers, on total revenues running well over £300 million.

In 2007, when Adam left ABP for Carillion, he had to resign from six other port-related directorships and a port-linked property company. Collecting non-executive directorships was a way of life for him – the Companies House records show at one time or another he has had 150 director and non-executive director posts. The Carillion move came a year after ABP had been taken over by a consortium led by Goldman Sachs, who brokered a £2.8 billion buy-out of ABP.[6] So by the time he was 50, Richard Adam had been around the accounting block a time or two, and was ready to become the chief architect of Carillion's jaw-dropping accounting tricks, which established 'smoke and mirrors' balance sheets everywhere that Carillion was in business.

That would make him millions but, in the end, ruin the company. By the time he left Carillion, Richard Adam had served as finance director for almost ten years. He had allies – notably in the early years the standing chief executive John McDonough – but as far as most Carillion staff were concerned Adam was seen as distant, aloof and uncommunicative. People who worked in his department for years would comment about how they did not know his wife's name or whether he had kids. He was not the type of bloke with whom you would gladly go for a pint. There was speculation that he had been brought up in South Africa, which accounted for his somewhat strangled vowels.

There wasn't any doubt, however, about his vaulting ambition. Some staff poked fun at Adam, referring to him as 'Richard the Robot' behind his back. But everyone knew he had a stiletto of ruthlessness as real as any Mafia assassin when it came to his own ambition. In August 2010 Carillion's company structure experienced what might be described as a 'summer of the long knives'. Five leading executives at the top of Carillion's major business units left for new jobs, were given packages to go, or were made an offer to leave they could not refuse. This then left Adam free to convince other key members of the Carillion leadership that it would be useful to promote Richard Howson, under his control, to a newly created post of chief operating officer. Howson didn't need convincing; his hallmark had already been identified as brazen ambition as well.

Inside the business, people whispered that this exposed the Adam plan to make Howson the next chief executive when McDonough left. There were a number of other equally qualified candidates when the time came, but Howson had the Adam seal of approval and was an 'insider'. The following August, in 2011, it was announced that McDonough would leave at the end of the year and be replaced as chief executive by Richard Howson. One small confirmation of Adam's strategy came in *The Times* days after the collapse of Carillion. The report noted that even after Howson's appointment as chief executive, Adam would frequently interrupt Howson if he started answering financial questions in meetings with analysts and investors. 'Mr Adam dominated discussions with investors over and above the chief executive,' one company insider said. 'It was like he was the guy calling the shots.'[7]

Adam spent a considerable amount of his working time in the London office of Carillion at 25 Maddox Street, off Regent Street. The premises had been inherited in one of the Carillion takeovers. Adam's office there was above a Ladbrokes bookmaker's shop. That could be considered as paradoxical because Adam was no gambler. He only considered 'sure things'. Howson was one of them – Adam knew that Howson would be a reliable acolyte who would do what he was told for years to come.

Among Adam's last acts at Associated British Ports was to appoint his successor there as finance director, one Zafar Khan. Khan had been deputy finance director at ABP, answering to Richard Adam for five years. *Accountancy Age*, the accountants' in-house journal, heralded Khan's coming appointment as ABP's finance chief with a glowing endorsement from Adam: 'Zafar has played an important role in the development of ABP over the past five years, and I am confident in his ability to lead the finance function, in support of the next stage of the group's development.'

Khan would become ABP's finance chief in March 2007. He'd be there for four years before becoming Carillion's finance director for their Middle East and North Africa division. Then, in 2013, he became his old boss's right-hand man for the second time. Zafar was reliable – like Howson he could be depended upon to do his leader's bidding. That included closing his eyes and signing off accounts that even those accustomed to the construction industry's way with numbers believed were 'straining at the boundary of reality'.[8]

There are qualifications to this. If you visit the offices of *Construction News* in London's East End, the journalists Zak Garner-Purkis and David Price, who have been ahead of the curve on the Carillion story since day one, will offer some caveats about construction accounting standards. They will tell you that the whole construction industry is blighted by age-old, questionable accounting practices, never-ending sub-contracting chains and cut-throat contracting bids. So, in other words, Carillion is not the only construction multinational familiar with the ledgers of 'creative accounting'.

Firstly, let's consider 'goodwill' in big company balance sheets. The *Economist* recently defined the problem – 'Goodwill is an intangible asset that sits on firms' balance sheets and represents the difference they paid to buy another firm and their target's original book value.'[9] The estimated intangible assets go on the balance sheet as a gain. This is no small matter, because if we consider the 500 top European firms and the top 500 in America, by market value, more than half of them have a third or more of their book equity represented by goodwill evaluations. Carillion was a big 'goodwill' hitter after a series of acquisitions which started in February 2006 with the buy-out of Mowlem. However, Carillion's 2011 takeover of Eaga, the renewables company, is probably the best case-study of its goodwill hunting. It illustrates clearly where the practice of overestimating takeover 'goodwill' inevitably leads.

The *Financial Times* defines 'goodwill' in slightly different terms from the *Economist* – 'an accounting item that measures the difference between the purchase price paid for an acquisition and the net value of the assets actually acquired'.[10] So when Carillion took over Eaga, which then became Carillion Energy Services, it recorded in the 2011 accounts that the acquisition cost £306 million, and that the assets acquired had a goodwill value of £329 million – more than 100% of the cost of the purchase. Goodwill can include estimates of the value of the brand acquired, importance of the gains of market share, intangible reputation gains, contracts in the pipeline and a host of other positive money-value estimates. 'Estimates' is an important word in this circumstance.

One of the more quantifiable elements in the intangible assessment of goodwill, according to Professor Karthik Ramanna of Oxford University's Said Business School, is 'the conjectural future profits that an acquiring manager hopes to realise through an acquisition'.[11] As Ramanna puts it, thanks to accounting methods, recording 'hope value' has become a significant element in corporate balance sheets across the globe.

This allows a return to the question of the stewardship of corporate governance in Carillion, led by Richard Adam, the chief executive Richard Howson and the board's endlessly unquestioning non-executive directors. The 'fog of goodwill'[12] at Carillion, as the *Financial Times* describes it, never dissipated. By 2016 goodwill accumulations in the accounts reached £1.6 billion. At the time that was more than a third of the company's total notional assets.

Here, let's introduce, for the purpose of simple explanation, the fictitious Joe Brown, who runs Joe Brown Plumbers Ltd. Let's note that in 2015 Joe decided to buy four new vans for the business and the plumbers who work for it. Each van cost £8,500, paid in a cash transaction from the bank. So on the capital costs debit in the Joe Brown Plumbers Ltd accounts, he can record a debit of £34,000. In the assets/liabilities side of the accounts he can similarly record an increase in the held assets of the business of £34,000 for 2015. The point here is that in his 2016 accounts, Joe's accountants will have to record a depreciation of the assets the four vans represent, because they will fall in value, in market price, and there will be wear-and-tear reductions and so on. Impairment is the correct accounting term for the assessment of the reduced value of Joe's vans.

So to return to Eaga/Carillion Energy Services (CES), it seems reasonable to expect that the books would show impairment of the £329 million goodwill year after year, as the reduction of the values involved went down. Not so – for whatever reason, KPMG, the Carillion auditors, accepted that the goodwill value of the

Eaga acquisition remained at £329 million from 2011 across the succeeding five years to 2016. By then, revenue at CES had tumbled to £43 million and total losses in the disastrous takeover had grown to an astonishing £350 million.[13] Yet despite this, Carillion was allowed to maintain the original goodwill values year after year after year.

It is important to point out here that annual goodwill accounting assessments are not simply a case of companies submitting 'hope values' to their accountants for verification, who then with a wave of a pen sign them off for another year over a good lunch, even if there are grounds for suggesting that this may have become custom and practice for impairment assessment with Carillion and KPMG. There is an established impairment test which has to be carried out. However, the current accounting procedures allow companies some flexibility in the presentation of these accounts. This means that an acquisition like Eaga can be bundled with what are called, in the trade, 'cash generating units', as part of an accurate value of current concerns.

As the *Financial Times* noted: 'Not only does this process minimise the chance of an impairment, it depends heavily on the willingness of the auditors to challenge the numbers plucked out by management . . . There is no objective market value for the asset, so you mark it up to a model. And if it's bullshit, well, it is up to the auditors to call it out.'[14] Eaga insiders say that KPMG and Carillion maintaining these goodwill figures was 'a total fiction', not least because everyone at Eaga was astonished at the over-valued buying price of £306 million in the first place. At Carillion's staff meeting in 2011 to salute the takeover, Richard Adam was introduced at the meeting by a senior manager, Dominic Shorrocks, who was believed to be destined for greater things at Carillion. But Shorrocks knew the Eaga numbers and believed they didn't add up. So in a flight of fancy he introduced Adam to the meeting as 'Richard, the Paul Daniels of profit and the Ali Bongo of the Balance Sheet'.[15] Carillion used to hire the Magic Circle Conference Centre near Euston Station, in London, for staff meetings. This never happened again after the Ali Bongo magic quote. Dominic Shorrocks' Carillion career did not last long either after his magic-themed introduction. Shortly after it he was invited to do his own disappearing trick by Adam and Co.

The reason the assessments for goodwill are so important for company executives is that goodwill is a vital determinant of the accumulated and realised profits in the balance sheet. In turn this affects 'distributable reserves' – the term used to determine the size of shareholders' funds available for dividend payment. Or, to use a definition shortcut, goodwill affects total available shareholder funds, which determine how much you can pay each year in dividends to shareholders. According to a *Financial Times* analysis in 2015, Carillion had £373 million in shareholders' funds which allowed a dividend payment of £77 million. Had Carillion written down the total goodwill in its accounts, it could only have paid out a dividend of £44 million. In turn that would have affected market confidence and would have been 'a red flag to investors'.[16] So, keep up the goodwill, if the auditors can be convinced. The reason that this is so important in the boardroom is that executive bonuses are linked to dividend payments as an indicator of business achievement – the share price and dividends underpin executive remuneration.

That's why in 2011 – the year of the acquisition of Eaga, and the goodwill that mushroomed with it – the earnings of Carillion's top three executives almost doubled. The chief executive John McDonough, chief finance officer Richard Adam and the chief operating officer Richard Howson saw their collective earnings rise to £3.35 million – up 43% on 2010 levels.

So much for goodwill's part in the 'creative accounting' practices which undermine the reliability of the books in the construction industry in particular. What of so-called 'aggressive accounting'? Due to the nature of large-scale construction contracts which can take years for delivery and thus for final payments being made, companies have to find a way of showing an up-to-date valuation of their accounts. 'Aggressive accounting', ruthlessly deployed by Carillion, solves those complexities by booking the value of contracts into the balance sheet as soon as possible after the deals are signed, and often, long before the receiving company has been paid a penny by the client. This is linked to the much earlier emergence of what is known in the accountancy trade as 'fair value accounting'. When the Glasgow Bank went bust in 1878 with unlimited liabilities, the result was ruin for executives and investors. As a safeguard to avoid such calamities in the future, there was the development of the limited liability company. But, in turn, for the limited liability safeguard, businesses had to produce annual accounts to allow investors and clients to have a measure of the financial health of the enterprises concerned. This allowed investment decisions to be made on theoretically reliable public information. These 'limited liability' accounts were based on historic costs for assets and liabilities and profit and loss.

In the mid-1960s, accountants and professors at business schools in the US began to question whether the old system presented a fair value, up-to-date picture of the company's financial standing. Nonetheless, these question-marks remained only theoretical for succeeding decades until the 1980s. Then came the Savings and Loans crisis in the US, which would cost the US Treasury more than $130 billion in a bonanza of bank bail-outs – history does repeat itself in the banking world, again and again. The S and L crisis, as it became known, was partly blamed on the old accounting systems because the banks involved had out-of-date, dare we say unreliable, books with investors making decisions on those presumed facts with disastrous effect. Accountancy had to change, and fair-value accounting, linking asset valuations to current market prices reflecting today's economic reality, took hold throughout American business from the mid-1990s. As usual, in matters of business, Europe dutifully followed suit. In 2005 the International Financial Reporting Standards were approved by the European Union which conditioned the fair-value shift in Europe. No doubt it seemed a good idea at the time.

Time was when the role of the auditor was to check and verify facts. Now the fair-value system allows for future earnings and profit predictions to be developed by computer models and noted in annual reports and accounts as though they are fact. In today's construction industry, as has been noted, it is now common practice for accounts to book potential income and profits for any building project the moment a contract is signed. This before a single payment has been made by the client into the construction company bank account. The *Financial Times* series on audit in crisis in the summer of 2018 concluded: 'In the UK in the past three decades, standard-setters have progressively dismantled the system of historical cost accounting, replacing it with one based on the idea that the primary purpose of accounts is to present information that is "useful to users." The process allows managers to pull forward anticipated profits and unrealised gains and write them up as today's surpluses.'[17] Lastly, if you add cut-throat contracting to this, the wonder becomes not why Carillion went down but why it lasted so long and which company is likely to be the next one approaching catastrophe? Major construction companies continually bid at truly perilous margins to gain contracts to keep the flow of cash coming in, even using 'loss leader' bids to stay in the market, in the hope that tomorrow will bring better days, bigger margins and bigger profits.

To get to that point, everyone in the great game recognises the necessity that the supply chain of sub-contractors in the contract must be sweated mercilessly to create continual cash-flow and, where possible, a profit margin. The former chair of the European Parliament's Economic and Monetary Committee, Sharon Bowles, told the *Financial Times* in 2019 that all these dubious practices have created a circumstance where 'the un-anchoring of auditing from verifiable fact has become endemic'.[18] Nonetheless, to use a criminal justice metaphor, there is a difference of degree between assault and murder. In that context it might be said that those in charge at Carillion definitely murdered the company's accounts. At one crisis Carillion board meeting, in May 2017, there was open questioning of how Richard Adam's accounting methods 'maintained margins', or profits, which turned out to be wholly unrealistic. Insiders at Carillion say Adam was the numbers man and the rest of the Carillion bean counters did what they were told. If Adam didn't like your numbers he told you to change them to more agreeable totals to match expectations of Carillion results.

If Carillion's business history is inspected, it is not difficult to conclude that Richard Adam was the company king for creative accounting, who made the figures look much better than they were on acquisitions, masterminded better-than-real bottom lines by exploiting 'goodwill' intangibles, and deployed 'aggressive accounting' ruthlessly to deliver Never-never Land growth and profits forecasts. All legal, of course, but which made Carillion into 'an unsustainable corporate time-bomb'.[19] Take the final full accounts for 2016, published on the day Richard Adam cashed in – 1 March 2017. Here, on glossy pages, were tomorrow's profits added up for today. The title-page might be seen as giving it all away – 'Making Tomorrow a Better Place'. On page 1 under the heading '2016 at a glance' the income stream sub-paragraph 'High quality order book and strong pipeline of contract opportunities' declares:

- £4.8 billion of new orders and probable orders
- High-quality order book plus probable orders worth £16 billion
- Expect over £1.5 billion of revenue from framework agreements not yet included in orders, probable orders or revenue visibility
- Substantial pipeline of contract opportunities worth £41.6 billion.[20]

These accounts were signed off by Carillion's new finance director, Zafar Khan. Although Richard Adam remained in post in the 2016 financial year until 31 December 2016, he says he had nothing to do with the preparation of these accounts. He told the Carillion parliamentary inquiry that the preparation of the audited accounts in Carillion 'takes place in the period of January and February leading up to the announcement of the results in March'.[21] Company insiders say that the account preparations for layout and pictures started in August 2016.

Whether Mr Adam added up any of these figures remains to be seen. Nonetheless, in the annual report Adam gets fulsome praise from the chair of Carillion, Philip Green: 'Richard Adam, who joined the board as group finance director in April 2007, retired on 31 December 2016. Richard made a major contribution to Carillion's development and success through his outstanding financial leadership and he retired with the Board's grateful thanks and best wishes for the future.'[22]

In fact everyone was happy with the 2016 accounts and indeed the prospects for the future. Peter Meehan, the senior statutory auditor from KPMG, approved the accounts submitted by Carillion, in these terms: '1. Our opinion on the financial statements is unmodified. We have audited the Group financial statements of Carillion plc for the year ended 31 December 2016 ... In our opinion:– the financial statements give a true and fair view of the state of the Group's and of the Parent Company's affairs as at 31 December 2016 and of the Group's profit for the year then ended; – the Group financial statements have been properly prepared in accordance with International Financial Reporting Standards as adopted by the European Union.'[23]

Perhaps we should not be surprised at such encomiums. In the 19 years that KPMG audited Carillion's books they never issued a single qualified audit opinion. In that time they were paid £29 million in audit fees. By December 2017 Carillion had issued three profit warnings concerning their accounts which amounted to a total hit of £1.2 billion on what the company was supposed to be worth. Those not accustomed to the fine words of the grandiose Big Four auditors of our time, KPMG, PwC, Deloitte and EY, might describe that as a £1.2 billion hole in the accounts down which the company was about to plunge. When those particular chickens finally came home to roost, the acting chief executive, Keith Cochrane, was petitioning for liquidation in the High Court of Justice on 15 January 2018. The game was up.

Richard Adam says it wasn't him. Nothing to do with him. He says that when he was in the organisation it had liquidity, was operating successfully, and had enough financial flexibility to deal with any shocks that it had experienced in his tenure. The Joint Parliamentary Committee concluded somewhat differently. They say that when Adam sold his shares he was in the know of the approaching catastrophe: 'Richard Adam, as Finance Director between 2007 and 2016, was the architect of Carillion's aggressive accounting policies. He, more than anyone else, would have been aware of the unsustainability of the company's approach. His voluntary departure at the end of 2016 was, for him, perfectly timed. He then sold all his Carillion shares for £776,000 just before the wheels began very publicly coming off and their value plummeted. These were the actions of a man who knew exactly where the company was heading once it was no longer propped up by his accounting tricks.'[24]

When Richard Adam sold his Carillion shares in March and May 2017 the average share price he gained was £2.12p. After the first profits warning in July the Carillion shares had slumped to 57p. Good timing, you'd say, because Richard Adam says he never saw it coming. Rudi Klein, the chief executive of the Specialist Engineering Contractors' Group, thinks not. You are not long in his company before his liking of the ironic becomes clear. He told me: 'Richard Adam telling us that he cashed the shares because they became due and nothing else is like the Russian poison crew telling us they went on holiday to Salisbury so they could see the cathedral. They expect us to believe them? Does Richard Adam expect us to believe him?'

The GMB is one of Britain's top three unions. Since 2016 Jude Brimble has been the national secretary in the union for the Manufacturing Section, so she knows all about Carillion. When I asked her about Richard Adam's share dealings, she told me angrily that if any of her union members had abused the system like the Carillion directors they would have been locked up: 'They'd be jailed for fraud, but then there seems to be another law for Britain's top executives that doesn't apply to the rest of us. They just walk away after filling their boots. In Richard Adam's case that meant a £1 million final pay off, as far as I know. It's outrageous, and something ought to be done about it. No ifs, no buts.' Brimble says that British oligarchs like Richard Adam are all about 'show me the money'. She argues that there is no chance that Adam didn't know the Carillion crash was coming. Then she asked: 'If things were otherwise and everything in the garden was rosy, surely Richard Adam would have held on for bigger and bigger return?' Brimble continued: 'These top people are always in the financial papers telling us how they deserve their rewards due to their business acumen, their acute abilities for deal making that delivers the bounty for their shareholders. Richard Adam never saw it coming? Don't make me laugh.'[25]

When the Joint Parliamentary Inquiry of the BEIS and Work and Pensions Committees was held into Carillion, Rachel Reeves was its imposing chair. She is as unequivocal as Jude Brimble. 'He got out at the best possible moment. He played his part in preparing the 2016 accounts and then made sure he was out the door before the Annual Report came out, before the revelations about the major contracts came out. Richard Adam was out of there cashing in every penny he could as soon as he could.' It seems Adam has a bit of a habit of getting out at the right time. In June 2014 he was appointed as a non-executive director of Countrywide plc – Britain's biggest estate agency. He was chair of the Audit and Risk Committee on a salary of £55,000 until his resignation as a non-executive director at the end of December 2017.

In the early years of Adam's tenure things went so well that the annual reports were metaphorically predicting that the golden rain of profits at Countrywide would be never-ending. There was no problem then of Countrywide carrying more than £200 million in debt, and 'goodwill' totalling £471 million, in its balance sheet. These figures were largely historical, based on its previous acquisition strategy. Between the end of 2015 and the end of 2016, the goodwill valuation didn't change. Then the bombshell dropped – Adam reported in the 2017 accounts that his committee had focused 'on the impact of the deterioration in the Group's trading position with respect to goodwill and other impairments and going concern and viability'.[26]

In 2017 three significant things happened in Countrywide's Audit and Risk Committee. It announced an impairment of goodwill of £193 million in the main company accounts and thereby reduced goodwill in the books from £472 million to £279 million; it warned that this, combined with current debts, risked the future of Countrywide's 'ability to continue as a going concern', and Richard Adam resigned. By August 2018 Countrywide had issued a number of profit warnings as shares plummeted. Like Carillion, Countrywide's future had been overvalued. The 2017 annual report and accounts showed a £208 million loss. In late

August 2018 shareholders voted in favour of a share issue to raise an emergency bail out of £140 million. Still, Richard Adam was gone by then. Long gone.

CHAPTER 2

Beware the Ides of Mercer

> 'Given the size and quality of our order book and pipeline of contract opportunities, our customer-focused culture and integrated business model, we have a good platform from which to develop the business in 2017.'
>
> Philip Green, Chair of Carillion,
> Annual Report and Accounts 2016

Mariana Teodorescu spent most of her life in Brasov, Transylvania, the heartland of Romania. She survived World War Two, when she remembered the Germans coming and then going and then the Russians doing the same. But in the Russian footsteps came a communist Romania. That would end in the horrors of the final years of Nicolae Ceauşescu's secret police dictatorship. Mariana celebrated his downfall, not least because it opened Romania's borders, which allowed her eldest daughter, Lida, to find a new life in Glasgow, in Scotland. That meant a regular supply of precious US dollars sent from Glasgow to Brasov, often secreted in the cut-out middle pages of old paperback novels. In those times US dollars were the 'legal tender' of Romania's currency black market.

In April 1992, a new investment bank, Caritas, arrived in Brasov. It didn't take Mariana long to find out that it was promising an 800% return on all deposits left untouched, for three months, in a Caritas account. As luck would have it, towards the end of that year Mariana had dollars to invest. She also had the conviction that the best way to deal with this temptation was to give in to it.

What could go wrong? Here was the new chief of Caritas, Ioan Stoica, promising a way out of the desperation of day-to-day life in a Romania trapped somewhere between Ceauşescu's communism and the IMF, which was ensuring the birth pangs of capitalism would be accompanied by crushing austerity.

Mariana traded $50 for 50,000 Romanian lei with Brasov's black market spivs and opened the account. She was following the footsteps of hundreds of thousands of Romanians who had done the same and, three months later, had come home laughing all the way from the bank with their money multiplied eight times. By the spring of 1993 Mariana did the same after her Caritas three months was up – 400,000 Romanian lei ($400) to the good. Mariana was one of the lucky ones. Caritas was a Ponzi scheme. A year or so after Mariana's pay-out, the cash-flow of new deposits dried up. By this time more than a million Romanians had invested the equivalent of $1 billion in Caritas banks across Transylvania. When the cash-flow of new deposits dried up – as they always do in Ponzi schemes – the pay-outs stopped. By August 1994 Caritas was bust and Ioan Stoica, the saviour with feet of clay, was heading for jail.

Ponzi schemes (also known as pyramid-selling schemes) are illegal. They are a form of fraud, operating by luring unsuspecting investors with promises of huge returns on investment but which use the funds obtained from the most recent investors to pay profits to previous ones. Eventually the new investors dry up, and those late in on the scheme get double-scammed, receiving no profit and losing their investment too. Ponzi schemes got their name from Carlo Ponzi, an Italian conman who is credited with running the first such pyramid investment scheme in America, in 1920s Boston. Ponzi's cover for his investment pyramid was supposedly buying special mail-reply coupons in Europe which were much cheaper than US stamps. The pitch then was that the coupons would be traded in America for much greater sums: invest with Ponzi and your troubles would be over. This was the cover, it never developed in any real sense. When folk invested to buy the coupons their money went straight into Ponzi's racket. Of course, when the first Ponzi pay-outs were made, doubling people's money in three months, and news of that spread, the reach of Ponzi's scam knew no bounds. By the summer of 1920 he was sitting on a pile of deposits reaching $3 million. But the first Ponzi scheme, like all the rest, went bust when the flow of new cash ran out. If you are swindling Peter to pay Paul, that racket has to collapse when you run out of 'Peters' with new money to pay all your previous 'Pauls'.

By the time Richard Adam left Carillion in December 2016 the whole enterprise had become an elaborate, big-business Ponzi scheme, which could only continue to exist by maintaining cashflow into the business, at all costs. New contracts were taken on at rock-bottom margins to use the new income to pay for the old debts mounting on previous contracts; so-called 'aggressive accounting' put money in the balance sheet, in revenue and profits, which had not actually been made, based on optimistic forecasts; then the construction industry's so-called early payment facility was exploited to turn it into loans from creditors to Carillion. Finally, the merciless refusal to make proper payments to the employee pension fund, when added to these other scams, built the Ponzi flow of cash to keep the books looking like the money was rolling in. The figures presented by 'the Paul Daniels of profit', Richard Adam, made Carillion look like some demented, deluded debtor who counts the money on his credit card bill as personal income. The 2016 annual report and accounts were the last complete accounts issued by Carillion. The glossy brochure's front page carries a dramatic aerial shot of the Midland Metropolitan Hospital which at that time was under construction in Birmingham. Inside the front cover are the bragging rights:

> This state-of-the-art hospital, which will have around 683 beds and 13 operating theatre suites, has been designed to the best international standards that will make it highly patient-focused and support the efficient delivery of high-quality clinical services, as well as achieving the highest standards of sustainability. Carillion will invest £13 million of equity in the project, as well as building the hospital at a capital cost of £297 million and providing hard facilities management and maintenance services

worth approximately £140 million over the 30-year life of the concession contract.[1]

How did that turn out? Not well. When Carillion went bust in January 2018 the Midland Metropolitan project collapsed with it. At the time of writing, by the second anniversary of Carillion's collapse in January 2020, how the project is ever going to be completed remains an open question. On page 5 of the 2016 accounts there are more vainglorious declarations to follow the boasts about Midland Metropolitan:

> We have a high-quality order book . . . worth £16 billion, framework contracts that are expected to generate up to £1.5 billion of revenue and a substantial pipeline of specific contract opportunities potentially worth £41.6 billion . . . We have implemented a consistent and successful strategy of focusing selectively on winning contracts where we can achieve our objectives for revenue, margins and earnings. We also have a strong track record in reducing our cost base and improving efficiency through a number of on-going programmes.[2]

The truth is different. The accounts show that between 2015 and 2016 the value of Carillion's assets – the figure for the worth of the company – dropped by almost £300 million, or nearly 30%.[3] In 2015 the net assets were worth £1,016 million; by the end of 2016 that total fell to £730 million. In 2016 the company's cashflow that year nose-dived by almost 30% also. The negative cash position slumped from –£170 million in 2015 to –£219 million in 2016. That is to say, by the end of December 2016 the company 'overdraft' was £49 million higher than the previous December. The wheels of Carillion's Ponzi scheme were kept turning by increased borrowing year after year. Instead of 'having a strong record in reducing our cost base' as the accounts proclaimed, the truth was that company debt had long since spiralled out of control. Over the nine years from December 2009 to January 2018, Carillion's total debt, in loans and other borrowings, increased from £242 million to an estimated £1.3 billion – which, staggeringly, is more than five times the total at the beginning of the decade.[4]

However, these borrowings were not used to enhance the asset base of the company to build real sustainable growth. Instead they ended up as Ponzi deposits, ostensibly to keep the balance sheet in the black. This was the equivalent of keeping the family income going by piling debt on the family credit card. In fact, while Carillion's debts rose by almost 300% between 2009 and 2017, assets grew by a miserable 14%.[5] The perils of any balance sheet with huge elements of 'goodwill' on it have already been noted. It is startling that the largest single item on Carillion's 2016 balance sheet was goodwill. The 'consolidated balance sheet' recorded 'intangible assets' of £1,669 million – of which goodwill made up £1,571 million.[6] However, it is fair to say that these interpretations of the books have the advantage of hindsight. Certainly they were nowhere to be seen among the observations in the accounts by Carillion's chairman, Philip Green (no relation to the notorious Philip Green of the BHS scandal). The chairman's statement in the 2016 accounts noted:

> Given the size and quality of our order book and pipeline of contract opportunities, our customer-focused culture and integrated business model, we have a good platform from which to develop the business in 2017. We will accelerate the rebalancing of our business into markets and sectors where we can win high-quality contracts and achieve our targets for margin and cash flows, while actively managing the positions we have in challenging markets.[7]

In Voltaire's satire *Candide* one of the main characters is Dr Pangloss. He is the tutor of the central character, Candide. In the novella Pangloss is satirised as the epitome of foolhardy optimism, with his belief that 'all is for the best in the best of all possible worlds', a parody of the views of Gottfried Leibniz, a German philosopher of Voltaire's times. In fact the full title of the book reflects this – *Candide ou L'Optimisme*. Arguably, Philip Green was Carillion's Dr Pangloss. Or did he get away with such misrepresentation of the facts because of Carillion's auditors 'turning a blind eye' to such 'foolhardy optimism' as they perused the draft account statements? Or did Philip Green make a habit of saying one thing and doing another?

Carillion's first board meeting of 2017 may hold a clue or two. It was held at the end of January in the Maddox Street offices, off Regent Street in London. Initially, the new finance director, Zafar Khan, gets it in the neck from other directors in the meeting regarding Khan's report on current trading. This had been circulated to board members after the December meeting. Keith Cochrane, then a non-executive member of the board, huffs and puffs and tells Khan that the Khan report 'does not respond to the questions raised' when it had been commissioned.

Philip Green then delivers what can be described as a schoolteacher's reprimand for the new boy trying to fill Richard Adam's shoes. He tells Khan that 'transparency and clarity' are critical in the company's financial affairs, especially if there is a deterioration in its financial position. Now, there's a hostage to fortune, you might say. Green tells Khan 'It's imperative that you understand that's what is required . . . The board shouldn't be in a position where it's having to work out where we are from the papers you present.' He then peremptorily instructs Khan to produce a cash plan for the end of the first quarter which should be updated monthly.

So it's not been a good day so far for Khan on this, his first anniversary of being appointed to the board. He was on his own now with no Richard Adam as a shield from the flagrant contempt of some of the other board members. A soothsayer attending this board meeting might have predicted that even if the obsequious Khan was not looking for trouble, trouble was surely looking for him.

Green's haughty 'It's imperative that you understand . . .' reflects his enduring high opinion of himself. Carillion staff who moved in Green's circles remarked that invariably when he entered a function hosting business people, politicians or establishment dignitaries, he would immediately ask them who among the gathering were the most important people he should meet. Green was overjoyed to be appointed as the chairman of Sentebale, Prince

Harry's African HIV charity, based in Lesotho and Botswana in Southern Africa. He served HRH as the Sentebale (the word means 'Forget me not') chair for seven years, stepping down in February 2018. When it emerged that Green's invitation to Prince Harry's wedding to Meghan Markle was in jeopardy, due to the fall of Carillion, an acquaintance of Green's observed: 'Philip will be crestfallen. Toadying up to establishment types is his lifeblood.'[8] One Carillion insider said that it was impossible to be in Green's company for more than fifteen minutes without him name-dropping, even though Prince Harry had told him not to do that.

Green was an Olympian social climber. The story goes that at a Carillion staff event in 2017 he remonstrated with the staff organisers because his name-badge did not include his CBE honour printed beside his name. A new name-badge had to be printed. He was awarded his CBE in June 2014 for his business and charity work. Of course, Green fully understood that his social standing and business acumen more than justified his high opinion of his own worth. In the seven years he was a non-executive director at Carillion he 'estimated' he was paid 'about £900,000'. His final salary as chairman when Carillion collapsed was £220,000.[9]

But back to Zafar Khan and the 26 January board meeting, because there was more than one reprimand coming his way that Thursday. Zafar should have known, even by then, that there might have been those on the board who were less than delighted at his appointment. He had to advise the meeting regarding the board's 'Preliminary view on the 2016 final dividend'. Khan had the audacity to suggest that the board might consider holding the final dividend 'in the light of the desire to conserve cash and reduce debt'. Mistake. A big mistake which provoked general disquiet on the board and which seemed to pose the question for the board members, 'Does he know what he's talking about?' One board member reminded Khan that the board had had a policy of a progressive dividend over the 17 years since the demerger from Tarmac in 1999. He asked what sort of signal would such a hold on dividends send to the markets. The taciturn Scotsman Andrew Dougal, chair of the audit committee, said there was little doubt that the reaction would be 'extremely negative'. Keith Cochrane then threw Khan a metaphorical lifeline. 'It might be appropriate to send a message to the market about debt reduction at the right time. But this is not the right time,' he said.

The reality is that only the declaration of £1,669 billion of 'intangible assets' in the company balance sheet is allowing the company to stay afloat. There is a tangible looming financial crisis, given credence by the 2016 accounts which record what will become the biggest debts in the company's short history. In these circumstances Zafar Khan, the newly appointed financial director, suggests a possible hold on dividends. These are the facts. The other six directors drown him out in a chorus of denial. They remonstrate with Khan – 'The dividend will be paid!' Exactly how much will be paid out will be determined at the February board meeting. But make no mistake, the dividend will be paid. There's another small item taken at the January board meeting which proved that Zafar Khan was right – even if it was presented as reason to believe that all seemed to be for the best, in this the best of all possible worlds. The board minutes note that there was a new loan on the books of some £112 million. In the final months of 2016 the board of Carillion made the decision to go to the German money markets to raise money: 'The German bond issue had been completed with funds to flow during the day at an equivalent of £112 million, denominated in sterling, euros and US dollars.'[10]

The chair of audit, Andrew Dougal, noted the board's congratulations on getting this done. The startling reality, however, was that a flagship UK, FTSE 100 company, with a stated turnover of £5.2 billion in its most recent financial accounts, and with a potential supply-chain of contracts worth £41.6 billion, had had to go cap in hand to Frankfurt, Germany, to borrow £112 million to help it pay off other previous loans which were due to be redeemed in 2017. Really? The chairman's statement in the 2016 accounts declares: 'The Group continues to have substantial liquidity with some £1.5 billion of available funding, including £112 million of five-year funding raised on the German Schuldschein market. The latter was secured in January 2017 to replace the £116 million of existing funding that is due to mature in 2017and 2018.'[11]

There we have it – Carillion has to access new loans to pay off old ones. This, as already noted, is like taking out a new credit card at higher rates than your old cards, so you can use the new card to pay off the debts piling up on the old ones. Richard Howson would say blithely on a later occasion that he wasn't aware that going to the German markets was an 'unusual way of sourcing finance'. Yet irrespective of what it signifies, the accessing of 'the German bond' seems to be cause for celebration among the seven board members present at the January meeting.

A month later the February board tidied up a lot of outstanding business. Following the January discussion the first tranche of what promised to be the highest ever dividend was agreed. Fifty-five million pounds of a total dividend of £79 million would be paid out in June. All the directors' reports and balance sheets for the Annual Report and Accounts to end December 2016 were to be published at the May AGM. They were signed off and the unflinching auditors, KPMG, who had served continually for 19 years, were re-appointed. Job done.

Then a couple of weeks later, Emma Mercer came back from Canada. She would turn out to be an extremely unlikely rebel with a cause inside Carillion. Between January 2014 and March 2017 she had been the chief finance officer and senior vice president for Carillion's £600 million operations in Canada. She carried a bit of heft in the organisation for 'stepping up to the plate' in Canada. She also had impeccable credentials to be a member of the Carillion top brass.

Mercer joined Carillion in April 2008, a matter of months after its biggest-ever acquisition, of the construction giant, Alfred McAlpine, for £565 million. So she would have learned how much 'goodwill' was loaded on the books for that deal. She was around again in 2011 when the next acquisition took place – the £306 million takeover of Eaga, with £329 million of goodwill then entered on the balance sheet. Funnily enough, it turned out that the balance sheets for the Canadian operations carried substantial 'goodwill' in the project accounts too. Mercer was also a senior insider for years when the deficit on the pension fund was building relentlessly and Carillion was becoming notorious for holding its sub-contractors to ransom through its carefully devised late-payment systems. There is no record of her speaking out anywhere against any of these iniquitous business practices. Mercer was a loyal financial servant in the court of Richard Adam, the Carillion finance director, for ten years.

She also had the favoured imprimatur of being almost thirteen years at KPMG before joining Carillion. She left KPMG as a senior manager who, Carillion sources say, was seen even then as a potential high flyer. Then, after her successful stint in Carillion's Canadian proving-ground she comes back to Carillion UK in March 2017 and accuses the powers that be of fiddling the books. Boom! It's worth noting that these were high stakes. As we have already described, in effect, by then, Carillion had turned into a Ponzi scheme; in fact the mother of all Ponzi schemes. The Annual Report and Accounts for 2016 published in March 2017 – the same month as Mercer's return – show that Carillion's global turnover was £5,214 million. The UK revenue was around 70% of the global figure – £3,784 million. In turn, Carillion's public-sector contracts in the UK accounted for 45% of its total UK revenue, or £1,719 million. There were 423 public-sector contracts. The top five were 10 contracts with the Ministry of Defence worth £510 million; 22 with Network Rail worth £372 million; 25 with the NHS worth £287 million; 11 with Highways England worth £140 million and five with devolved governments worth £135 million.[12] This was a lot of money. Emma Mercer returns from Canada and inside six weeks she's stridently into accusation mode. The problems emerge following her discovery of the use of an accounting device known as 'negative accruals' on a number of Carillion's major construction contracts.

Carillion had been here before. In the financial year 2008/09 it had come to light that negative accruals were being used extensively in certain company returns. This accountancy practice allows debts owed to the parent company to be treated as discounts on its total debts, even though not a penny of the outstanding claims on creditors have been paid. Good custom and practice dictates that debts owed should be identified in the 'creditors' part of the accounts. The negative accrual process instead assumes the payment of certain debts and offsets that figure against the company's total debts.

This accounting measure is entirely legal, but it's a balance-sheet smokescreen because it hides the real scale of debts. It assumes the payment of debts, even though they have not been paid, and treats them as income by setting them against balance-sheet debts. This, in turn, reduces the scale of the parent company's liabilities and more importantly improves its ratio of debts against equity held. It is an accounting sleight of hand which makes the accounts look better than they actually are. It's a balance-sheet relation to goodwill which is, in effect, fictitious capital, dressed up in the accounts as though it were real money. Negative accruals count money you are owed as though it has been paid by setting the figures against debts and liabilities.

Carillion banned the use of negative accruals in its 2008/09 accounts. Thereafter it became a golden rule in the company that they could not be used in balance-sheet calculations. When she returned from Ontario, as the finance director for construction, Mercer started looking at the accounts of one of the major construction contracts – Carillion's £335 million Royal Liverpool Hospital project. She was after all, the director responsible for Carillion construction. She found out that negative accruals were accounting for tens of millions of set-asides in the books at the project. Further investigation raised questions about how widespread this was across all Carillion's major construction projects. Later, when Mercer was asked by the chairs of the House of Commons Joint Committee Inquiry into Carillion what had caused her concern, in the first place, she replied: 'Carillion had a policy that claims had to be recorded as a separate receivable on the balance sheet as an asset. Negative accruals are where these claims are not recorded on the asset side of the balance sheet but rather are set off against the cost of the project on the liability side . . . The reason Carillion had a policy against negative accruals is because there is a risk that their use can mean that some of the measures we monitor such as percentage of costs complete, receivables by project or the level of uncertified revenue by project are less transparent.'[13]

This is perhaps a crafted euphemistic way of saying 'using negative accruals is dodgy'. Seriously dodgy. In the fullness of time,

Mercer would be vindicated. In May 2017, an internal Carillion inquiry would establish that the Liverpool contract was faced with a write-down on forecast profits of £49 million, of which £47 million were negative accruals. A further review of the Liverpool March 2016 accounts would show that the books had over-valued the Liverpool contract profits by £53 million.

On 15 April 2017 Mercer went to see her boss, Adam Green. He was the managing director for construction. Green was regarded as a 'really decent bloke' by most Carillion workers – 'never afraid to get his hands dirty'. Mercer and he did not know it then, but the 15 April meeting would be the crack of the starting pistol for what would become the eventual downfall of Carillion. One construction worker said: 'Adam tried his best to take ownership of what went wrong when the ship was going down. Even if we never understood that at the time. This isn't an exaggeration – in six months he aged right before my eyes.'

Mercer told Adam Green about the negative accruals in Liverpool and said that she was 'not comfortable with the figures'. This is in its own context an extraordinary move, because the entire long established business custom and practice of Carillion was that criticism of the decision-making at the top was something that was never to happen. Within Carillion, Mercer was generally regarded as serious and totally focussed on the work, partly because her manner carried a certain authority. Not everybody shared that positive view – some found it difficult to work with her. However, when she suggested to Adam Green that the negative accruals practice might involve 'several projects' and the concerns might go well beyond the Liverpool project, he took her seriously. Even although she didn't see it that way herself, the loyal lieutenant of the Carillion board, and of the former finance director Richard Adam, had just become a whistleblower.

Adam Green went to Richard Howson, the chief executive, and raised Mercer's concerns. Howson decided to palm this off on Zafar Khan. He told Khan that Mercer wanted to present her concerns at the next Carillion Project Review meeting on 26 April. Howson instructed Khan to see Mercer to help her organise the presentation.

Mercer and Khan, after a cursory investigation, established that there were at least nine projects with substantial negative accruals on the books – including the flagship projects at Royal Liverpool Hospital, Battersea Power Station and the Aberdeen roads project. When Khan and Mercer presented their findings to the Project Review Meeting they were heard politely, but nothing was decided about what needed to be done. Mercer wasn't going to take no for an answer. A week later, on 3 May 2016, she raised her complaints with Carillion's head of HR, Janet Dawson, not pulling any punches.

By now there were two issues at stake for Mercer – the accuracy of Carillion's accounts and the preservation of her own reputation. She was going to be 'catching' for Carillion Construction finances, so she was going to make sure that when this all came to light she wasn't going to be left being blamed for the developing fiasco. Dawson understood the stakes. On the same day, following the Carillion AGM, Dawson spoke to Richard Howson about Mercer's concerns. The penny seemed to drop. He was due to go to Qatar for more discussions on the troubled Carillion contracts there, but agreed he would fix a meeting for 5 May with 'Mrs Mercer' for his return. Howson later spoke to Philip Green, the company chairman, who he asked to notify the rest of the board. The initial prevarication about Mercer's findings was now replaced with the axiom, 'We better get something done about this. Bloody hell!'

Compared to the Stakhanovite norms pervading today's boardrooms, Richard Howson appears as a bit of a throwback. He didn't do 24/7. Instead he favoured using endless conference calls to play catch-up and get things agreed. When he first became Carillion's chief executive he had to be cautioned about using his rather self-deprecating line of introduction: 'Me, I'm Richard Howson, I'm just a builder from Yorkshire.' He would soon shake off that lack of self-confidence and rapidly developed the honed interest in personal remuneration which seems to have been characteristic of Carillion top executives. One City fund manager, who advised Carillion on the markets, concluded: 'With Howson you could never lose the impression that somehow he was permanently out of his depth. That was disconcerting, not reassuring the way chief executives are supposed to be.' For the greater part of his business life as chief executive, Howson worked out of the Wolverhampton headquarters of Carillion or the Maddox Street office in London. However, when circumstances allowed he liked to work in Leeds, nearer home, especially on a Friday. There were two offices in Leeds – one beside the Leeds United stadium at Elland Road and another near the railway station in the centre of town. The latter was Howson's personal, private office for which he had the keys. When he returned from the Qatar trip he met Emma Mercer there.

There is no record anywhere in the Carillion papers about what was said. There was a board meeting scheduled for the following Tuesday – 9 May. Howson asked Mercer if she could head up an investigation team on the accruals difficulties. He then contacted Robin Herzberg, the head of risk, Adam Green, managing director for construction, and David Holmes, the commercial director, and asked them to join Mercer to bottom out the problem contracts, so that a report could be made to the board the following week. Herzberg had been hands-on in the negotiation of all Carillion's major Private Finance Initiative (PFI) contracts; Holmes was overseeing the Aberdeen roads project and Green was the top man in construction. Howson's response to Mercer wasn't panic but it was moving in that direction. The figures Mercer was working with probably raised questions immediately for Howson about whether the 2016 accounts, signed off to 31 December 2016, could still stand. They'd been published at the AGM which had taken place two days earlier. The follow-up question was whether, legally, the board would immediately have to announce its investigation of potential problems in its accounts to the Stock Exchange.

According to Howson he 'held various discussions with Mrs Mercer and the team . . . that I had tasked with examining the issue over that weekend'.[14] The board held a telephone conference meeting on Tuesday 9 May at 7.30 am. This would turn out to be pivotal for the future of Carillion and its executives. The decisions taken would be crucial in the unfolding of the collapse. After this day the Genie was out of the bottle. And it couldn't be put back in.

Despite her prominence in the proceedings before the board, Emma Mercer was not in the teleconference call. Howson briefed the board members about the recent developments and the work carried out by the sub-committee to date. He identified three possible options. These were: to disclose the position immediately to the Stock Exchange; work with KPMG to establish if the accounts still stood or not; whereby, if, following this second option, the 'year-end accounts were able to be upheld, that no disclosure be made'.[15] One interpretation of this might be that it is the business version of the declaration of a verdict before the trial had taken place.

On the line there was general comment from a number of the directors, and then Zafar Khan was asked to give his view. His annual salary was £425,000 – £8,000 a week. Plus hefty potential bonuses on top. At this point he'd been the chief finance director of Carillion for five months, and before that, for almost four years, the group finance controller and second-in-command to Richard Adam. He told the board that until he spoke to Mrs Mercer he had not been aware of negative accruals being widely used in the major accounts. He admitted that 'there had been incompetence and laziness in the accounting review of the contracts and in recognising the position.'[16] By any standards, this seems a remarkable admission from a man who had been second in command of Carillion's finances for more than four years.

Cue Alison Horner. Since 2011 she had been the chief people officer for Tesco plc, and a board member there. In December 2013 she was appointed a non-executive director of Carillion's board, as a member of the company's audit committee, which approved all the accounts.

In May 2014 she became the chair of Carillion's Remuneration Committee, or RemCo as it was known. That was the internal committee which approved the salaries and bonuses of the Carillion directors which turned them into oligarch millionaires. In 2016 Horner collected £61,000 in fees as a non-executive director and an additional £10,500 for the RemCo chair role. She was one of the more hard-working non-execs. In 2016 she attended 19 meetings, as a member of five sub-committees. And ten board meetings.[17] That's two and a half grand a pop.

When Howson made his report to the board on 9 May, with the options indicated above, Horner was the first to call for an independent outside review. In 2014 she had been the chief people officer, or HR director, to use another term, when Tesco had its own accounting scandal. Tesco was found to have been putting income through its accounts that had not been earned. As a result the company had to issue a corrected statement of its August 2014 profits to the stock market. In late September that year, Tesco disclosed that its profits had been overstated by £250 million. The Serious Fraud Office called it 'false accounting on an industrial scale'.[18] In 2017 the SFO agreed an out-of-court settlement through which Tesco had to pay £129 million to avoid criminal prosecution. That emerged after a whistleblower at Tesco sent the company's newly appointed chief executive a report on what was going on.

All this must have been preying on Horner's mind as the 9 May Carillion teleconference progressed. After Robin Herzberg, the head of risk, summarised the report submitted by the Mercer sub-committee, Horner interjected about her experience at Tesco during the £250 million scandal. She said, 'The key question is disclosure ... I feel that an independent view is required,' after suggesting that Mrs Mercer 'appeared to be a whistle-blower who did not feel she had been listened to'. Horner also said that she was wary about an in-house review with KPMG, implying that they might be part of the problem, not part of the solution. Then she said 'that a decision appeared to have been taken to hold a position when that may not have been the right thing to do'.[19] The intent is clear, if stated somewhat opaquely – staff are being instructed to make the numbers fit even if they don't. This was a direct attack on the integrity of those who had produced the 2016 accounts – including Carillion staff and the auditors, KPMG.

The board minutes note: 'Mrs Horner was concerned that individuals were directed to routes which were inappropriate and the position regarding Mr Adam's instruction as noted in Mr Herzberg's paper ... Mr Khan confirmed that in his view an instruction to hold the margin could not have meant to maintain it come what may.'[20] The initial Herzberg sub-committee report has never been made public. However, it seems reasonable to suggest that Alison Horner's remarks that 'individuals were directed to routes that were inappropriate' refer to instructions being issued to staff by Richard Adam regarding the deployment of negative accruals. Zafar Khan's comments above appear to confirm that Richard Adam had, at some point, issued 'an instruction to hold the margin' – accountant-speak for retaining the rate of profit shown in the returns. Without sight of the initial Herzberg sub-committee report this remains conjecture.

That aside, what the 9 May minutes seem to confirm beyond any reasonable doubt is that Richard Adam was directly involved in the determination of some of the contents of the 2016 accounts. This contradicts the statements he made on 6 February 2017 to the Joint Parliamentary Inquiry into Carillion. The minutes record the following exchanges:

> *Antoinette Sandbach* MP: Although the accounts were signed off by a different accounting officer, Mr Khan, for 2016 – all the detailed preparation would have been done while you were still CFO, in relation to the Carillion Accounts?
>
> *Richard Adam*: It would not for 2016, no.
>
> *Antoinette Sandbach*: You were not working as the CFO until December 2016?
>
> *Richard Adam*: I was, but the preparation of the audited accounts predominantly takes place in the period of January and February, leading up to the announcement of the results in March.[21]

After Horner had raised her questions at the board, Keith Cochrane, who was still a non-executive director at this point, supported her call for an independent review. He said what was going on seemed 'to ring alarm bells and raise red flags'. Significantly, Cochrane, at this point, said that there would be a case for a much broader review beyond the issues of negative accruals. He added, 'The position raises some fairly substantial questions around the ability to manage large contracts properly, and the broader question of culture. There seems to be a risk of over-optimism, the "glass-half-full thinking".' Cochrane had been on the board since July 2015. This was putting a marker down for the future. Alison Horner then re-emphasised that once the accounting misrepresentation had come to light at Tesco, the board announced that a review of the accounts was taking place and then, thereafter, announced the results.

Slaughter and May, the Carillion lawyers, were asked to give an opinion. The nub of the matter was whether the board needed to declare the need for an investigation and, further, that it was now proceeding; or to wait for more full findings to inform what was to be done. As usual in lawyer-speak it's an 'on the one hand, whilst on the other' answer. C.W.Y. Underhill, Slaughter and May's advisor to the board, stated that: 'It was not an instance of an obvious material mis-statement – a mis-characterisation of something on the balance sheet was not a mis-statement – and one might conclude that if you are confident having done the work that has been done that you don't have to re-state the accounts you don't need to announce.'[22]

That must have come as some relief to all those concerned. It was decided that plans should be made for what was termed 'a four-level position':

- What was now to be called the Carillion Working Group, comprising Herzberg, Mercer, Adam Green and Holmes, should make further investigations regarding the financial position;
- that KPMG be invited to investigate the determination of the 2016 accounts and the results of the further investigations of the Carillion Working Group;
- that a totally independent review be established; and
- that a further sub-committee comprising Andrew Dougal, chair of the audit committee, and Keith Cochrane, oversee the progress of the other three approaches.

That independent review edict only lasted a matter of hours before
further discussions, among board members unknown, decided that
an independent review was not required. The head of Carillion's
audit committee, Andrew Dougal, would later explain that it was
felt an independent review would take too long. In other words,
in the scope of this second-stage review, KPMG was going to be
allowed to mark its own homework.

The board had another teleconference meeting on 15 May. The
report from the Mercer Working Group confirmed the worst,
although by this time the prospect of the findings being calamitous was already understood. The results of the accounting
'incompetency', previously identified by Zafar Khan, came to a
£170 million hole in the forecasts. Worse, this was in only three
major projects which had been subject to detailed investigation.
The board minutes note that, according to the latest paper from
the working group, Liverpool required £49 million to be found (of
which £47 million were negative accruals . . . Battersea had £44
million to be found (£24 million of which were negative accruals
. . . and Aberdeen had £77 million to be found (£18 million of
which were negative accruals).

These were outstanding claims combined with negative accruals
which had been entered in the accounts but had not been realised.
That is to say, not been paid. So the board members were confronted with a £170 million problem which meant they could not
now be sure if the profits declared in the 2016 accounts still stood.
They had to draw up 'recovery plans' for the three projects. These
plans had to establish whether the outstanding claims would be
paid or whether they could find other claims or other values that
could offset the £170 million of negative accruals that had been
discovered. Otherwise the 2016 accounts could not stand. The
potential effect of that was what was causing creeping sweats of
alarm. When Tesco had restated their profits in the 2014 scandal,
their share price had collapsed by 12% in one day, costing the
company £2 billion and putting its future in jeopardy. This was
now the spectre haunting the Carillion board, and the real reason
for these desperate measures. They knew that if the recovery plans
could not square the £170 million circle, Carillion was almost

certain to become holed below the waterline. They were suddenly in do-or-die territory.

At this stage two figures were beginning to emerge who would be decisive in the boardroom battles to come. Emma Mercer was now being seen as a crusader who had fearlessly challenged the board's apparent impunity. At her sub-committee she had declared that much of the difficulty the company was now facing was the result of 'sloppy accounting'. Thus, it looks like she was determined to take on Carillion's auditors, as well as taking the board to task about its financial mismanagement. In the annals of Carillion's history this was extraordinary. As one Carillion insider said: 'You didn't go "off on one" calling the board to account. Nobody did that in Carillion.' The House of Commons Joint Report on Carillion recognised the role played by Mercer, who turned out to be 'the only director prepared to concede that Carillion were engaged in "aggressive accounting".'[23] The report declares: 'Emma Mercer is the only Carillion director to emerge from the collapse with any credit. She demonstrated a willingness to speak the truth and challenge the status quo, fundamental qualities in a director that were not evident in any of her colleagues.'[24]

Thus it cannot be gainsaid that Emma Mercer, 'the whistle-blower', demonstrated great courage and integrity in bringing the 'negative accruals' malpractices to light.

Keith Cochrane was the second figure emerging in the new power struggle. He was the former chief executive of the Scottish engineering firm, the Weir Group. Due to the obvious failings of the board executives on the money, Cochrane was now well placed to begin to dictate future strategy. He and Dougal's sub-committee, which was now called the Accounting Review Committee, would have the last word on the work of the other investigations. At the 15 May teleconference Cochrane warned that there had better be no more cock-ups. He said when the recovery plans were presented to KPMG they had to be 'credible, with a realistic chance of recovery, not simply an assumption that they would all fall in our favour'. Thus he distanced himself from what had gone on before and issued a threat about future performance. Philip Green, until now the prevaricating chairman, would soon have to decide where he stood regarding Cochrane and Mercer and their persistent critical salvoes.

The board deciding to allow KPMG to mark its own homework turned out to be a good move. Peter Meehan was the senior partner at KPMG in charge of the Carillion external audit. Meehan was there to present the findings of the group of KPMG auditors who had been tasked to review the recovery plans for the negative accruals and other outstanding costs. Specifically these 'independent' KPMG auditors had to make the call on whether the rescue plans could actually lead to the recovery of sums outstanding, or whether they could find other offsets to cover for them. Thereafter, the same KPMG auditors had to advise if their findings meant that the 2016 accounts could stand. In his report to the board meeting of 23 May, on his own auditors' findings, Meehan noted: 'KPMG concurred with the output of management's review, and remained satisfied that the profit recognised on construction contracts at 31 December 2016 was appropriate. There was no impact on the 2016 Accounts.'[25]

There must have been audible sighs of relief in the boardroom at that point. The importance of these reports meant the meeting was held in the London offices and not as a conference call. Nonetheless, Meehan's report on the KPMG findings did not amount to a gold star on the homework which you could take home to show your mother. He noted that there were, for example, problems with construction contracts not keeping auditors up to date, so that, for example, often the October findings were simply updated to December rather than being inspected afresh. There had been significant movement between the October and December positions which were not properly reflected in the papers at contract level. Or, to go beyond KPMG-speak, the left hand was not making sure the right knew what it was doing. Meehan also found that the use of negative accruals conflicted with a 2008/9 'golden rule' to prohibit their use. He did not believe that 'there was an intent to deceive, but rather [the difficulty] was a result due to incompetence, negligence, or sloppy accounting'. So despite accounts being skewed, rules being broken and evidence of incompetence, negligence and 'sloppy accounting', the conclusion was there was no need to do anything on disclosure. The accounts did not need to be amended.

In his eye-opening book *Bean Counters: The Triumph of the Accountants and How They Broke Capitalism*, Richard Brooks recalls the words of the American socialist writer Upton Sinclair: 'It is difficult to get a man to understand something when his salary depends upon him not understanding it.' Many might say that the epigram seems appropriate to these KPMG conclusions. Not least when considered along with the auditors' nine key recommendations made to the board. Meehan acknowledged that these were a matter for the board, but insisted that the key point was that it was imperative that the company worked with 'one version of the truth'. KPMG had just dug the Carillion directors, and perhaps themselves, out of their immediate hole and everyone knew it. The KPMG report was agreed unanimously. The chairman, Philip Green, asked if there were any further questions. There were none. Green said the board noted and agreed KPMG's position that there was no need for any restatement of the 2016 accounts. It had been a close-run thing.

So close, in fact, that a matter of days later decisions were taken to do something about the rising debt. Following discussions between the board and the audit committee, it was decided to press forward with a rights issue. The aim was to make a share issue to the markets, which, while it would dilute the current share value, would raise cash to reduce the debts. The move was meant to create a swap – shares for income to reduce the perilous debts. On 25 May Carillion's leading brokers, Morgan Stanley, along with the lawyers Slaughter and May and others, were instructed to start preparing for the potential rights issue. The work was named Project Salmon. If the rights issue could be underwritten, the target was to announce it with the mid-year trading statement due on 10 July. Normally the underwriter in a rights issue is a powerful bank or finance house, where an agreement will be set for the bank or finance institution to guarantee to the company making the rights issues that they will purchase a certain percentage of the shares on offer, to increase the share sale beyond what the stock markets buy up.

It was also decided to conduct further financial analysis of the major contracts, given the disquiet about the figures produced by the Carillion Working Group. That would serve the double function of a rigorous financial review, which would be needed in any case if a rights issue went ahead. Although Emma Mercer had instigated the negative accruals investigation, it was Robin Herzberg, head of risk, who had been the lead in reporting on that to the board. Step forward Mrs Mercer. It was agreed that 'this analysis of key contracts should . . . be undertaken internally, principally involving Mrs Mercer'.[26] KPMG were also instructed to conduct further inspections in conjunction with the Mercer review, in what became known as the Enhanced Contracts Review. This was to be undertaken in June, in addition to the normal process of contract monitoring by senior management leading to the half-yearly statements.

Perhaps all these developments were put in hand not by design but coincidence. Perhaps. Their consequence would be that as the weeks in June passed, Emma Mercer would know before anyone else on the board how the numbers were falling. So would Keith Cochrane. He was on the co-ordinating committee which allowed him to ask.

CHAPTER 3

Something with a Bit of an Edge

'I have always been a believer that chief executives have life cycles, and there comes a point when it gets "samey", for you and for the business. I still have the desire to go and do something else; I'll probably look for something with a bit of an edge to it.'

Keith Cochrane, former CEO the Weir Group,
Sunday Times, 25 September 2016

Keith Cochrane joined the Carillion board in July 2015. He was the chief executive of the Glasgow-based engineering concern, the Weir Group, at the time. He 'stepped down' from Weirs a year or so after joining Carillion. Cochrane joined Weirs in 2006 as their chief financial officer (CFO). Three years later the board promoted him to chief executive officer. In 2007, when he was still the CFO, Cochrane organised the £328 million purchase of a Texas shale company, SPM. It produced pumps for the fracking business. That meant that in the latter part of the decade, Weirs was into the fracking bonanza when fracking boomed. 'It's hard to believe,' Cochrane told one journalist when talking about the Weir Group business history, 'our North American business was growing at 7% a month!'

The Weir Group returns prove it. In one year the revenue from the boom climbed from £1.6 billion in 2010 to £2.3 billion in 2011. Cochrane's pay boomed as well – up from £1.26 million in 2010 to £1.62 million in 2011. Weir Group shares hit an all-time high in 2014. That was before the world oil crisis kicked in – later in the same year, oil prices plummeted from $115 a barrel to $30 a barrel in a matter of months. The Weir Group's fracking pumps business plunged into crisis in parallel. Fracking is clearly a land-based operation. Relatively it is much easier to turn off the taps on fracking than it is to do so on oil wells in the North Sea or any other ocean-based exploration. So that's what the big oil companies did. Temporarily, they shut down much of their fracking operations and concentrated on serving oil markets from conventional oil sources. As one seasoned business insider put it: 'That was the cost-effective thing to do with oil prices tanking. But that meant double trouble for Weirs.'

Weirs suffered a double whammy, with mineral commodity prices collapsing at the same time as oil. Commodities, particularly copper, plunged in price, which meant that ore extraction 'tanked' as well. The result was that world-wide demand for Weir Group's pumps used in the minerals business slumped alongside the fracking pumps' collapse. Cochrane had his hands full with two major elements in the business going down simultaneously.

For the next two years Cochrane had to stabilise the global business, laying off thousands of workers and selling assets across the world. By 2016 Weir Group operating profits were almost half the boom time of 2011 – down from just over £400 million to £214 million. By then revenues had also dropped from £2.3 billion to £1.8 billion. That's a 20% drop. The figures might tell the story of why it became inevitable that Cochrane would 'step down'. One business source put it this way: 'He told everyone he was leaving of his own free will to seek new challenges, as they say. But in my experience these guys don't do walking away. They've got relentless drive at the top, and it's usually counted in millions.'

It's fair to say that other insiders would take a different view. One told me that Cochrane was a 'good tough businessman but a straight-shooter. He wouldn't cut and run. That wasn't his style. He would have stayed to steady the ship and then pick his own time to move on.' The insider maintained that Cochrane always held a view that 'any chief executive anywhere has a shelf-life'.

The truth probably lies between the two opinions. Circumstances had changed and the board concluded they needed a new CEO to face the new challenges. Cochrane thought he had arrived at the point where it was time to move on. The deal was done. The detail is significant because his leaving the Weir Group would see him free to step into the breach when Carillion bombed. There is a certain repeating pattern between Cochrane's stepping down from the Weir Group and the rest of his business career. He might be seen as a boardroom Jose Mourinho, in the sense that football manager Mourinho's appointments seem to have dazzling seasons of achievement which eventually become defeats piled upon defeats; followed inevitably by his departure. Cochrane began his business life at Arthur Andersen, the one-time global accountants, before they got caught fiddling the books at Enron.

He was hands-on as the accountant for the flotation of the Megabus company, Stagecoach. It was owned by Brian Souter who, even then in the 1990s was one of Scotland's top business entrepreneurs. Souter head-hunted Cochrane after the Stock Exchange flotation and Cochrane then became Souter's right-hand man in the business. In a matter of years Cochrane went from finance director to one of Scotland's youngest chief executives, early in 2000, at the age of 35. Cochrane was well-positioned at this point to salvage Stagecoach's billion-and-a-half dollar acquisition of America's biggest bus monopoly, Coach USA. That deal had gone pear-shaped. However, the hoped-for transformation did not work out and Souter and Cochrane parted company. In 2002 Cochrane stepped down.

Then came the Scottish Power years. Cochrane was head-hunted by the then chief executive of Scottish Power, Ian Russell, and spent a number of years there. He looked to be in line for the top finance job, but there was a boardroom blood-letting which ended with Russell's departure. After that the top finance job went to an outsider from the consultants McKinsey. It was time for Cochrane to step down and move on to new challenges, again. This time it was to the Weir Group in 2006.

He left Weirs in September 2016 after being the chief executive there for seven years. According to media reports, in his time as chief executive he was paid £15 million; the sums add up, given the seven-figure salaries and benefits packages he picked up for most of those years, including his last, in 2016. Cochrane was in on the curve that for the last decade has seen chief executives' earnings increase by four times as much as national average earnings. Of course if asked, Cochrane would say, with the usual big-business executive justification, that his rewards were no more than the going rate for the job. 'All the other kids on the block have got a bike, so why not me?' to coin a phrase. There is another view, of course. When asked about Cochrane's earnings at the Weir Group and then at Carillion, GMB Scotland's leader, Gary Smith, was caustic in his reply: 'These so-called top guns and all their weasel words defending their telephone-number pay packets to the last penny – it's greed on an industrial scale. They never put their hands up to confess that. Even if they talk about top pay averages. Put it this way, the average of an outrage is still an outrage.'

Keith Cochrane resigned as chief executive of the Weir Group on 30 September 2016, although his contract stood to the end of the year. To the end of September his base salary was £562,500. When the October to December figures are added that makes his base salary for 2016 £861,031. His bonus payments for the year were £498,104. As for the rest of the executives, that figure was docked that year by 10% as a clawback for 'unprovided liabilities of £17 million in the China business due to poor product performance and inventory management'.[1] So the bonus figure reduces to £448,294. That takes salary and bonuses to £1,309,325. Benefits like health care, insurance and car allowance of £12,761 make up additional income which is just over £17,000. Although he is 'stepping down' there is still a huge payment in lieu of notice of £472,788. That takes his 2016 valedictory payment to £1,799,192. In 2017 Cochrane gets further bonuses due under contract for that year of another £356,756.[2] However, the golden goodbye doesn't end there. The annual report to the year end of 2018 noted that in April 2019 Keith Cochrane would receive another shares bonus. This was signed off in 2016 and would pay out £410,000 in a shares cash-in from his personal shares bonus scheme. The 2018 annual report published that figure. Under the bonus terms Cochrane must hold the shares for two years. Then he can cash in. Thus, four years after his 2016 departure from Weirs he'll have an additional £400,000 plus coming his way. If Weir Group shares stay at the average of £15.05 till then, that rounds up the grand total of Cochrane's golden goodbye from the Weir Group to £2.56 million. These figures give a master-class about the way in which top pay in the UK has gone stratospheric in the last ten years whilst the average pay for the average worker, in real terms, has scarcely shifted, if not gone back.

For the purposes of like-for-like comparison, let's consider Keith Cochrane's last year of work at Weir Group. Cochrane's 2016 earnings come to £34,600 a week. This individual example shows the way the ratio of chief executive pay compared to the average pay of their workers has skewed exponentially in favour of the CEOs. In 2016, the median gross annual salary in Britain was £27,645, or £531 a week.[3] By 6 January 2016, Keith Cochrane has already been paid the total of what the average worker in Britain earned that year. It is safe to say that in July 2017, when he took on the job of interim chief executive of Carillion, it was not because he needed the money.

It should be understood that Cochrane's earnings are not simply a consequence of some personal dedication to enrichment. Not that this is not a pervasive driver among Britain's boardroom elites. Rather the most significant factor is the shift which took place in the late twentieth century from stakeholder capitalism to shareholder capitalism. This linked the company share price to the rewards paid to chief executives. If the former went up and up, it opened the gates to undreamed-of bounty for the executives. The managers of monopoly capitalism, in a matter of a decade or so, were transformed into evangelists of profit, shareholder capitalism and their own burgeoning bank balances. That process is reflected in 2016 in Cochrane's £34,600 a week.

Cochrane's remuneration at the Weir Group, compared with other chief executives, is not extraordinary. For example, the controversial pay awards made to the chief executives of Royal Mail and BT have been referred to already in the Prologue. In fact, Cochrane's rewards are typical of executive pay. They follow

the long-term trends of bigger and bigger pay packets for chief
executives, the increasing element of share options in the hundreds
of thousands of pounds within total pay, and the growing gap
between average company pay and chief executive rewards. The
House of Commons Business Committee's report on executive
pay, which was published in March 2018, notes that the average
pay of the FTSE 100 chief executive rose from £1 million 20 years
ago to breaking the £4 million barrier that year.

Nevertheless, Cochrane's earnings take him comfortably into
the British oligarchy club. He passes the second test of knowing
the right people. As testimony to that it can be noted that Keith
Cochrane CBE was a paid advisor to the Secretary of State for
Scotland, David Mundell, in an influential government position
for three years until 2018; in 2016 he was elected a Fellow of the
Royal Society of Edinburgh, and, at the last time of asking, he was
the chair of the Committee of Glenalmond College in Perthshire,
which *Tatler* magazine terms 'the Eton of the north'. The third
qualification for oligarch status is a propensity to loot the state,
of which more later. Cochrane's CV undoubtedly puts him in the
heavyweight division of Carillion's board. The rest of the board,
by comparison, are fighting at lightweight. This would prove to be
decisive as events unfolded.

After the Mercer/KPMG investigations there was an initial
review at a Carillion board meeting early in June 2017. The report
'Lessons Learned from the Accounting Review' was presented by
Zafar Khan. Even by his standards of opacity and obfuscation
the 'Lessons Learned' document makes for gruesome reading. On
accounting standards, 'doing the numbers' was now recognised as
a problem: '. . . high level instructions such as that to "hold the
line" [i.e. maintain declared profits] may if crudely implemented
have unintended consequences.' So management had to ensure
that any such issues had to be 'sensibly understood and implemented'. The prohibition of negative accruals as an accounting
device was emphasised. Then, on staff being pushed to make the
accounts reflect the desired returns, it was emphasised that they be
encouraged to challenge instructions which 'are either impossible
to carry out, which feel ethically unacceptable or which could lead

to any embarrassment to the business'.[4] The need for accounts to display 'one version of the truth' was again stressed, which confirms that previously more than one version of the truth seems to have been commonplace.

Finally, the Khan paper called for a review of values which should make changes where necessary 'such that staff fully understood that behaving with transparency, honesty and integrity is as important as achieving, improving and delivering'. Thus the two-page 'lesson learned' report turns into a savage indictment of the way the company was being led from the top. These cursory observations challenged chairman Philip Green's remarks in the annual report of 2016 that 'we have a good platform from which to develop the business in 2017'. Green must have forgotten the conclusions of Khan's paper when he was asked at the Joint Parliamentary Inquiry, in February 2018, about the values of the board. 'Honesty, openness, transparency and challenging management robustly but in a supportive way,' came his reply. Two days after the 'Lessons Learned' discussions, Carillion paid out a £55 million dividend as the first part of a planned £79 million total dividend. The seemingly unbreakable priority for paying dividends to shareholders, come what may, held firm. Given that the financial plight of the company had been identified, at least in the preliminary findings of the contracts reviews, how could such recklessness be justified?

The question is all the more pressing, given that the directors were told by the Pensions Trustee the previous December that the deficit on the pension fund was going towards £990 million.[5] Moreover, at this time, in discussions with the trustee, the board had argued they could only pay £23 million annually to reduce the deficit, instead of the £35 million the trustee had demanded. So only £23 million for the pension deficit, but £55 million down, out of £79 million planned, for the shareholders. The cumulative totals in these matters are just as revealing. Over the six years from 2011–2016 the company paid out £441 million in dividends, compared to £246 million in pension scheme deficit recovery payments.[6]

The give-away which explains such skewed business priorities is the shift to shareholder capitalism. Since its founding in 1999, Carillion's dividends had gone up for 16 years, year after year. The dividend paid is seen as a sign of the health of the company, which maintains market confidence and therefore the share price. The share price and profits are key indicators for the remuneration of executives in their salaries and bonuses. If the board had not paid the dividend, that would have put all the usual excessive rewards of the executives in jeopardy. So, to repeat the question, how could the board have decided to pay out the £55 million in these circumstances? Greed, is the answer. If asked, the average shareholder might have intoned: 'Remember, you scratch my back and I'll vote to fill your boots.' And the devil can take tomorrow. This short-termism is symptomatic of the failings and greed that determines the outlook of British capitalism's ruling elites.

Towards the end of June the spectre of a two-headed monster was coming Carillion's way. The investigation of the possibility of a rights issue to bail out some of the debts was coming to a conclusion, and the size of the hole in the accounts was getting nearer to determination in the second-stage management and KPMG internal inquiries. There was going to be bad news. In due course it would confirm that Carillion was now haunted with an approaching catastrophe. Maybe the time was right for new blood on the board. At the end of June 2017, the board announced that Baroness Sally Morgan of Huyton was to become a non-executive director on the Carillion board. The official notice was posted on 1 July 2017. Morgan had been a significant part of Tony Blair's inner circle that created the New Labour project. She described the original group as Blair, Alastair Campbell, Peter Mandelson and the political guru of New Labour, Philip Gould.

In the mid-1990s she was just outside the inner circle, but by the time Blair won power, in 1997, she was a fully paid-up member. Between 1997 and 2001, Morgan was Blair's political secretary. In his autobiography Blair says Morgan 'could reach parts of the political firmament that others couldn't'. That, according to Blair, included a special relationship with 'the women in the Parliamentary Labour Party'. Presumably for these services to politics and all-round human decency, Morgan was made a life peer in June 2001. After the peerage she was promoted to Director of Government Relations at 10 Downing Street. So she stayed in the inner circle after Alastair Campbell had left. Her somewhat splendid title meant that if you wanted to see Tony Blair, you had to go through Baroness Morgan and, in addition, when newspaper editors, MPs or trade union leaders needed to be mollified after this or that strop, it was Morgan who calmed them down and brought them round.

This was a long way from her role as the Labour Party's full-time organiser for the National Organisation of Labour Students in the 1980s, when she was in her 20s. In 2005 Morgan decided to quit full-time party politics and resigned from her Downing Street post. Then she cashed in her chips. It looks like she signed on the dotted line for boardroom non-executive directorships whenever and wherever she got the offer.

She joined Carillion in 2017. The £30,000 she would get from Carillion for the six months she was on the board would take her earnings for that year beyond the £200,000 mark. When she was officially appointed to the Carillion board on 1 July she was already the chair of Royal Brompton and Harefield NHS Trust on £65,000 a year; she was already a director at Dixons Carphone Warehouse on £55,000; and already on the board of Countryside Properties plc being paid £45,000; further, she was reportedly also an advisor to Lloyds Pharmacy for fees of £30,000. That leaves the baroness's take for the year just £25,000 shy of a quarter of a million quid. Baroness Morgan's income is set out here as another example, this time of how, within the conventions of current practice, most board non-executives, following their own chief executives, are also distanced from the economic realities of everyday life.

Nevertheless, despite this emergence as a scion of capital, not everything Baroness Morgan touched turned to gold; notably Southern Cross Healthcare. At one stage Southern Cross Healthcare was the biggest provider of care homes in Britain. By 2010 it had more than 300 care homes with the number of elderly residents nearing 30,000. This scale of operation had been forged by the American private equity colossus Blackstone, which took

over the company early in the 2000s. They built Southern Cross
on a programme of ruthless acquisitions of competitors, risky sell-
offs of its own properties and lease back, and huge borrowings
to make the asset-stripping financial whirligig go round. Oh, and
on the minimum wage for care staff. A couple of years after the
Blackstone cowboys sold up and left with their moneybags bursting, Southern Cross collapsed in a pile of debt it could not pay
off, rents it could not meet, and a cash flow that had dried up.
With the baroness on the board. In 2011 when Southern Cross
was engulfed in crisis, the leader of the GMB union, Paul Kenny,
lambasted the role of private equity in the scandal: 'More is known
about the Mafia than about the antics of private equity. This is
a financial exploitation process that does not care if it exploits
elderly people in care.'[7] At that point Baroness Morgan was one of
the longest-serving board members of Southern Cross Healthcare.
Over her five years on the board she was paid almost a quarter of a
million pounds. Baroness Morgan and a quarter of a million seem
to go rather well together in her business career. She resigned in
July 2011 when Southern Cross was on the brink of going under.

This adventure might have troubled a militant trade union leader
but not the Carillion board. They were wedded to the Tories at
this point. Big style. Between 2011 and 2016 the chairman, Philip
Green, had been an advisor on corporate social responsibility
to Prime Minister David Cameron, strange as it may seem now.
'Green' and 'advisor on corporate social responsibility' is a spectacular oxymoron. Green was also a reliable rent-a-quote for the
superiority of the Conservative economic model whenever asked
to speak out or sign up to letters to the editor. He was on first-name
terms, if you believed him, with several Royals. By this time, due
to his established links with Cameron, he would have been able
to reach Theresa May. Keith Cochrane knew David Mundell, the
Secretary of State for Scotland in May's cabinet, and, at this time,
had been the lead advisor to Mundell for three years. Cochrane's
brief was to keep Mundell in the loop about how government
policy was being perceived by the movers and shakers of Scottish
business. But, as importantly, what his Scotland portfolio also
included was to promote the work of the devolved Scotland office

to the entire government. That meant he had a permanent invite to the offices of most Cabinet ministers, at any time. So given this, why would the board go for the Labour baroness? Maybe, given what was shaping up to be dangerous times, it was thought that Baroness Morgan would open the doors to the Labour aristocracy if that was needed. Maybe. Also, wasn't the board all a bit macho-male? An impression which would be toned down by a feminine face on the website.

However, the real reason Morgan became the chosen one is likely to be much more prosaic. She knew Richard Adam. The former finance director of Carillion and the baroness go back a way. The two of them had been appointed on the same day, 17 December 2015, to the board of the housebuilder Countryside Properties plc. They were on the same board, on the same audit committee, on the same nomination committee at Countryside for years. 'Need someone to open doors to Labour? I've got the very woman,' Adam may well have said. So as the shadow of crisis loomed into view, Carillion turned to the who-knows-who 'chumocracy' of British capital. As the *Economist* describes it, 'The country's model of leadership is disintegrating. Britain is governed by a self-involved clique that rewards group membership above competence, and self-confidence above expertise . . . Thus meritocracy morphs into crony capitalism.'[8]

Funnily enough, Baroness Morgan didn't turn out to be a saviour for Carillion. Instead, in December 2017, as Carillion was near collapse and needing all the friends it had to speak up and demand a rescue, Morgan asked three questions in the House of Lords – about the numbers of children in Britain being home-schooled. She should have gone to her first Carillion board meeting on 5 July 2017, but due to 'existing commitments' she was unable to attend.

Throughout June of that year, Carillion's brokers, the merchant bankers Morgan Stanley and Stifel, had been full on trying to put a package together for a rights issue that could fly. They worked intensively with senior managers and key figures on the board towards the 5 July deadline. What they were trying to do was put together a proposal for current investors and new investors that was compelling enough to get them to invest substantial amounts of money into Carillion. The investment proposition had to include a credible plan to reduce Carillion's debt to a sustainable level, as well as deliver a future strategy for the business that was sufficiently powerful to galvanise new investment. The board and senior management flunked the test. The night before the board, the Morgan Stanley and Stifel bankers met with Philip Green and told him all bets were cancelled. Later on, Green ensured he would 'shoot the messenger', in this case by systematically strangling the use of Morgan Stanley's services in favour of other brokers from this point onwards. As one Carillion source explains, 'Everyone could tell you that Green only wanted to hear good news. And woe betide the bearers of bad tidings.' Morgan Stanley later explained its case which proved to be a call-out of the board and, in effect, a funeral notice: 'If investors did not have the confidence that Carillion's senior management had a sufficiently compelling investment proposition and the ability to deliver it, the rights issue would be unlikely to succeed. By early July our firm was increasingly of the view that Carillion's senior management could neither produce nor deliver an investment proposition that would convince shareholders and new investors to support the potential rights issue.'[9] In the evening meeting, Morgan Stanley told Green that investors were convinced that Carillion could neither produce nor deliver an investment proposition that stood up. Consequently, the brokers said that they could not recommend a rights issue and therefore could not underwrite one either. It's likely the bankers received short shrift thereafter.

You could not make up what happened at the board meeting in London the next day. Green gave the board the news that the two banks – Morgan Stanley and Stifel – could not underwrite the proposed equity issue. He said Carillion were now engaging with HSBC before asking Peter Moorhouse of Morgan Stanley to speak. Moorhouse now had time to expand on what had been said the previous evening. In bank-speak he told them that since the word was out about the contracts review, and the possible blow-back, potential investors were not interested and had looked the other way. So it was goodbye to a share issue. And the board knew then that was also goodbye to Plan A, a debt for equity swap. What Moorhouse actually said to them was: 'The executive directors and advisers have worked hard to enhance the investment case but it is materially short . . . the expected impact to the share price from the contract review given the current market rating means that the investment case is insufficient to support an underwriting.'

Green told the board that they would now just proceed with Plan B – they'd make the announcement to the Stock Exchange on 10 July as planned, but drop any mention of the rights issue carry-on. It is worth quoting the board minute: 'The Chairman reported that in the light of the decision of Morgan Stanley and Stifel, it was proposed that the board should endorse "Plan B" – essentially that the proposed announcement should proceed subject to amendment of detail, and obviously excluding the references to the proposed rights issue.'[10] After Moorhouse and the other bankers from Morgan Stanley and Stifel left, the board discussed how they were going to present the programme for selling off assets to the markets, which was now the last refuge for any substantial reduction of the debt. The chief executive, Richard Howson, told them also that there was no chance of HSBC coming up with an offer to underwrite a rights issue before the Monday announcement. Then there was general outrage about what Moorhouse from Morgan Stanley, and Mr Arch of Stifel, had said in the meeting. 'How dare they!'

This takes us into the realm of adamantine denial of the real situation. The substance of the discussion was why had the bankers reached this preposterous decision to walk away from the rights issue, since nothing had changed from late May when they said that the share deal was viable and they expected to underwrite it. If nothing had changed and if the two banks wouldn't now support the board, then they'd find someone who would. Outrage gave way to petulance: 'Whilst it was necessary to continue to work with them as brokers in the short term, that would clearly change in the future,'[11] was the declared aim of the board.

At this meeting these guardians of reason raged against the inconsistency of their one-time banking friends and promised commercial vengeance. They were prepared to acknowledge everything but reality. This is all the more dumbfounding because it is irrefutable that a number of the board members at this time had an understanding of the likely scale of the write-down. In a letter to the chairs of the Joint Parliamentary Inquiry, Cochrane confessed that by the end of June 'the whole board had access to the contract review prepared by management and the report prepared by KPMG on that review, both of which were extensive.'[12] When Cochrane gave evidence to the Parliamentary Inquiry he said that the general numbers were known at the end of June, if not all the detail: 'The first time I heard of the size of the number was at the end of June. The first time I saw the papers was the weekend before I was appointed [as interim chief executive]. That was when I had the detail, because prior to that, it had been work in progress.'[13]

Here Cochrane is referring to the papers from the audit committee on the numbers and details of the write-down, presented to board members on Saturday 9 July – four days after the 5 July board meeting. At that point the board could no longer avoid reality. That realisation, however, was in remarkable contrast to Philip Green's remarks which close the section of the 5th July board on the proposed rights issue. Green capped all that had just gone before, piling incredulity on incredulity. He delivered a salvo in advance of the Stock Exchange announcement the following Monday: 'In conclusion the Chairman noted that work continued toward a positive and upbeat announcement for Monday, focusing on the strength of the business as a compelling and attractive proposition.'[14]

Rachel Reeves MP, who chaired the Joint Parliamentary Inquiry on Carillion with vigour and insight, commented that this seemed to indicate that Green had 'no grip on reality'. The inquiry would eventually conclude that Green's assessment proved he was 'delusional'. With the benefit of hindsight, given the crash, it was indeed out of touch with reality for Green to draw such conclusions. But here we might make a qualification. Green is a British oligarch. He has stood at the top of mega-corporations for years, made a multi-million pound fortune and, albeit that he knows Carillion is in trouble, he is convinced that he, and his board, will not be denied success by some faint-hearted bankers.

Throughout the whole Carillion debacle, Green never once doubted that he was the man who could lead the company, the board and the staff back from the brink. This is the ideology of the oligarch. Multi-millionaires who have made their money in business are never crippled by self-doubt. Green was the chief executive of P&O Nedlloyd, the container-shipping company, for two years between late 2003 and late 2005. About 18 months into that journey, P&O Nedlloyd was taken over by the world's biggest container-shipping line, the Danish AP Moller-Maersk. They paid a very generous $2.9 billion for the acquisition. The result was that when Green departed from the newly merged concern at the end of 2005, his pay-off package of salary, bonus and shares amounted to £5 million. He didn't need any other incentive to jump ship. At the time Green was asked by a *Telegraph* business journalist about the £5 million – 'not bad for such a short voyage?' Green replied with a bow in the direction of shareholder capitalism. 'When I think about the money I'm making I think about the $1.3 billion of shareholder value created since I took over.'[15] That is grade-A oligarch-speak.

At the time, as a devout Christian and one-time chair of the Bible Society, Green insisted that 'the more money you've got the more money you should give away'. Green put some of his money into South Africa. He caught the Africa bug in the mid-1990s, when he was chief of operations for Europe and Africa at DHL, the global shipping and courier company. Today, Green and his wife Judy are still founders and patrons of Hope through Action, a South African charity which supports sports and community development in two African townships in the Cape. The Greens – Philip, Judy and their two daughters – have a house in the exclusive Val de Vie estate in Paarl, in the South African winelands, about 40 miles east of Cape Town. The original venture for a Hope through Action project was a community sports centre built at Mbekweni, the African workers' township outside Paarl, not far from the rather more prosperous Val de Vie. Green once organised the 'world's biggest charity polo event' for Prince Harry's Sentabale charity in Val de Vie.[16] He resigned as chairman of Sentabale after the Carillion scandal.

Green was in the right place at the right time when Maersk acquired P&O Nedlloyd. He's made a habit of that even when he's been sacked. Before he joined P&O Nedlloyd he rose to chief of operations at the communications giant Reuters. Unluckily for him, after a £498 million loss in 2002, the Reuters chief, Tom Glocer, decided on a company restructuring. That went top to bottom at Reuters and included the ousting of Green. There was some pain relief in his £1.25 million pay-off in June 2003. The levels of executive pay at Reuters had caused a furore at the April 2003 AGM, but the deals for executive pay-offs still stood when Green was 'stepping down' – one year's salary, bonus and pension. In 2002 Green's top line was £836,000. That took him to the £1.25 million hand-out in 2003.

Taking only the two pay-offs from Reuters in 2003 and from P&O Nedlloyd in 2005, being in the right place at the right time had netted Philip Green £6.25 million. He would probably describe this as just deserts for a man of his abilities. In today's world your average bricklayer earns good money, not least because of the shortage of those in the trade in the UK economy. For the purposes of averages, let's take a bricklayer earning £40,000 a year over 45 years – today's brickies on big contracts can earn £2000 a week, but we are considering average pay here. Looking at these two pay-offs for Green and comparing them to our brickie's 45-year earnings, what conclusion do we reach? The answer is that Green's two deals are three and a half times what a bricklayer would make in an entire lifetime.

By the time of the P&O goodbye, Green was well on the way to the oligarchy. He was part of the UK's business establishment and his wealth was trending towards incalculable. If it was needed, his next post is the clincher. He became part of the privatised water company, United Utilities plc, which was previously the publicly owned North West Water. Cue what his business friends would call 'maximising shareholder value', and what most union shop stewards would call 'looting the state'.

Green parachuted into the United Utilities board as their chief executive in February 2006, a matter of months after his P&O Nedlloyd goodbye. The early annual reports indicate the new chief executive's priorities. The first is to divest the company of any interests which are beyond the core business of water. So in his 2007 annual report, the first for a full year, Green declares: 'We are initiating a sale process for our electricity distribution assets with a view to maximising shareholder value.'[17]

After the electricity arm has been flogged off, Green's declarations in the 2008 report are somewhat more forthright. He notes in his CEO's statement that the first priority is still the return to the core water business, then adds: 'The second has been to set a capital structure and dividend policy appropriate for the future of the group. Following the sale of United Utilities Electricity, principally comprising our electricity distribution assets, and the review of our capital structure, we intend to return £1.5 billion to our shareholders, adjust our gearing to a level more appropriate to the business and implement a new dividend policy.'[18] In 2009 there was the delivery of another £1.5 billion bonanza for shareholders. Thereafter, for whatever reason, the annual reports for the rest of his time there – 2009, 2010 and 2011 – only post 'total dividends per share'. Nevertheless, that still allows a reasonable estimate of the total shareholder returns when Green was United Utilities' chief executive. In the five years between 2007 and 2011 that is around £7 billion.[19]

The scale of these returns is reflected in Green's own remuneration. In salaries, bonuses, benefits and share options that amounts to £8,261,200. To put this into perspective, the average brickie we referred to earlier would have to work for 206 years to get anywhere near that earnings total. In 2011 Green's final payday for five years of selling water was £2.63 million, including the cashing in of share options worth £827,000. This story of reward is a classic case of maximising shareholder value whilst at the same time exposing how the British oligarchs are capable of looting the state like their Russian counterparts.

Green was born into a middle-class family in Folkestone; he graduated from the University of Wales Swansea and collected an MBA at University College London. Clearly Green turned out to be pretty good on the numbers for his own wages, but he didn't always get the numbers right. Green's first venture in UK business was with the home-furnishing group Coloroll. He stayed there for ten years. In 1990 he was the managing director when it went bust. The year before that, as one of the three pension trustees with the firm, he signed off on a deal using company pension fund money to buy a luxury flat from Coloroll's then chief executive at a grossly inflated price. In 1994 all three trustees were found guilty of a breach of trust and maladministration by the Pensions Ombudsman. Compensation was ordered to make good the losses to the fund from the scam. It's unlikely that was ever paid, as Coloroll was bust by then.

Anyway, by that time Green was working for DHL. Close one. Green says he became a better manager as a result of the Coloroll experience. He accepts the ombudsman's criticism from that time, but says the trustees were 'not well advised in the Coloroll situation'. He told the Parliamentary Inquiry that he had learned the lessons about getting quality legal advice in his time at Carillion. Thirty years later, however, it seems that the lessons Green learned at Coloroll didn't stretch to reducing Carillion's calamitous pension deficit.

Green was a non-executive director of Lloyds TSB between 2007 and 2008. So his membership of the main board gave him a grandstand view of the 2008 banking crash. In September 2008, as the shock wave of the Lehman Brothers collapse was thundering across the US and world banking system, Lloyd's board made its first moves to take over the collapsing HBOS – once heralded as 'the new force in banking', but no longer. No more. In many quarters the deal was regarded 'as one of the most recklessly ill-judged of recent times'.[20] In the end Lloyds TSB and HBOS were conjoined not by a takeover, but by the 2008 banking bail-out. So when Philip Green made the numbers they didn't always add up.

By the end of the 5 July 2017 board meeting in the Maddox Street office, decisions were taken that something had to be done before the 10 July Stock Exchange statement. Something had to be done to convince the shareholders and the markets that Carillion's board was ready to face up to the calamity confronting it. No matter how late it was. The day after the meeting, Phil Wakefield was at a Carillion management meeting in Liverpool. It was a regular meeting to review the Liverpool hospital project. Wakefield had been managing director of Carillion's building division for almost 13 years. In that time he'd been the lead on several of Carillion's major construction projects. His mobile phone went in the middle of the meeting and he stepped outside to take the call. He returned to the meeting, gathered his papers and briefcase and left. He'd just been sacked. And he wasn't going to be the only one to carry the can.

CHAPTER 4

Tobogganing to Disaster

'It's greed on stilts, pure and simple.'

Frank Field, Joint Chair, House of
Commons Carillion inquiry

Pinning down the precise details of what happened next is challenging. It's established that the board was expecting the worst when the final shakedown on the contracts figures was determined. It's also established that Howson was present at the 5 July board meeting – in fact he was charged with trying to bottom out the possibilities of HSBC underwriting a rights issue. By the time of the emergency board meeting on 9 July, the day before the 10 July trading update, Howson had gone. He didn't attend that meeting. It's also known that by this time Keith Cochrane had told the chair, Philip Green, that he would step in as interim chief executive if the board approved the sacking of Howson and his replacement by Cochrane as interim chief executive. At this stage, it seemed that Green had already fielded a number of calls from investors telling him they knew about the likely write-down and demanding that something had to be done. Howson had got to go.

The day after the 'rights issue' board meeting there was another meeting on 6 July. It appears that certain board members attending the 5 July meeting were asked to stay on to attend the 6 July meeting, though not all of them. Unusually, the minutes of the 6 July meeting have never been published. Most likely, the 6 July board considered a series of proposals which mapped out what was to be done. It is here that decisions were taken, at least in principle, notably in favour of the sacking of Howson and his replacement by Cochrane, as well as initial findings on the pay issues for both of them. Measures to retain staff through 2017, given the emerging crisis, were also agreed. Obviously, decisions had to be taken to determine the agenda for the 9 July meetings before they took place.

It was decided that the full board meeting would be preceded by an audit committee meeting to deliver the breakdown on the findings of the inquiries involved in the Enhanced Contracts Review – that's the final details of the write-down. There would also be a special remuneration committee on the same day which would make recommendations on Howson's pay-off and Cochrane's interim deal, and related pay issues. Sometime during the day a nomination committee would be called to approve the changes to the directors. All these issues would then come before a plenary session of the full board, scheduled for the London offices at 5.45pm on the 9th.

Philip Green met Richard Howson the day after the 6 July board meeting. Green told him about the scale of the problem confronting the company with the write-down, the anxieties of a considerable section of the investors and the fact that the board felt that in the circumstances Howson had to go. Green asked Howson to step down. Green would confess later that it was one of his regrets that he did not sack Howson earlier. Green softened the blow by telling Howson that although Cochrane was now to take over as the interim chief executive, the board wanted Howson to stay on as chief operating officer – mainly to help bring in the money that was outstanding on a number of big contracts in the Middle East.

Being the chief executive of Carillion was a long way from Settle Comprehensive School, in North Yorkshire. That's where Howson went to high school. Thereafter, he got a degree in construction management from Leeds Polytechnic. In 1999, he joined Carillion as an operations manager in the original de-merger from Tarmac which created Carillion. He was one of the first entrants into the Carillion Leadership Programme, which boosted his company credentials. He rose through the ranks, and by 2007 had become managing director of Carillion's Middle East operations.

This was a career-making move, even although the Middle East contracts would ultimately become among Carillion's most problematic. Howson stayed in that role for three years before becoming chief operating officer in 2010. This move was planned by the former finance director, Richard Adam, who was grooming Howson for the chief executive role.

People in the business were astonished when Howson was appointed as chief executive, at the end of 2011, not least because he was only in his early 40s at the time. 'Folk thought he was too young for such a big job, too wet behind the ears. But it soon became clear that he wasn't there to lead the company but to do Richard Adam's bidding,' one senior manager said. Rachel Reeves in her exchanges with Howson during the Carillion enquiry soon recognised 'his love of money and the good life and all that came with it'. Still, she thought his zeal for looting the company was not as keenly developed as most of the others. Her abiding impression was that he was never up to the job, which lends credence to the idea that Howson was promoted beyond his capabilities so that he was always in thrall to Richard Adam. 'When he was sacked as chief executive, he got a job with the company to bring in the money from the Middle East contracts,' Rachel Reeves says, 'but when I asked him "Mr Howson, how did that go?" he had to say he didn't bring any money in. Nothing. He thought he was really good at this stuff but he was out of his depth.' The assessment of Howson in the final report of the Carillion Joint Parliamentary Inquiry is equally withering: 'As leader of the company he may have been confident of his abilities and of the success of the company but under him it careered progressively out of control . . . Right to the end he remained confident he could have saved the company had the board not decided to remove him.'[1]

The single jarring truth is that Howson was part of the problem. Any idea that he could have been part of the solution is fanciful when you run the numbers on Carillion's balance sheet at this time. Howson couldn't even get any of the Middle East money in. Howson worked for Carillion for just over 22 years. He joined as a design co-ordinator when he was in his late 20s. This longevity gave him a certain credibility in the eyes of a section of the staff since he had come through the ranks. However, his reputation and the respect he had as a 'Carillion man' in time gave way to a perception among many staff that he had turned out to be little more than yet another upstart on the make. That said, it should be noted that his concern for personal remuneration was matched by that of the rest of the Carillion board; and like them he was spectacularly rewarded for failure. After the collapse the British tabloids dubbed the directors 'the Carillionaires'. With just cause.

In 2016, his last full year at Carillion, Howson's earnings topped £1.5 million. That included a base salary of £660,000, bonuses worth £245,000, half paid in cash, and a pension contribution of £231,000. This for a year when the company's income dropped, its debt spiralled and the published company accounts were judged, at best 'misleading', and at worst 'a fiction'. This too for a year in which Howson himself admits he spent most of his time not leading from the front but visiting the Middle East trying to get the sheiks there to cough up what he said they owed Carillion. In 2016 Howson's take was 17% up on his earnings for 2015. In that year his total earnings topped £1.25 million. His base salary then was £610,000, bonuses £293,000 and pension payments £214,000. Over 2015 and 2016 then, years of mounting decline, Howson's bonuses alone were worth £538,000. In the same period Richard Adam, the director of finance, had bonus payments of £355,000. So in these two years Howson and Adam booked £893,000 in bonuses. That's just south of £0.9 million.

Nonetheless, there was retribution for this enormous trousering of funds. In the light of the subsequent collapse of Carillion, and what we now know, presumably almost all the £893,000 has been retrieved as a result of Carillion's punitive 'clawback' provisions for corporate failure? No. Not a single penny. The Carillion board had already made sure that couldn't happen. The board has long been accused of poor governance and a lack of foresight in its leadership of the company. True, with one conclusive exception. Early in 2015 the Carillion executives had sufficient foresight to protect their future bonuses, in perpetuity, in case their own forecasts of everlasting plenty turned out to be wrong. In 2014 the business watchdog, the Financial Reporting Council (FRC) introduced a requirement for companies to include 'clawback provisions' in their company codes so that bonuses paid for any period could be subject to 'clawback' or recovery if subsequent events justified that. At this point the Carillion governance code included the possibility of clawback in some 'circumstances of corporate failure'. Given the FRC's recommendations, Carillion's Remuneration Committee (RemCo) duly altered the clawback provisions in the company governance code. That was on 26 February 2015. The governance code was now to be governed by 'events of gross misconduct' and 'material mis-statement of the company's published accounts'. The 'circumstances of corporate failure' were replaced by these new conditions. This meant the RemCo recommendations, which were subsequently approved by the board, actually reduced the possibilities of clawback of bonuses. In fact, the rule changes actually made the payment of bonuses possible even if the company was threatened with economic collapse, provided the payments were approved by the board. The comedian Mark Steel in the *Independent*, in January 2018, emphasised the point in his own style of plain English: 'Some people have accused the board at Carillion of lacking foresight, but this seems unfair, because . . . the board changed their policy to protect executive bonuses so they would still be paid in the event of the company going bankrupt. And that seems packed full of foresight.'

When this scam became known at the Joint Parliamentary Inquiry, Frank Field MP said, 'It's greed on stilts, pure and simple.' The new terms which stood post 1 February 2015 were actually applied to Richard Howson's settlement, when he was paid off in July 2017. Carillion's economic crisis didn't affect his 2016 bonuses due, in his case, to the board's apparent ability to predict what might happen in the future and to protect themselves legally and financially accordingly. Alison Horner, Tesco's head of HR, was chair of the Carillion RemCo when the changes were made. She challenges the interpretation that the rule changes made clawback much less probable. She argues the opposite – that the changes actually made clawback of bonuses more likely. However, it is prudent to judge things not by what people say but by what they do.

In September 2017, the Carillion RemCo actually considered clawback of the bonuses paid for 2016 and concluded that they had no legal grounds to make that possible. In fact, the same committee recommended the introduction of additional new triggers for clawback to make it potentially much broader in scope. This included additional terms of indictment involving 'reputational damage, failures of risk management, errors in performance assessments and any other circumstances which the RemCo believed to be similar.'[2] It seems if they had to fix the governance code it must have been bust. Horner's stated opinion doesn't stand up to the test of the real-world outcomes, to put it in its most forgiving form. She was severely criticised in the Joint Parliamentary Report on Carillion. It says: 'She failed to demonstrate to us any sense of challenge to the advice she was given, any concern about the views of the stakeholders, or any regret at the largesse at the top of Carillion.'[3]

2016 provides a quintessential example of 'largesse at the top of Carillion' and Alison Horner's culpability for it. Carillion's remuneration policy was established at the AGM in 2014. This meant that, due to its time limits, it had to be renewed at the 2017 AGM. Hence Horner's RemCo spent part of 2016 evaluating the current policy and making recommendations for change. These had to be sent to shareholders and investors at the end of 2016, in preparation for the 2017 AGM's approval. In the light of the calamitous deterioration of Carillion's finances, already noted elsewhere, it might cause some surprise that one of the RemCo's proposals to investors was that they should support an increase in potential bonus payments to directors from 100% of base salary to 150% of base salary. Horner described the proposal to one shareholder in 'just tick the box' terms: 'This increase to the limit is intended to ensure that there is flexibility in the remuneration policy . . . to continue to provide competitive remuneration packages in order to attract and retain Executive Directors of the calibre required . . .'[4] The get-out clause was that the increase to 150% was for 'sometime in the future'. It was not for immediate effect.

The sense of entitlement which saturates the executives at the top of Carillion thus proves to be everlasting. Their own personal history of continual demand for ever-greater financial reward speaks volumes about how, for them, there is never enough. Even in the shadow of a crisis we can almost hear the cry: 'More. More. I am entitled to more!' Far from challenging the greed, Horner, day after day, sought to provide explanations as to why it was totally justified. On this occasion her banal advocacy for the latest demands of avarice failed. When notification of the proposals reached the investors they were at first astonished, and then outraged. They block the bonus hikes. Horner and Co have to concede: '. . . after feedback from some of our shareholders . . . the committee has decided not to include provision for additional quantum in the bonus'. For once. For 'additional quantum' read a potential 50% rise in bonuses for the Carillion bosses.

Richard Howson was one of the 'Carillionaires' who benefited from Horner's blind eye to Carillion's 'largesse at the top'. When Carillion collapsed, he and his wife, Geri, had a £1.5 million, five-bedroom former farmhouse outside Skipton in the Yorkshire Dales. They also owned a six-bedroom chalet in the upmarket ski resort of Chatel in the French Alps, near the Swiss border. Some time ago *The Times* noted that Howson and his wife had a property portfolio which included an additional 12 properties.[5] Howson has not replied to requests for comment. His LinkedIn profile seems to suggest he may now be working in the USA, where it's said his brother has a construction business.

When Howson was sacked, he wasn't left, like most of the Carillion workers and subcontractors, standing outside the padlocked gates of a building site wondering where his next wage was coming from. The largesse continued for him in the scale of his 'golden goodbye'. Moreover, what happened at Carillion's offices in London on Sunday 9 July would provide more evidence that this 'largesse at the top' was also characterised by a resolute belief in an entitlement to every penny of it. Entitlement is as real to the credo of the oligarch as personal superiority, a Rolex and driving a Merc.

The Carillion Remuneration Committee met at a quarter to four in the afternoon of Sunday, 9 July 2017. Alison Horner, Baroness

Morgan and Andrew Dougal were present as RemCo members. The chair of Carillion, Philip Green, and Janet Dawson, head of HR, were also in attendance as observers. Nothing broke the unity of purpose. By this time everyone remaining on the board knew what had to be done. Most of the proposals had already been discussed beforehand, so it was a case of nodding approvals and 'after discussion it was agreed', as the minutes show. Howson was to step down as chief executive but would be retained in employment for a period as chief operating officer (COO) tasked with retrieving money owed on major contracts in the Middle East. His remuneration as COO would be the same as it had been for the chief executive position – £660,000 base salary, annual pension of £231,000 and £17,000 a year for his car allowance. There would be no bonus payable for 2017. His COO payments would be made until that contract was terminated at the end of September 2017.

At that point his 12-month notice period would begin on the basis of these sums, paid monthly, over the following 12 months, until October 2018. But if the board thought stuffing Howson's mouth with gold would avoid a shouting-match they were wrong. Howson's entitlement gene kicked in. On the termination of his contract he wanted his 12-months' notice paid up-front in a cash lump sum. Similarly, he wanted his share-related bonuses paid in the same way, when they matured.

The RemCo of 9 July also discussed Keith Cochrane's remuneration as the interim chief executive. The RemCo approved a base salary of three-quarters of a million pounds for the new interim chief executive. That was £90,000 more than Richard Howson's salary. Cochrane, fresh from his £1.8 million Weir Group pay-off for 2016, knew he was a man entitled to that. There would also be 12 months' payable in lieu of notice, 'due to the interim nature of the role'.[6] Any indication of his acceptance of the £750,000 salary was qualified by questions he had raised about his bonus and payment for a London flat. Both Cochrane and Howson had matters arising from the RemCo proposals. The final parts of the RemCo agenda on further financial proposals were agreed without qualification. We know that Carillion's situation was dire. We know that there was a hole in the accounts amounting to hundreds of millions. We know that they were about to sack the chief executive. We also now know that on 9 July 2017 the Remuneration Committee recommended increases in salary for the senior management team as well as lucrative 'retention bonuses' on top to make sure they would stay with Carillion.

Lest this is considered as unlikely in the circumstances, it might be worthwhile to quote the memorandum: 'It was proposed in the light of the very considerable burden likely to fall on certain roles that the committee should consider ensuring that salaries were very competitive for those roles. The increases considered and approved were . . .'[7] The details are not disclosed: instead, what follows in the memo is a blank box; the reports are permeated with such blank boxes, or their variation, black box redactions, all embodied under the justification of 'commercial confidentiality'. Certainly in Carillion's case this is nothing more than an accounting cloak to cover up regulatory failure, excessive financial rewards and what in many cases would turn out to be fraudulent practice. In Carillion for 'commercial confidentiality' read 'escape from public accountability'. Time after time.

However, the RemCo was to serve up more than just salary aggrandisements. The next agenda item approves the payment of 'retention arrangements' to the same senior managers who had just been promised the salary hikes. The retention arrangements proposed that if they signed up to stay with Carillion until 30 June 2018, and did not resign prior to that date, they would be awarded bonuses of 100% or 60% of current salary, according to their grade; that's on top of the salary, bonuses and benefits already set. For the avoidance of doubt, this means that many of the senior managers who had been in charge of delivering a crisis write-down in profits, in the hundreds of millions, were to get sizeable salary increases and huge potential bonuses to keep them at the company. It's been established that the agreed salary hikes gave senior managers at Carillion annual remuneration of 'up to £240k with 100% bonus'.[8] Had Carillion survived, this means that a sector managing director, who stayed for a year, had just been promised £480,000 before other awards. There is one qualification, which is that these terms only applied to those who had not been sacked immediately after the crash. And that fate did apply to a considerable proportion of the top managers. Those who remained were poised to cash in on the others' misfortune. Nonetheless, this means that one sunny Sunday afternoon in London, in July 2017, in an hour and a half, Horner, Morgan and Dougal, with Green and Dawson watching, agreed to sign up to added millions in Carillion salaries and bonuses. By any stretch of the imagination, any Carillion outsider would surely find these new executive priorities difficult to comprehend, to say the least.

That is all the more confounding because when Horner, Morgan and Dougal launched the salary and bonus bonanza they will have known about the scale of the financial Armageddon about to be reported in the update to the Stock Exchange the next day. They will have known the top line had become a possible write-down touching £900 million. Andrew Dougal had attended the audit committee which preceded the RemCo meeting. There's one possibility that lets them out of the dock. That the new interim chief executive, Keith Cochrane, had taken up the reins of power before his actual appointment, and told them to do it. He knew he could save the day and was determined to take all necessary steps to do so. One who has known him since Cochrane was chief executive at Stagecoach says Cochrane is extremely conscious of his own reputation and, in turn, has a high opinion of his own abilities and achievements in business. The source says, 'He will have thought "I can turn this around". He will have been conscious of how success with Carillion would raise his reputation after the less than glorious departure from the Weir Group, and he will have thought he could drive Carillion to recovery.' The executive added more, suggesting that Cochrane may have seen the situation as a 'win-win'. 'He thought he was the man to deliver the Great Escape. But even if it turned out that Carillion still looked like going over the edge, Cochrane was convinced there would be a government bail-out. Win-win.' And finally it came down to ego – 'I've known Keith Cochrane a long time. He will have seen himself in the big picture, in the *FT* and *The Herald*, under the headline "The Man Who Saved Carillion". That's Keith.'

On Saturday 8 July the chair of Carillion's audit committee circulated the committee papers containing the Enhanced Contracts
Review (ECR) and supporting papers from KPMG. These were in
advance of the Sunday meeting of audit in London the next day.
Three-quarters of all Carillion contracts had been reviewed. Out
of these 58, there were further enhanced reviews of the 11 most
complex contracts. The reviews had involved Carillion's internal
team as well as the company's commercial operations and contract specialists. KPMG had provided additional reports on the
findings of the ECR. Saturday 8 July was the first time Cochrane
had seen the results of all the final reviews. This time round
everybody knew how important it was to deliver accurate assessments. There could be no fudge this time – that had been going
on for too long. However, even though there had been plenty of
talk about the deteriorating situation in the previous weeks, the
final countdown must have come as a shock. The starting point
for the enhanced review had been the reported £170 million
gap in the accounts identified by the 'negative accruals' investigation. The audit papers now recommended a write-down of
£695 million.

Cochrane studies the figures on Saturday. He's been in chief
executive mode for days now. It's already been discussed at board
level that there needs to be a strategic review of the whole business, which will include plans to exit from key contracts and
key markets as emergency measures on the debt. Cochrane figures this will mean that the estimates in the review for income
need to be reduced because 'it will be much more challenging
to collect cash' when Carillion is departing from key contracts.
When your leverage goes down in the building game people
delay paying or stop paying altogether. As a result, Cochrane
also thought the review needed to be more pessimistic on what
would constitute the 'likely worst scenario'. This, combined with
the reduction in cash from projects means he reaches a figure of
£150 million to make sure there is real robustness in the numbers
in the coming trading update. On the Sunday morning Cochrane
meets Zafar Khan before the audit committee meeting. They
agree to put Cochrane's amended figure of £845 million to the

audit committee. It gets approved. Later in the day the full board approves the write-down, the changes at the top and a strategic review of the business. It was too late. Carillion was tobogganing to disaster.

CHAPTER 5

The 'Perfect Storm'

'If you have a company that burns through £850 million of cash in one year, having apparently for many years generated reasonable amounts of cash flows, then there is clearly a case to answer. The notion that this all happened in the matter of a couple of months in early 2017, to our mind, is incredible.'

Murdo Murchison, Kiltearn Partners,
House of Commons Inquiry, 'Carillion',
7 March, 2018, Q1006

By most recollections on 10 July the conference call for all senior managers in Carillion was early in the morning, not long after the Stock Exchange notice had been posted at 7 am that Monday. There had been some rumours flying around inside the company about Howson – 'Look, keep this to yourself, but Howson's been sacked.' Regardless of this, however, a large majority of those in on the call did not know what was going on. They didn't have a clue about Howson. They knew nothing of the £845 million. Cochrane starts the call by saying that people might be surprised to hear his voice. He tells them that he is now the interim chief executive. He explains: 'The board have decided that Richard Howson should step down, although Richard will continue to support the company in the next period, especially to help us get money in from the Middle East projects.' One staffer spoke for many when he said, 'We were all expecting to hear Howson's dulcet tones and there's this Scottish bloke instead. Most of us were thinking "Who the fuck's this?"'

Cochrane tried to give assurances. He told the staff that there would not be any large-scale redundancies but emphasised that there was a need to face facts – 'We need to sort out the mess.' He said that there was going to be a strategic review of the company's long-term priorities which would provide the plan for a total restructuring. He insisted that 'We need to become fitter, more sustainable. We've got to stop doing things that are a waste of time. Concentrate on things we are good at.' Since this was back in July 2017 and the conference call was pretty sharp and to the point, people who were there don't remember much of the detail. However, one thing that gets mentioned frequently is that there was definitely no comprehensive reference by Cochrane to the £845 million. He referred to the trading update but then spoke more about how the shorting of Carillion's shares had seriously damaged the company.

A workable definition of shorting is betting on a company's share price falling so that a killing can be made if it does. You might call it using special methods of share purchase to make money out of predicting failure.[1] Stocks go down, your money goes up. By the summer of 2017, short-selling of Carillion's shares had captured almost 30% of the company stock. Cause for concern, because it means a lot of investment houses were betting a lot of money on Carillion's woes getting worse, which would cause the share price to go down and down. In the conference call Cochrane told the staff that these practices undermine confidence in a company like Carillion. 'This isn't allowed in Europe,' he said, 'it's something you get in the UK. Once the big investors smell blood, more and more move in for the kill.' He told the staff that the only way to overcome this would be to make much better decisions about the contracts that Carillion bid for. He added then that too many of the contracts that were then in trouble got there because of poorly prepared, rushed bids.

He spoke about major contracts that were causing problems, but did not give detailed information on names or numbers. This monthly dial-in would become a feature of Cochrane's leadership from then on. Towards the end of the call he said he was confident that things could be turned round. People recall that he also made the demand that would be repeated at every future conference call: 'You guys have got to get the cash in!' There were no questions from those listening. There never were at Carillion conference calls, with the exception of the occasional obsequious 'soft balls down the wicket' in the Howson era, which would allow him to extol this or that business achievement or talk about contract miracles that had been delivered. Howson's regular dial-ins were part of Carillion's management communications establishing a business culture such that nobody ever wanted to be the bearer of bad news. Emma Mercer had been the first to break that tradition in April, and now Cochrane in July. And how.

From then on Cochrane retreats to his office at 25 Maddox Street, above the bookmakers, in London. There he surrounds himself with his own coterie, made up of the new advisors he recruits, like Lee Watson from Ernst and Young. Initially the Cochrane appointment raised hopes among the staff that he might be the man to turn things around – for example he creates an email suggestion box system for staff to write in with suggestions to improve the business, which sets him apart from the previous regime. However, that doesn't last long. Cochrane's voice is heard on conference calls but he is seldom seen by the rank and file. It's not long before the rising hope that Cochrane was going to get to grips with the business dissipates. The troops begin to doubt their new general. It seems he isn't going to be their Napoleon, after all.

The update posted to the Stock Exchange on 10 July 2017 would make for some astonishment. Even if many of the warning signs had been well recognised beforehand – the shorting of the stock being an example – the scale of the interim declaration was beyond most expectations in the City of what was coming. One City analyst, Sam Cullen, told the business media, 'People suspected a write-down was coming. But everyone was shocked at the scale of it.' The top line of the update delivered by finance director, Zafar Khan, referred to Carillion's most recent review of the business: 'The review has resulted in an expected contract provision of £845 million, of which £375 million relates to the UK (majority three Public Private Partnership (PPP) projects) and £470 million to overseas markets, the majority of which relates to exiting from markets in the Middle East and Canada. The associated future net cash outflow is £100-150 million, primarily in 2017 and 2018; average net borrowing is now expected to be £695 million (full year 2016 £586m).'[2] In addition, the company had to announce it was parting company with its chief executive (Howson), its UK contracts boss (Wakefield) and three of its highly-placed financial directors.

After speaking to Carillion staff on the conference call, Cochrane's next report is at St Paul's, in London's Aldgate, for an 8.30 am start. Cochrane tells them there's to be a strategic review, but it's already been decided that Carillion is coming out of Canada and the Middle East – including Qatar, Saudi Arabia and Egypt – exiting from construction PPP contracts, and immediately disposing of global assets worth £125 million. The business is going to be repositioned more strategically in the services and facilities management sector. And that 'no option is off the table'. The message for the City cognoscenti was in the usual Stock Exchange business-speak. If it had been delivered in plain English Cochrane could have said bluntly: 'There's a £845 million gaping hole in the books, where we've just found out our forecast revenue is down by that amount. So we're getting out of international contracts, we're getting out of all that PFI government stuff which is now costing us a fortune, and we're flogging off £125 million of our property holdings all over the place to reduce our debts immediately; our borrowings this year are up to £685 million, more than £100 million up on the whole of last year, so we've sacked the chief executive and four other directors. And, by the way, we're broke. So we're going to concentrate on where we make money – support services and financial management.'

Throughout Monday 10 July the City had its say. Carillion's share price dropped by 40% in that one day. It was down a further 33% on the Tuesday, and dropped another 27% on Wednesday the 12th. In 2015 Carillion shares stood at 350p. A month before the write-down they were still worth a little more than 200p. At the close of play on the Wednesday they were trading for 57p.

That meant that in three days what was a £5 billion turnover global business was worth less than £250 million on paper. On 13 July *Guardian Business* headlined: 'Carillion has no future without a rights issue of at least £500m'. The Carillion board knew that was never going to happen, given the failures the Morgan Stanley brokers had reported in the previous week. Cochrane told the analysts that four individual projects carried about half of the total £845 million provision. He declined to name them, claiming that doing so might jeopardise getting cash in for what was owed. Later investigations put numbers on the catastrophe:

- Carillion faced losses of £91 million on the Aberdeen bypass roads project – the bid price was too low, it was a fixed price contract, inadequately resourced from day one, and no-one had factored in problems with water courses, peat deposits and avoiding oil company pipelines.
- £83 million losses were now forecast on the Royal Liverpool University Hospital – design problems had caused cracked beams and other structural deficiencies in the building and a lack of due diligence before the project started compounded those issues financially
- The Midland Metropolitan Hospital was going to be £48 million out in 2017 – design problems had delayed the build by 17 months, including inadequate load bearings on ward floors and the increased costs that resulted
- There was Carillion's facilities management contract for 52 public sector prisons in England and Wales. The £200 million project over five years was losing £15 million a year – initial tender assumptions were wildly out of context and there had been issues because it was a 'first generation' outsourcing. Carillion had never run prisons before
- The Doha downtown regeneration project, in Qatar, originally worth £395 million, had become a major dispute about who owed what to whom. Carillion claimed Msheireb Properties, the contractor, owed some £200 million; they said they didn't.

So just how did we get here? Time and again the directors would assert that the write-downs were a result of a sudden collapse in revenues from these major projects in the UK and one from abroad. The truth is that the new financial crisis was a product of long-term business problems which were camouflaged by accounting scams. In fact, the way Carillion's accounts were presented amounted to a great charade. In October 2017 Carillion's lenders commissioned the consultants FTI to review the business. FTI reported on accounting practices which 'enhanced reported financial performance above underlying operating performance.' That's accountant-speak for cooking the books. And the charge sheet is extensive. The great charade was created by:

- including profits from share sales in PPP and PFI projects as though they were part of operating profit and cash flow; in other words, share sales were treated as income
- counting the profits from Carillion's joint ventures with other companies into Carillion's cash flow as though they were produced by Carillion alone; in other words, for example on a joint venture with Amey, all the profits were recorded in Carillion's books
- managing the books at year end by using capital transfers to make net debt in the books look better
- taking out short-term loans with joint-venture partners which would be paid back after the accounts were published to make net debt look better at year end
- developing the early-payment facility (EPF) which concealed the true scale of borrowings, since the EPF money was off the balance sheet; in effect the EPF allowed Carillion to delay paying its suppliers, which made it look as if they had more money than they actually had, creating the illusion that it was their money
- securing large advance payments on new contracts and whacking them into the books before the profits had actually been earned.[3]

That list prompts big questions: Who done it? And when will

they be prosecuted? Or will greed and malfeasance carry on with impunity?

During the House of Commons Joint Inquiry, the chair, Rachel Reeves MP, spoke about such accounting scams in a more direct manner for those of us not completely accustomed to the technicalities of high finance. She said: 'I have always been a more avid reader of fiction than non-fiction, but I wonder whether the KPMG audited accounts should be moved in the library from the non-fiction to the fiction section.'[4] Murdo Murchison of Kiltearn, the Edinburgh-based investment fund managers, spoke at the Joint Inquiry. He told the former Inquiry member, Heidi Allen MP: 'What was brought to the table in July last year was evidence of misstatement of profits over a prolonged period of time, evidence of aggressive accounting and evidence of extremely poor operational management which was completely at odds with the way the business was presented to the marketplace.'[5] Of course it wasn't just about the accounts. There was a malignant symbiosis at the very heart of Carillion. The accounting rackets affected how the business was run and the desperate 'dash for cash' business operations were then reflected in decisions about what would be disclosed in the accounts and what didn't need to be. The wheel turned faster and faster, spinning to the tune of 'Anything Goes'. Hereby hangs a tale about Carillion and Battersea Power Station, and another one about houses for serving Armed Forces families.

The construction magazine *Building* tells this story about the Battersea Power Station project. It comes from a London-based contractor in the construction business. He was looking for staff for a new project and noticed that one of the applicants came from Carillion, which by then had gone bust. 'No harm in having him in, and having a look-see,' he thought. So he called the applicant in. It turns out the jobseeker had actually been a Carillion subcontractor before the collapse. We'll call him the candidate to avoid any confusion. Carillion's Battersea project was for the redevelopment of the power station into high-end luxury flats. The first phase was 800 flats in what was known as Circus West.

When the candidate was being interviewed, the contractor asked if he knew about the Battersea contract and what had gone down.

The candidate had been an approved subcontractor for that actual project. His firm was on the Carillion list for the tender. One day, Richard Howson, the Carillion chief executive at the time, phoned him and told him that the bad news was that Carillion hadn't got the contract. Howson told him that Carillion had bid £500 million for the job but that was £50 million more than the client's figure so they had lost it. Then the candidate went on to tell the contractor that some days later Howson called him back. The good news was that Carillion was in after all. They had cut their pitch to £450 million to meet the client's estimate and the deal was done. Howson said that he'd cut the price because part of the deal was that the client was going to pay Carillion £16 million up front in cash. The Carillion subcontractor says he was gobsmacked.

Later, when *Building* heard this story, one of their journalists got in touch with the chief executive of the Battersea Power Station project, Rob Tincknell. He told *Building* that Carillion had 'done a brilliant job', but tellingly he said he didn't know if Carillion had made any money. In July 2018 *Building* noted that the Battersea Power Station story sums up everything you need to know about the whole Carillion debacle: 'That might have sounded ludicrous a year ago, but it doesn't seem so ludicrous any more . . . the way Carillion did business – the losses it was racking up, the blind optimism about getting money in it thought it was owed . . . the hapless performance of some of its executives . . . their "we were surprised as anyone when it went under" chutzpah, and the fact that a £5 billion turnover firm had just £29 million in the bank when it collapsed – mean it's not just unsurprising that it went under, it's incredible that it lasted so long.' [6]

Then there's the Carillion Armed Services housing contract, which exemplifies the fix that Carillion finished up in – in other words how the chickens of taking on contracts at lowest price in services they knew nothing about came home to roost. The repair and maintenance project for 49,000 houses for Services families became an exemplar of Carillion's broken model. Carillion, along with partner Amey, won the new contract in 2014. However, it was really Carillion that ran the business as the 'hands-on' partner.

That involved organising the 'moving in and moving out' process
for Services families. That meant homes and furnishings had to be
made good for new families moving in after others had moved out.
And then repairs also had to be done on demand, which meant
that Carillion was responsible for the maintenance of these properties – everything from boilers to back doors, pest infestation to
plumbing problems. Of course, this contract was going to be yet
another jewel in the crown of two road-builders from the private
sector delivering smarter services for Services families than the
previous MoD providers. Outsourcing would be the answer to the
MoD's prayers.

Except that it didn't work out that way. Firstly, the MoD had
sold the new contractors a total shambles without actually making that clear in the contract spec. Two years into the contract,
things had got so bad that the National Audit Office (NAO) and
the House of Commons Public Accounts Committee had both
been pressed to hold inquiries; both their findings lambasted the
'horrendous' state of the housing services being delivered. Both
inquiries also reported that the crisis in the standards of MoD
homes was likely to be affecting the numbers of Forces person-
nel both joining and staying in the Services. These failures could
be seen to be undermining the safety of the realm, no less. Liz
Phoenix was married to a Royal Marine. Her testimony before the
Public Accounts Committee says it all:

> *Q10 Chair*: Just to be absolutely clear. What's it like from
> your perspective?
>
> *Mrs Phoenix*: We are still seeing people with mouldy and
> damp homes, rat infestations. The big one is no heat-
> ing for weeks on end, even months on end, due to parts
> not being received, no-shows or even engineers turning
> up, banging on the boilers with spanners and walking
> away, leaving people with no heating and no hot water.
> Families are being left with no cooking facilities. It's up
> to CarillionAmey to ensure that the properties have white
> goods and cookers in them.

Q11 Chair: Sorry, are you saying people are moving into properties without white goods?

Mrs Phoenix: Sometimes the cookers are not working or they are in such disrepair that they cannot be used. CarillionAmey staff are telling forces families to go out and buy McDonalds or pizzas, and I find that totally disgusting. These are the things that need to be said. The annoying thing is that in February, when all this was brought up with the Defence Secretary, we were told that things would improve. I'm sorry, but in my personal view and the view of other families, there have not been improvements.[7]

The National Housing Prime Contract, as it was known, was worth £626 million over five years. The MoD estimated that it would save the department £192 million in comparison to the previous costs. It told the Public Accounts Committee that the CarillionAmey bid was the cheapest but 'that it bid against the same set of standards as other companies and the contract was subject to competition'.[8] The Conservative MP Anne-Marie Trevelyan told the committee that after she had spoken out about the crisis she received more than 1,000 complaints from Services families in a year. Carillion told the committee that the systems it created to deal with 30,000 complaints a month had been overwhelmed – there were not enough trained staff, subcontractors were failing, and the new IT system, introduced to replace the old one which was 'at the end of its life', was not 'up and running'. Carillion's MD in charge was Richard Lumby, who had a good reputation in the company. In fact after the £845 million crisis emerged, Keith Cochrane used Lumby as a troubleshooter for a number of the major government contracts, to try and get turnaround.

In his evidence to the Public Accounts Committee, Richard Lumby apologised. He was honest and straightforward, which is much more than can be said for the Carillion directors when they appeared before the House of Commons inquiries later on. Lumby told the Public Accounts Committee that in the last

18 months of the contract, Carillion 'absolutely let ourselves down'. He apologised for 'failing' the families involved. Then he told the committee, 'We have undoubtedly dropped a clanger – many big balls – in the last 18 months. We are incredibly sorry for where we have done that and caused significant failure for them and discomfort.' Mr Lumby admitted that it had to be recognised that Carillion was 'not a housing contractor'. In the Public Accounts Committee Inquiry there was a further exchange between Richard Bacon MP and Richard Lumby that exposes the Services Accommodation contract as all the more typical of Carillion contract cock-ups. They had pitched too low to get the contract and the cash flow it would guarantee, and two years into it Richard Lumby could tell the committee Carillion were still not in profit. The exchange started with the MP asking Lumby about what Carillion had been paid so far:

> *Q160 Mr Bacon*: Between November 2014 and to the end of March 2016, the Department had paid £115.3 million to CarillionAmey under the contract. Have you made a profit?
>
> *Richard Lumby*: No.
>
> *Q161 Mr Bacon*: You haven't. You have made a loss?
>
> *Richard Lumby*: We are not in profit. Our investment has been far greater than we expected. We have continued to commit to that. We have clearly got some backlog. We have taken some penalties. We have put some more people in place. We are doing that because we have to do it. We are compelled to do it, and we want to deliver a service to the Service families.[9]

Lumby was as good as his word and the services to the families did improve in the following two years. A subsequent update report from the NAO acknowledged the improvements, but noted that there were still many targets which had not been reached. Just over half of the families surveyed said they were satisfied with the service when they were surveyed. The NAO expressed the view that the government had seriously misjudged CarillionAmey's capacity to deliver a service which they 'accepted they were not equipped to deliver'. According to the Labour MP Chris Evans, who was then on the Public Accounts Committee, a week after the £845 million profit warning the government extended CarillionAmey's contract for the Forces families housing for a further two years. Evans says it should have been terminated, not extended. Of course the UK's 'outsourcing' Conservatives wouldn't see it that way.

The two Richards' stories – Howson and Lumby – taken together provide irrefutable evidence of Carillion's *leitmotiv* of cutting corners – in accounts, in bids and in business. Yet for years and years they got away with it. That could only happen with complicity – the complicity of their auditors, KPMG and Deloitte. We have already detailed what we might now call 'the Emma Mercer whistle-blowing' about how the use of negative accruals played out. It ends up establishing that the accounts are £170 million out. That needs to be reconciled with the rest of the balance sheet or the 2016 accounts will need to be called in and re-stated. One way and another the balance sheet is reconciled by the Carillion directors and KPMG declares the 2016 accounts can stand – 'the profits declared are appropriate'. So the 2016 accounts, published on 1 March 2017, were 'true and fair', and Carillion was a 'going concern' according to KPMG. Four months later there's a write-down of £845 million. The 'going concern' was gone pretty soon after that. The balance sheet was about to take a massive hit because quite simply the sums didn't add up. The verdict of the MPs on the Joint Inquiry about the KPMG failures was unequivocal: 'KPMG was paid £29 million to act as Carillion's auditor for 19 years. It did not once qualify its audit opinion, complacently signing off the directors' increasingly fantastical figures. In failing to exercise professional scepticism towards Carillion's accounting judgements over the course of its tenure as Carillion's auditor, KPMG was complicit in them.'[10]

2018 was not a great year for KPMG. An investigation into its audits for Carillion in 2014, 2015 and 2016 had been set up by the audit watchdog, the Financial Reporting Council (FRC) after the Carillion collapse. Then, come May 2018, there was the lambasting of the auditors in the Reeves–Field Joint Parliamentary Inquiry. A month later, the FRC reported that KPMG was the worst performing of the Big Four auditors (KPMG, Deloitte, PwC and EY) following an 'unacceptable deterioration' in the quality of its work. The FRC found more than half of KPMG's audits for FTSE 350 companies required considerable improvements. No doubt that finding had been influenced by another FRC report published a week earlier that determined KPMG had botched several audits for the software firm Quindell. In 2014, Quindell's profits in its 2013 accounts were investigated. In those accounts, KPMG had approved an £83 million profit. After the investigation this had to be amended, in a later restatement, to a £68 million loss. That's a £151 million turnaround – hardly a couple of slips of an account-ant's pencil here and there. KPMG was fined £4.5 million by the regulator for failing to find that 'the financial statements were not free from material misstatement' – the books were cooked and somehow they missed that. In August 2018 there was more cen-sure, and a £3 million fine, after KPMG admitted misconduct in its audits of the fashion house Ted Baker in 2013 and 2014.

Then, just when they might have been thinking that things couldn't get much worse, their trading update to the year ending September 2018 surprisingly showed a profits surge to £365 mil-lion. That meant that in the year when KPMG was centre-stage in the Carillion cover-up, the average pay for its 600-plus partners soared by £100,000 to £600,000. The chairman and senior part-ner Bill Michael's personal earnings were £2.1 million. The letter Bill Michael wrote to the Reeves–Field Inquiry shows that between 2008 and the end of 2017, when KPMG continued as Carillion's external auditors, their fees totalled £18.66 million.

Deloitte were Carillion's internal auditors. They were engaged to advise on risk management. Given the outcomes they were clearly not successful. Carillion paid Deloitte £7.5 million for that service. Consultancy fees and corporate finance fees logged another £2.8 million, making a grand total of £10.3 million. The risk portfolio included Deloitte advising on debt recovery. It is therefore some-what surprising they were unaware that Carillion was in dispute with the Doha property company in Qatar over who owed whom £200 million. Rounded up, from 2008, Deloitte and KPMG were paid £29 million to assist in what became the Carillion collapse.

Rachel Reeves MP and Frank Field MP were the driving forces behind the House of Commons Work and Pensions and Business Committees Joint Inquiry. It started taking oral evidence at the end of January 2018. Rachel Reeves says it was a matter of astonishment to her that six evidence sessions, and five weeks later, not one witness had said there were problems with Carillion before March 2017, when the 2016 accounts were published. Up to that point there had been a parade of 17 witnesses, including Stephen Hadrill of the FRC, Richard Ellison, chair of the Carillion Trustees Pension Fund, every director of Carillion, Howson, Adam, Khan, Cochrane, Green, Horner, Mercer, KPMG's Michelle Hinchliffe and Peter Meehan, and Deloitte's Michael Jones. The log-jam was broken when the investment managers from Blackrock, Standard Life Aberdeen and Kiltearn gave testimony. Murdo Murchison of Kiltearn suggested that the notion that the collapse happened over a matter of months in 2017 was preposterous. So how come not a word was spoken like that before he sat in front of the MPs?

To paraphrase Samuel Johnson – maybe the sight of the metaphorical hangman's noose concentrated minds and kept everyone else on message. And the message was clear enough. There was a cataclysmic collapse in four or five major contracts in a matter of months after March 2017 which resulted in the £845 million write-down. Nobody could have seen it coming, so nobody is to blame. There was a 'perfect storm'. There was no escape. Zafar Khan says he was 'surprised' when the write-down emerged; Philip Green talks about 'the extent and speed of the deterioration'; Howson says, given what they knew at the time, it was correct to sign off the 2016 accounts. 'We are all in this together', don't you know. Bill Michael, chairman of KPMG, was right on message on 2 February 2018 when he wrote to Reeves and Field to defend KPMG: 'An audit opinion is an audit opinion on a company's accounts at a particular time . . . In some industries, construction being one, an accumulation of adverse developments in specific areas of the business can quite quickly cause a precipitous decline.

It does not follow automatically from a company collapse either that the opinion of management was wrong, or that the auditor did a bad job.'[11] It's at times like these that having *alma mater* ties through school, or university, or completing your CA qualification at one of the Big Four, kicks in. Take Bill Michael's representative on Carillion's earth, Peter Meehan, KPMG's head of external audit for Carillion. The same Peter Meehan who signed off the 2016 accounts. This chap – and most of them were chaps – would speak for everybody when it became necessary, he'd stay on message and explain that the crash was sudden and surprising and no-one could have seen it coming. As the accountants' nemesis, Professor Prem Sikka, is fond of repeating, 'When all is said and done this is, after all, the chaps investigating the chaps.'

During the Joint Parliamentary Inquiry, the chair, Rachel Reeves, tackled Meehan about his 'perfect storm' explanation. She asked, 'You honestly expect people to believe that between March and July all this happened and, up until then, things were going well . . . nothing could have been foreseen?'[12] Meehan replied that there were a series of significant adverse events on a small number of contracts. Right on message. Pressed later by Reeves on whether he would have done anything differently if he had his time again he replied: 'The answer is, for everything I reflect on, me and my team all did the best we could and the best job. I stand by the opinion that we gave on the 31 December 2016 accounts.'[13] Earlier, in the same proceedings, Peter Kyle MP challenged Michelle Hinchliffe, head of audit at KPMG, and Meehan about this approval of the 2016 accounts. Told that KPMG had approved the published balance sheet based on Carillion management's records, he retorted: 'For me it comes down to this; I would not hire you to do an audit of the contents of my fridge, because, when I read it I would not know what is actually in my fridge or not.'

Who could have predicted the perfect storm? Not Peter Meehan. Not Michelle Hinchliffe. Not the directors. Not the accountants. Not the advisors. No-one. So how could it be that everyone associated with the £845 million debacle delivered the same cover-up sentences? There just might be a clue in the actual 10 July 2017 Trading Statement issued to the Stock Exchange. On page 3 it notes that the contacts for the media are Liz Morley and Sam Cartwright of the PR giant Bell Pottinger, with their mobile numbers attached. So Bell Pottinger, which would be swallowed up in one of the world's biggest accounting scandals a matter of months later, were on PR point duty for Carillion trying to explain away the £845 million catastrophe. In fact, it is wholly possible that while Bell Pottinger were on the Carillion case at the briefing in St Paul's, in London's Aldgate, another arm of their own business was fighting for its life in a media circus elsewhere in the city. There, Bell Pottinger were attempting to deal with their own growing media controversy about a cut-throat Bell Pottinger PR campaign in South Africa. It had aimed to defend the corrupt regime of President Jacob Zuma and his business links with the Indian millionaire Gupta brothers, by playing the race card in a way which resurrected the old divisions of apartheid.

In December 2016 Bell Pottinger, affectionally known as 'BellPotts' in the PR business, were appointed as Carillion's PR advisors on investor relations. Before we consider the company's fatal South African adventure we might note some of those on the 'BellPotts' client list before the Carillion board fell into their embrace. The list includes Oscar Pistorius, the Olympic 'Blade Runner', at the time he was charged with the murder of his girlfriend Reeva Steenkamp; the Assads of Syria; the Pinochet Foundation of the blood-soaked Chilean dictator, Augusto Pinochet; and the governments of Egypt, Bahrain and Belarus. Top of this list is the $540 million contract Bell Pottinger had with the US military for making covert propaganda videos, passed off as Arabic news channels during the Iraq war. And, of course, the former Tory leader, Margaret Thatcher, whose rise and rise was plotted by Bell Pottinger's co-founder, Lord Tim Bell.[14]

Carillion's previous PR firm had been Finsbury PR, chaired by founder Roland Rudd, who is the brother of Amber Rudd, the former Tory Home Secretary. It seems Finsbury were heavily favoured by Richard Adam. When he left Carillion, late in December 2016, there was a push for change from which Bell Pottinger emerged triumphant. It isn't easy to ascertain how the Bell Pottinger deal was done, especially as no-one on the Carillion board or connected previously to Bell Pottinger is prepared to answer questions. What is clear is that the Bell Pottinger big sell must have come from the top. The board needed to approve the decision, as this was a key appointment for communicating with investors and potential investors. That included getting investors on-side with board proposals. The appointment could not have been approved without the support of key board members – most importantly Philip Green.

So to South Africa, where, at the time of the emerging scandal Green had his second home. In January 2016, Lord Tim Bell, co-founder of Bell Pottinger, who died in August 2019, went to meet the Gupta brothers in Johannesburg. In post-apartheid South Africa the Guptas' business empire dwarfed even the capital held by South Africa's old money in minerals, chiefly gold, nickel and aluminium. But the Guptas' crusade wasn't a miracle of free enterprise. Instead it had been built on connections with South Africa's Godfather president, Jacob Zuma. The notorious double act became known in South Africa as 'the Zuptas'. Such was the stench of corruption surrounding them and their shakedown business dealings that the idea of 'state capture' emerged as a way of explaining what was going on: 'State capture goes beyond simple corruption. It involves the systematic ransacking of institutions, so that the nation's laws and regulations, as well as the people in positions of power, work for the financial benefit of groups or individuals. The singular aim of state capture is to facilitate the plunder of state resources for the benefit of politically connected individuals and their corporate vehicles.'[15]

These definitions link the Carillion oligarchs, looting the British state, with a PR outfit defending those perpetrating the same looting of the state in South Africa. By April 2018 the charge list against Zuma from the South African prosecutors had reached 700 cases. Zuma, still living in South Africa, and the Guptas, from their new residence in Dubai, deny all the accusations of bribery, corruption and state capture made against them. Bell says he opposed any Zupta deal, but he was over-ruled. 'Why don't we defend the Zuptas with a return to the old apartheid accusations?' must have been the Bell Pottinger pitch. They would develop the message that if you criticise Zuma or the Guptas, in effect, you are back on racist apartheid territory. The argument would be made explicitly that the Zuptas are black and represent the economic emancipation of the blacks of South Africa, which is now being challenged by the age-old power of 'white monopoly capital'. Simple. A huge section of the South African media were sold the pass – in more ways than one.

Towards the end of 2016 Bell Pottinger had whipped up a political storm where 'white monopoly capital skulduggery' became the rhetorical riposte to the growing clamour for something to be done about the racketeering of the Guptas and Zuma. In November 2016 the former South African public prosecutor, Thuli Madonsela, published a report indicting the Guptas for widespread bribery and corruption of officials, involving state contracts running to hundreds of millions of rands. She also noted that Bell Pottinger had attempted to stir up racial anger in South Africa, mounting a 'hateful and divisive campaign to divide South Africa along the lines of race'.[16] The point here is that at the time when this controversy was raging in South Africa, Carillion appointed Bell Pottinger as its PR advisors. Less than a year later, on 4 September 2017, the UK's PR regulator found Bell Pottinger guilty of four breaches of the PR code of conduct and expelled the company from membership for five years. The regulator described Bell Pottinger's work in South Africa as 'the most blatant instance of unethical PR practice I've ever seen'. By this time all the prestigious clients had gone. Carillion dispensed with BellPott's services on the same day as the regulator's report was published. Scarcely a week later Bell Pottinger was in administration and went bankrupt soon after.

The Bell Pottinger deal tied Carillion into a chain that also included KPMG, who were the auditors for the Gupta business empire. In March 2019, KPMG's Jacques Wessels was struck off as an auditor by the South African Regulatory Board after he admitted six charges of misconduct, which amounted to an 'egregious form of dishonesty'. There seems to be a lot of it about in KPMG. The charges on the Gupta audit included using a state-funded dairy farm business, owned by the Guptas, for money laundering. Wessels also signed off accounts for the farm, which had a £500,000 spend on a Gupta family wedding, put through as legitimate business expenses.

So one way and another the Bell Pottinger hire has the look of another example of calamitous serial bungling by the Carillion directors, who never seemed to miss the opportunity to make the worst of a bad job. In October 2019 the President of South Africa, Cyril Ramaphosa, made that case even more significant. He announced at a *Financial Times* 'Africa Summit' in London that the cost of corruption in the ten-year rule of Jacob Zuma had now been estimated at an extraordinary $34 billion or 500 billion South African rand. That is roughly equivalent to 10% of the annual value of South Africa's GDP. Jacob Zuma and the Guptas will struggle to protest their innocence against the scale of these accusations. That said, maybe the money lavished on Bell Pottinger by the Carillion board was well spent, because the Bell Pottinger 'perfect storm' message served the needs of the Carillion directors for a cover-up for a long time in the UK.

Rachel Reeves is crystal clear on that. She told me: 'They can't say there was a problem before March because if there was they should have told their shareholders – that is the problem they have. They are trying to present to the outside world, to their investors, that everything was OK. Now if they did that whilst they knew it wasn't, I think that would be criminal. It would be criminal to present something that was knowingly wrong. So they can't.'[17] Reeves acknowledges that the House of Commons Select Committee system has its limitations: 'Maybe a Select Committee isn't the best way to get to the truth, because they are not going to say in public "Look, hands up, we should never have published those accounts" . . . They are not going to say that; they are not going to say, "Yeah, we knew there were big problems".'

Philip Long scoffs at the idea that the Carillion directors never saw the collapse coming. He should know; in 2018 he retired as head of corporate recovery for Pannell Kerr Forster after being hands-on in insolvency for almost 40 years. When we meet in London he's got extracts from the Carillion 2016 accounts in his briefcase. Speaking of which, he says that 'not fit for purpose is the nicest way of putting it'. He refers to the fact that the directors signed off the accounts published on 1 March 2017. 'All was fine, according to the reports in the accounts from the chair and the finance director – in fact as far as everyone quoted in the annual report is concerned. Including the auditors KPMG,' he says. He argues that the facts provide a stark contrast to the glowing future that was forecast. He refers to a copy of the consolidated balance sheet from the 2016 Carillion accounts – page 93. His first example is 'trade and receivables', which is the general figure indicating a company's trading strength. The accounts show the worth of 'trade and receivables' as £1.664 billion. The bad news is that a matter of months after that, the £845 million July 2017 write-down was posted. In other words, the July write-down amounts to half the notional worth of the company. 'You can't have that. This 50% collapse didn't just fall from the sky overnight. That can't happen in four months,' Philip Long says.

His second exhibit is on the same page – the net assets – another indication of what the company is worth. He points out that the net asset value in 2015 is £1.016 billion. In 2016 the net asset value is £730 million (£729.9 million to be exact). He says, 'So in the one year the value of the company plunged £286 million – that's going on for a third! So we are told the worth of the company drops by almost £300 million and nobody notices?' He says he finds it hard to believe that the directors at Carillion come July 2017 were walking around scratching their heads saying, 'Blow me, where did that come from?' 'They knew what was happening. They knew.' To develop the argument, it is worth repeating some of the facts from Carillion's financial history which have been already considered, but this time with the purpose of challenging the view of the directors, auditors and advisors that the collapse was born of a sudden 'perfect storm'. Of course there are none so blind as those who refuse to see. Consider only a few of the findings of the House of Commons Library researchers. In March 2018 they produced a briefing on Carillion. It states:

- Although the July 2017 profit warning marks the beginning of the end for Carillion, it is poor decisions in the years leading up to it that caused the company serious trouble.

- On 29 September 2017, Carillion's half-year financial statements revealed a total hit to the company's worth of £1.2 billion – enough to wipe out the profits from the previous eight years put together.
- In the five-and-a-half-year period from January 2012 to June 2017, Carillion paid out £333 million more in dividends than it generated in cash from its operations.
- Over the eight years from December 2009 to January 2018, the total owed by Carillion in loans increased from £242 million to an estimated £1.3 billion – more than five times the value at the beginning of the decade.[18]

Frances Coppola is an experienced economic commentator. She is a senior contributor to the American business journal *Forbes*. She draws on the House of Commons briefing paper statistics to show that Carillion was in dire straits long before the first profits write-down of 2017. She notes that whilst Carillion borrowings increased exponentially in the 2009 to 2018 period, they produced practically no additional cash revenues: 'For a company whose entire business model relies on increasing net cash flow, this is disastrous.' She supports the Philip Long view that attempting to explain the crash away as a consequence of unexpected deteriorations in a few contracts is make-believe: 'The truth is that Carillion was living on borrowed time from 2011 onwards. It survived so long because accounting standards enabled it to disguise its true financial position and auditors turned a blind eye ... Carillion had no money, no cash, no profits, no assets and no future.'[19]

The truth is that, far from a calamitous collapse over three or four months, Carillion's crisis was long in the making. We could start as far back as 2011 with the ruinous £300 million purchase of Eaga. But for the sake of brevity, fast-forward to 2015 and the Swiss bank UBS. In March 2015, the equity analysts there identified Carillion shares as a strong possibility for shorting – that is betting that they would drop in value. At that time the shares were trading at 348p, but UBS identified a possible short position of 250p to 235p. The UBS analysts made these predictions because, at that time, they identified the persistent downward trend in Carillion's share values; they warned about the scale of Carillion's mounting debts, its growing pension deficit and its accounting practices devised to conceal the true nature of its balance sheet. On 2 April 2015 the Carillion board meeting at Maddox Street had to consider the UBS report. Richard Adam, then the finance director, dismissed it, saying 'those issues could apply to any organisation'. Despite that, here is irrefutable proof that the principal vectors in Carillion's crash were being identified at least three years before it happened.

The board minutes record that, at that time, 9% of Carillion stock was shorted. This 'short' selling position would grow and grow in the succeeding years to the stage where, in late 2017, Carillion shares became the most shorted stock on the Stock Exchange. At the start of the year, 25% of the stock was shorted, which grew to a peak position touching 35% by the end of the year.[20] This shorting trend is an indication of a widespread belief, lasting for years, that Carillion was a 'basket case'. The National Audit Office report on Carillion identifies that shorting was first developing in 2012. The UBS 2015 report demonstrates without question that these indications of developing crisis were evident long before March 2017.

Similarly, the divestment of Carillion shares by Standard Life (now part of Standard Life Aberdeen with funds of £640 billion) is a tell-tale sign. In December 2015, Standard Life held more than 10% of Carillion stock. By the time of the July 2017 write-down, Standard Life had ceased to have any active shareholding in Carillion – all sold in 18 months. The two joint chairs of Standard Life Aberdeen told the Reeves–Field Joint Inquiry that they adopted this 'sell' position so far back because they had 'concerns on a number of issues, including strategy, financial management and corporate governance'.[21] So investment brokers sitting on the outside were more prescient than the directors in the inside? Perhaps the Carillion directors and friends, who explained the collapse as a result of a deterioration which came in months, had forgotten the crystal-clear crisis warning of the Standard Life disinvestment. Or did they decide to overlook it, to be better able to dissemble when the questions came about their own disastrous stewardship of the company?

Then take Zafar Khan. In his fumbling, stuttering performance in front of the Reeves–Field Joint Inquiry he was asked by Frank Field MP if he was surprised that 'the whole thing crashed?' Khan replied, 'Yes, I was surprised. I was surprised at the outcome that eventually came to pass.' That's on 6 February 2018. Two weeks later, in reply to further questions from the Joint Inquiry, Khan writes 'I do genuinely believe that it was the level of debt which had been allowed to grow in previous years which was the principal contributing factor to the difficulties Carillion experienced in 2017 as trading conditions worsened.' The 'perfect storm' defence has a calendar of events measured in months. Here Khan recognises that the financial time-bomb had been ticking for years. The 'Lessons Learned' document – 7 June 2017 – written by Khan after the 'negative accruals' imbroglio, identifies a number of key lessons. One of them is that Carillion staff must stand by 'one version of the truth' in all future business dealings. There are two versions here.

The 'perfect storm' line of argument raises serious issues about those who were nearest the 'scene of the crime' of Carillion's downfall, as Murdo Murchison said in evidence. The question remains: did their adherence to the 'perfect storm' cover-up, and stonewalling at the various House of Commons inquiries, mean that they were guilty of misleading parliament?

CHAPTER 6

The Empire Strikes Back

'Government accused of big business love-in over Manzoni Whitehall job.'

Guardian headline, 2 October 2014

Professor Rudi Klein has been chief executive of the Specialist Engineering Contractors' Group (SEC Group) for more than 25 years. He is also a barrister. To get to his office in London you take the Tube to Tower Hill, then walk alongside the walls of the Tower of London into East Smithfield Street. From there it's ten minutes' walk. His office is an old customs house in the former St Katharine's and Wapping docks. He's a big character, which becomes pretty obvious soon after you meet him. From the SEC Group offices, Klein lobbies on behalf of the largest sector of the UK construction industry – the specialist engineering sector, which is made up of SMEs in the main. He runs an unremitting campaign for the reform of what he calls the 'desperate practices of the construction industry'. He majors in government contracts introducing special conditions to weed out rogue contractors, project bank accounts being used on all public sector contracts, and the retentions system being abolished. Klein argues that the simplicity of mandating project bank accounts would create much more transparency about what should be getting paid out for all those involved in the agreed contract. It means that the Government sponsors can see what is going on and the subcontractors can see what is in the bank and thus the probable schedule for payment. This is especially important in circumstances where large companies, like Carillion, insist on retention payments – the holding back of a percentage of the sub-contractors' due payments until the job is completed satisfactorily. This seems reasonable, but in reality it has been abused to the point where the lead contractors use the retentions to hold the sub-contractors to ransom. As one sub-contractor told me, 'They tell you if you don't accept reduced rates for completing the job you'll never see the retention money.'

Rudi Klein was invited on to the government Carillion Task Force shortly after the collapse. It was supposed to learn lessons from the crash, but Klein thinks that the Carillion reports will probably join the 15 others that have been produced about the construction industry in recent years. 'Where?' 'On the shelf,' he says. He shrugs his shoulders. 'After every collapse there is another task force – after the horse has bolted. When Carillion went bust, they kept referring to it in the news as a construction company. It wasn't a construction company, it was a finance house. They didn't do construction, they did money. They didn't think the bubble would burst.' He talks about a pervasive unscrupulousness in business culture in the UK which is seriously damaging the British economy. He says the construction industry is a special victim, in this regard. 'Jarvis never paid anyone – look, years before Carillion,' he adds, referring to a previous construction giant which went bust. He tells the true story of a Jarvis subcontractor who rang a Jarvis manager to thank him for sending a cheque for payment. The manager asked: 'Did you issue court proceedings?' The subcontractor responded, 'No.' The manager then asked if he could have the cheque back. Rudi likes the tale and laughs loudly when he finishes it. You can see he is exercised about this. He's not kidding. 'Greed got Carillion to where they were. They believed they were too big to fail. They believed "the banks won't pull the plug on us, the Government won't put us under". 'Us' gets emphasised. 'It ended up a zombie company with no assets to speak of.'

I ask him what he thinks of the cover story from the Carillion directors and auditors that it was all a sudden collapse, that no-one could see it coming, so no-one could be blamed. He says that everybody in the industry knew that Carillion was in big trouble. Maybe the scale of the profits write-down was more than expected, but he argues that the confirmation of Carillion's broken business model, inherent in the 10 July declaration, was not. 'People thought something like this had been a matter of time,' he tells me. But we know that there was a united cadre for whom this was seemingly not the case – the directors, the auditors and the advisors. Then they were joined by the Government. According to the National Audit Office's Carillion report, the July announcement caught the responsible government department unawares: 'The size of the profit warning of 10 July came as a surprise to the Cabinet Office as it contradicted the information and commentary Carillion had given it, up to that point, as well as the publicly available financial information; and expectations of the market.'[1]

The fact that they were surprised is a surprise, given the much acclaimed framework the government had created to monitor the financial health of strategic suppliers some five years before. It defined a company as a 'strategic supplier' if it had contracts across several departments worth more than a £100 million a year. In January 2018 there were 28 of them, including Carillion. According to the system, each of these mega-concerns was given a risk rating of red, amber or green – the RAG scale as it was known. Red flagged 'significant material concerns'. Black, beyond that, embraced more serious failings, including 'financial distress' or 'serious underperformance on a contract'. These ratings were defined by the Crown Representatives who, in theory, reported to the Commercial Relationships Board (CRB) of the Cabinet Office every six weeks. There was a Crown rep, as they are known, assigned to Carillion as part of this Cabinet Office system.

The Crown reps are not full-time civil servants; rather they are more like advisory consultants. Almost all of them are part-time and many only work one day a week. They are often recruited for their experience in business, particularly the sectors of business where they are going to be the government's 'eyes and ears'. So if the strategic supplier is a large IT provider, ideally the Crown rep will be someone with considerable experience in the outsourcing of mega-IT contracts. The RAG system serves dual purposes. It is a key performance indicator for the work of the Crown rep, but also for the company being rated. From August 2013 until January 2016 Carillion's rating was coded green for 'no known issues'. In February 2016 there was then a downgrading to amber caused by problems with contracts in the MoD and for the HM prisons in England and Wales. Although there were continuing question marks about Carillion's payment systems, the rating stayed at amber for almost 18 months – 'it is only one or two contracts causing concern' – until the profits write-down in July 2017. This suggests that Carillion's escalating debts, pension deficits and the departure of its finance director on the one hand did not cause the Crown rep any concern, and on the other didn't create any red flags for the Cabinet Office politicians who were supposed to be 'hands on' for all major public contracts.

Who were they? The actual answer varies because of the 'revolving door' of ministerial promotions and sackings in Theresa May's government. Damian Green MP, as the first Secretary of State at the Cabinet Office, was, in effect, Mrs May's deputy. He had been promoted to the post after her disastrous performance as leader of the Conservatives in the snap General Election of June 2017. He stood in for her at PMQs and sat beside her on the front benches in the Commons, renewing close ties that had first bound them together when they were undergraduates at Oxford University. Green went out through the revolving door late in December 2017, after he admitted lying about the presence of pornographic images on his House of Commons computer, which had first been discovered many years earlier. So Green was the minister ultimately responsible for the monitoring of Carillion's projects until the very eve of its demise.

In May's January 2019 reshuffle, David Lidington MP took over from Green as the first Secretary of State at the Cabinet Office. He had been the Minister of Justice in May's government. He was elected as Conservative MP for Aylesbury in 1992 and had risen through the Tory ranks almost without trace. Critically, Lidington was appointed on 8 January 2018 – a week before the Carillion collapse. He was thus a 'rookie Cabinet Secretary', totally in the hands of the top civil servant, John Manzoni, who was Permanent Secretary to the Cabinet Office. Manzoni was also the chief executive of the Civil Service which, as a consequence of the twin powers, effectively made him the most powerful civil servant in Whitehall. Lidington recalls that he was appointed between 1 pm and 2 pm on the afternoon of 8 January. At some point that evening Manzoni put his head round the door of Lidington's office and said, 'I need to have a word about Carillion.' The choice of pronoun might be significant – 'I' not 'we'.

Before his ascension to the throne as 'King John', in February 2014 Manzoni was appointed to the Cabinet Office as Chief Secretary to the Major Projects Authority. So he knew about Carillion. He was recruited after working for 30 years in the oil business, including 24 years as global head of operations for BP. Lord Browne, who was formerly Manzoni's boss as the chief executive of BP, was a member of David Cameron's cabinet when Manzoni took up the Major Projects Authority post. In fact, the *Guardian* reported that Lord Browne was one of six members of the appointments panel who subsequently chose Manzoni as chief executive.[2] Both of them reflected the ethos of making the Cabinet Office and Civil Service feel the so-called cutting edge of the commercial world by recruiting business leaders to transform these government bureaucracies. Of course this was not a new practice – it was first instituted by the Labour Government led by Tony Blair, and then continued by successive governments. In October 2014, Manzoni was appointed as the first ever chief executive of the Civil Service and Permanent Secretary to the Cabinet Office, and has been in post ever since. He has made it a priority to recruit more business leaders to the higher echelons of the Civil Service. He created what he called 'a new career path' and correspondingly vastly increased pay scales, which he said were essential to attract big business talent. In this sense he has been the major mover in the creation of what is now well on the way to becoming the 'Civil Service oligarchy'.

Manzoni's chief commercial officer, heading up the Government's commercial capabilities and contract management within the orbit of the Cabinet Office, is Gareth Rhys Williams. Rhys Williams had a previous career as chief executive in a number of businesses. His most recent position was as CEO to PHS, an outsourcing facilities management company, and before that, his previous posts range from CEO of a FTSE 250 engineering concern, and earlier, CEO to a supplier of photographic and broadcast equipment and services. He was recruited in March 2016 to lead the transformation of the Government's commercial relations, particularly on its major contracts. With Manzoni as his immediate boss, Rhys Williams produced 'commercial blueprints' for all the commercial programmes within major government departments inside a year of his appointment. In a letter to the Public Accounts Committee he explained: 'The overall thrust of these plans is to concentrate more and better resources on early strategic work to ensure that we procure the right things; and also to ensure that we have the right resources to manage each contract through all its stages.'[3]

Rhys Williams is probably in the top ten of the best-paid executives in the Civil Service. In December 2017 government top pay announcements recorded his salary as £250,000 a year. If Rhys Williams sat down beside you on a train you probably would not think 'oligarch' or 'big business'. You'd most likely think 'grandee' and you'd be right. Rhys Williams is actually Sir Gareth Ludovic Emrys Rhys-Williams, 3rd Baronet of the Miskin, in the Welsh parish of Llantrisant. His grandfather, who was a Liberal MP, was awarded a hereditary peerage for political services. He was the one who inserted Rhys into the family name to give it its prerequisite double-barrel. Sir Gareth's late father, Sir Brandon Meredith Rhys Williams, was the Conservative MP for Kensington between 1974 and 1988.

If the Cabinet Office buck on Carillion stops with Manzoni and Rhys Williams, the derelictions of duty they should account for include the fact that the Cabinet Office had no direct phone calls or any official face-to-face meetings with Carillion chiefs for the five weeks before the July statement. Worse: when the statement was made public, the Cabinet Office only had reliable information on Carillion's central government contracts like the MoD, Ministry of Justice and the Home Office. It had no reports on Carillion's contracts with Network Rail, the NHS, local authorities and the school contracts in England and Wales. This means that come 10 July 2017, the Cabinet Office was oblivious to the real standing of 385 Carillion contracts that were worth £875 million.[4] So when Carillion's crisis emerged, the Cabinet Office running the Government, which was also responsible for overseeing its major contracts, only had reliable data on one in ten of Carillion's contracts.

Eight days after the £845 million write-down, the Cabinet Office's Commercial Relationships Board (CRB), run by Rhys Williams, discussed the situation and decided to recommend a downgrade of Carillion to a red risk warning – 'significant material concerns'. That red grading was finally approved by the CRB, and presumably Rhys Williams, two months later, after legal advice, in September 2017. According to Carillion's interim chief executive, Keith Cochrane, between July and September 2017 – critical months for Carillion's developing crisis – there was also no Crown rep linked to the company for that entire period. This was due to what the Cabinet Office initially explained away as 'normal staff turnover'. It was thus apparently acceptable to the Cabinet Office, Manzoni and Rhys Williams included, to respond to a developing financial crisis in Carillion and their own parallel staff crisis by resorting to 'normal' procedures' – 'Stay calm and use the approved appointments system.'

Earlier in this narrative the arrangements that the Carillion board made, late in 2016, to take out a £112 million loan on the German Schuldschein markets were considered. The loan appears in another context regarding the role of the Crown reps when Richard Howson is questioned about it, in February 2018, when he appears before a House of Commons inquiry, this time convened by the Public Accounts Committee (PAC). This is some time after Carillion has gone down. The committee questioner offers the opinion that playing the Schuldschein markets was 'highly unusual', and asks if the government knew at any time that Carillion was borrowing this money and in these circumstances. Howson replies: 'I can't remember whether we discussed it with our Crown Rep or not.' The Joint Inquiry report of the Reeves and Field Committees found that the assignment of a Crown rep to Carillion 'served no noticeable purpose in alerting the Government to potential issues in advance of the company's July 2017 profit warning'.[5] No noticeable purpose.

At the point of the profits write-down a clear conclusion can be drawn – the Government, Government ministers and top civil servants failed Carillion. They were never on top of the developing crisis. What then follows with the politicians and the civil servants in charge can be interpreted as a textbook example of 'covering your own back'. This was done by going into 'Carillion is a goner anyway' mode, to deflect blame from them for their earlier failures. In civil servant-speak they were saying 'Carillion was doomed, so even if we were a bit behind the curve before the profits warning, it made no material difference. It was going down the tubes anyway.' On 20 July – just ten days after the profits warning – the Cabinet Office called a summit of Carillion customers in all government departments. This was to play catch-up on all the major contracts where there were no reports on current standings. Arguably, the meeting had another purpose – the Carillion customers, in addition to reports on the current state of affairs, were instructed to provide Government with their contingency plans if Carillion went bust. This can be seen as the Government taking the first steps in preparing for Carillion's demise. The NAO report on Carillion considers the direction of Government policy after the profits warning: 'On 20 July it started to enhance government contingency plans for the possible failure of Carillion and told us it notified Carillion that it was doing so. It appointed law firm Dentons on 24 August. It also appointed PwC on 17 September to advise on contingency planning and dealing with the consequences of insolvency.'[6]

The Minister of Transport when Carillion crashed was Chris Grayling MP. On 12 March 2018 he told Lilian Greenwood MP, chair of the House of Commons Transport Committee, that contingency plans for all the Department of Transport ALBs (Arms Length Businesses) began immediately after the July 2017 profit warning. Further, he admits that the purpose was to co-ordinate contingency plans for a Carillion collapse. Grayling says: 'This included plans for a "day one" situation if Carillion were to enter liquidation.' His department not only reviewed all the ALB plans but 'refined and strengthened them to better understand the level of risk and the companies' planned response if Carillion were to enter liquidation'.[7] That's unequivocal. Thus it may have been overlooked that when the profits warning was made, a fatal dichotomy about Carillion's future began to develop. The key civil servants were advising the Government that Carillion was doomed and that requisite preparations should be made for its collapse, whilst at the same time, the Carillion directors were desperately seeking Government financial help to keep it going. The fact that PwC were hired in September 2017, four months before the collapse, and instructed to prepare for insolvency, is surely pivotal in this line of argument.

Putting the Carillion jigsaw together involves considering evidence which is revealed sometime in the future about events that took place in the past – the House of Commons Reeves–Field Inquiry takes place in the early months of 2018. But evidence given at that inquiry then explains what happened some time before, when there was the £845 million write-down which occurred in July 2017. We can proceed, on this theme, with another case in point. It is irrefutable that by the autumn of 2017 the top brass in the Civil Service had advised local government the length and breadth of the UK to prepare for the worst regarding Carillion. Consider a declaration from the head of procurement in the UK's second biggest council, Birmingham. Nigel Kletz, as well as being the director of Birmingham's commissioning and procurement was, at the time, also chair of the National Advisory Group for Local Government Procurement.

In March 2018 he's on the record at the Public Administration and Constitutional Affairs Committee (PACAC), in reference to the direction of Government policy after the July write-down: 'We got good intelligence from the Cabinet Office, Crown Commercial Service and through the LGA [Local Government Association] of the profit warnings and the risks to this . . . Luckily we were able to ready the alternative suppliers to take contracts on board and we did that in the autumn through the advice and advance warning we had.' Then he's asked for additional clarification:

> Q307 *Kelvin Hopkins MP*: In a sense, you saw a long way ahead that there might be problems with Carillion?

> *Nigel Kletz*: We were advised that that was the case.[8]

That's also unequivocal. David Simmonds was the Conservative leader of the LGA. He told the same committee that the Government had been in contact with the LGA since July. He said that, from then onwards, local government was advised to make contingency planning for the failure of Carillion a priority. The Cabinet Office had performed a dialectical U-turn – from knowing nothing and doing nothing, it was on Carillion's case and performing a guiding role in advising about what had to be done as Carillion hurtled towards its likely demise.

In December 2017, as word spread that Carillion was on the brink, MPs in the House of Commons started to raise questions about the risk reports that the Government, and relevant departments, had on strategic suppliers. The chair of the Public Accounts Committee, Meg Hillier MP, was asking for the information. That seemed reasonable, in the light of Carillion's growing crisis. Lidington's office stonewalled, utilising the usual cover-up grounds of 'commercial confidentiality'. The refusal to disclose was point-blank.

A month later, towards the end of January 2018, following the Carillion collapse, there was a special 'Humble Address' debate on Carillion in the House of Commons. A Humble Address is made in unusual circumstances when the House of Commons asks the Queen to intercede, usually with the sitting government, on its behalf. In this case the request was 'to give directions to the Chancellor of the Duchy of Lancaster [Lidington's office] that the assessments of risks of Government strategic suppliers by Her Majesty's Ministers, referred to in the Answer of 19 December 2017, and any improvement plans which Crown Representatives have agreed with such strategic suppliers, since 2014, be provided to the Public Accounts Committee.'

Lidington had to reply to the Humble Address debate in the House of Commons on 28 January 2018. He filibustered and stonewalled. Again. The Labour MP for North Durham, Kevin Jones, commented that Lidington 'just seems to be reading his speech'. There are no question marks about who would have prepared the speech – Manzoni or others in his office. The vote on the Humble Address was carried unanimously. Nothing happened, except that the vendetta between the Public Accounts Committee and Lidington and Manzoni intensified.

At another House of Commons committee, scarcely a week later, on 7 February 2018, there was another fraught exchange. This time it was at the Liaison Committee, which is made up of the chairs of all the House committees coming together:

> *Meg Hillier MP*: How many contingency plans are being worked up right now?
>
> *John Manzoni*: An appropriate number
>
> *Meg Hillier MP*: Double figures? Double figures is quite a range, Mr Manzoni – it is 10 to 99.
>
> *John Manzoni*: Yes.
>
> *Meg Hillier MP*: Between 10 and 99. Thank you very much.[9]

Eventually the related risk reports were released, after Hillier gave guarantees of protecting their confidentiality. But the rigmarole is a sign of a closing of ranks to protect controversial information, which always starts with deliberately introduced delays. The case stands that Cabinet Office prepared for Carillion's downfall from day one after the July announcement. In contrast, while the Cabinet Office and others were on track for the crash, the Carillion directors were clutching at straws to save it. One argument against the theory that the Government had decided that Carillion was going to the wall concerns the award of government contracts following the write-down. How can the theory that the Government abandoned Carillion stand, when Carillion won four central government contracts and three other variations of contract worth around £1.9 billion in the six months after the July warning? It may be that the Government was hedging its bets here, since all the major contracts had clauses which dictated that partners had to carry out the contract in the event of one contractor failing. That means that the Government could sanction what has been called by many politicians and commentators 'a concealed bail-out'; in other words the Government did not write a series of blank cheques guaranteed by public money to save the company, as it did in the 2008 banking crisis. Rather, it signed off massive contracts which would keep Carillion alive without it being seen as a Tory government dispensing public money to bail out a stricken private enterprise. It would be a win-win for the Government. If this helped Carillion to survive, that would be all to the good; if Carillion still crashed there had been no billions of tax-payers' money wasted on a failed rescue.

Two massive contracts for the high-speed rail project HS2 are central to these considerations. They were jointly worth £1.34 billion of the total £1.9 billion awarded in the July 2017 to January 2018 period. Both the HS2 contracts had Carillion in a common venture with the construction companies Kier and Eiffage. Here we come upon another paradox connected to the whole outsourcing pantomime. Part of the Government's defence regarding the contract awards is that the procurement process for the contracts involved had been started a considerable time before the actual awards were made, and if they had been cancelled following the profits warning, HS2 and others would have been on difficult legal ground. In addition, after the July warning, HS2 undertook additional financial assessments of the suitability of Carillion to undertake the contracts concerned.

Enter Ernst and Young, or EY as it is now known. From December 2015 HS2 had a two-year contract with EY to undertake due diligence of the bidders for a number of major HS2 contracts. In these circumstances, after the July write-down, HS2 contracted for a further financial assessment of the suitability of Carillion to be approved for the HS2 works. EY was awarded that contract. However, as has already been pointed out, after the July profits warning Carillion also engaged EY to advise on the restructuring of the business, which included the appointment of Lee Watson, from EY, as chief transformation officer. That project was identified within Carillion as Project Ray.

The Reeves–Field Joint Inquiry wrote to the Transport minister, Chris Grayling, asking for an explanation of what clearly appeared to be 'a conflict of interest' for EY. It was advising Carillion on its future restructuring at the same time as assessing for HS2 whether Carillion was in sound enough standing to undertake a billion-pound plus contract, along with two others, for HS2.

In time, it would be confirmed that millions were at stake here for EY. According to EY's submission to the Joint Inquiry, the two-year contract for analysis of contract bidders for HS2 resulted in fees totalling £197,001. £29,000 of this was the cost of the investigation of Carillion's financial standing after the July profits warning. In 2017 EY submitted fees invoices to Carillion for £14,047,298. This was made up of fees for Project Ray of £10.8 million and other costs. £2.3 million of the fees were unpaid when Carillion went bust. So, in 2017, Project Ray and other services from EY cost Carillion £11.75 million.[10]

It's a bit like being on the garage forecourt with the used-car salesman. He wants to sell you the 'only one owner' Landrover for plenty. He has a conflict of interest. He isn't going to tell you about the Landrover's front window which has a leak in driving rain, because he knows you won't buy the car. Maybe EY faced similar dilemmas – if Carillion fails the finance test, won't that affect its possibility of survival in the long term, which would also jeopardise the gargantuan fees we can make if it gets its 'going concern' box ticked? Chris Grayling said that logic did not apply. There was no conflict of interest, because the EY contracts for HS2 and Carillion were let on different days. Simple, really.

Grayling wrote to the chairs of the Reeves–Field Joint Inquiry: 'Immediately following the Carillion profits warning on 10 July 2017, HS2 Ltd commissioned an *ad hoc* report covering Carillion Construction Ltd and Carillion plc. This report was commissioned on 11 July 2017 and was delivered on the same day.'[11] There were follow-up questions from HS2 so that: 'The *ad hoc* report that EY completed for HS2 Ltd . . . concluded on 13 July 2017. EY did not alert HS2 Ltd of its intention or appointment to advise Carillion on restructuring at the time of its appointment on 14 July. It did so on overall completion of the final report on all shortlisted suppliers (which included the *ad hoc* additional report on Carillion which was completed on 13 July) submitted to HS2 Ltd on 28 July, ten working days later.'[12]

So there was nothing to worry about. This was, after all, 'the chaps giving out contracts to the chaps'. EY had surely long before learned the lessons of giving Lehman Brothers a clean bill of health audit before its 2008 crash. Besides, the letter to the Joint Committee was written on 13 June 2018. That was long before EY caused further concern by signing off the accounts of London Capital and Finance (LCF) when LCF was technically insolvent; it went down, months later, in March 2019, taking £273 million of the savings of its investors with it. The minister's reply absolving EY of any misconduct was also long before April 2019. That was when the Danish police opened an investigation into EY to see if they had broken money-laundering laws as auditors to Danske Bank, which is engulfed in a €200 billion money-laundering scandal surrounding the Bank branch in Estonia. But on 13 June 2018, when Chris Grayling wrote the letter about EY, there was nothing to worry about.

The two HS2 contracts were approved on 6 July, but Carillion did not announce the wins until 17 July. Similarly, two MoD contracts worth £182 million were awarded by the end of June, but not posted by Carillion on the Stock Exchange until 18 July. This remained a puzzle. That is until 21 July, when the Carillion directors sent out a briefing note to all its customers and suppliers. The delay in announcing the contract awards created a 'good news' platform which Carillion used to calm supplier nerves and hoodwink the markets. If they had announced the new contracts as the awards were certified, the sequence of events would have been 'good news' on contracts followed by the calamity of the £845 million write-down. This way it meant that what followed the write-down was 'Look guys, good news on new contracts.' The delay allowed Carillion to declare to the world that 'We continue to be committed to business as usual with all our partners, suppliers and stakeholders, including adherence to all payment terms.' Don't you know, every Carillion cloud ends up with a silver lining: 'Carillion remains well financed and trading within our banking limits' as the briefing note declared.[13] Even although this was untrue.

Rudi Klein of the Specialist Engineering Contractors' Group says hundreds if not thousands of suppliers must have been conned. The scam, this time around, aimed to create new business confidence – 'If the Government is signing off contracts in the billions, things must be alright, tip-top, tickety-boo.' Time passing would demonstrate that the 'new confidence' was a false dawn. Probably an illegal one at that. But that would be too late for the subcontractors, who piled new investments into their Carillion future, only for them all to turn to nothing months later. Literally nothing. 'They were selling the idea of "C'mon, guys, everyone has confidence in us – so should you",' says Rudi Klein. 'They duped people.' There was a Carillion hoarding on the site of the £335 million Royal Liverpool Hospital project. It had the usual Carillion logo emblazoned on it. But, a matter of days after Carillion collapsed, this sign had a blue felt-tip pen graffiti above the logo. It read: 'YOU BASTARDS'.

CHAPTER 7

Downfall

'This story is about more than the demise of one company; it's about the future of British capitalism.'

Liam Halligan, *Daily Telegraph*, 26 May 2018

The first Carillion board meeting after the July events takes place in London at the Maddox Street offices on 22 August 2017. It will turn out to be Zafar Khan's last full face-to-face board meeting. 'Hapless' seems to be a word which follows Khan about like a stalker he can't shake off. Mind you, it could be argued that he was 'hapless' in the right way, given that his final salary at Carillion was £424,000, with 100% bonuses if the figures on the balance sheet turned out well. In his report to the board that day Khan delivers some disappointing news. Operating profit is down on the same quarter the previous year; cost savings forecasts have not been reached and the expected level of income post the July statement has not been realised. That was it. Next business. He doesn't insist that the board should see all of this as a warning. Why would he? – the only thing Zafar can decide is not to decide.

On Wednesday 30 August, Keith Cochrane holds a board conference call on the plans to restructure the business and his proposal to bring in a specialist to assist with that. He also reports on the changes made at board level. Khan is invited to report on the financial position. He tells the board that in the next two months things will be tight but, based on the lending already in place, 'there is no need for new funding'. Before the weekend Khan has changed his mind. He tells Cochrane there has been a deterioration in the financial situation and that Khan's own revised figures, worked up in conjunction with EY (Ernst and Young) show they need new loans from the bank to avoid insolvency. In Zafar Khan's world, inside four days, it is possible to go from the ship is 'steady as she goes' to 'we might be holed below the waterline' – from no need for new funding to insolvency is looming. Cochrane speaks to Philip Green, the chairman, to get him to arrange an emergency conference call on the Sunday, 3 September. On the call Khan outlines the crisis. There's general alarm. It's decided that the banks have to be approached for a bridging loan.

The next day Cochrane again speaks to Philip Green. They are both appalled at the latest failings revealed by Khan. Cochrane tells Green he has lost confidence in Khan because he doesn't seem to be able to get close to the real numbers in Carillion's different business units. There is a pre-existing presentation with Carillion's bankers scheduled for the next day – Tuesday, 5 September. Cochrane tells Green that he doesn't think Khan is the man to be negotiating with the banks. He proposes that Khan should be sacked and replaced by Emma Mercer, who he thinks is obviously closer to the construction side of the business and a better bet for raising new finance from the banks. They agree. The die is cast for Zafar Khan.

Cochrane approaches Emma Mercer. He asks her to take over as the chief financial officer, from 11 September, which will allow time for the necessary arrangements to be put in place. It doesn't take her long to accept. Later, Cochrane has what Khan describes as 'a short meeting' with him. Cochrane tells him that the latest car crash on the figures, made clear on the 3 September conference call, has 'spooked the board'. They've lost confidence in Khan, he says. Cochrane also explains that he wants someone who has experience running the construction side of the business, and that Emma Mercer ticks that box. Mercer is promoted but doesn't become a board member. She has observer rights. Cochrane can call all the shots now. Unopposed. But his only allies at the top are those he has promoted or the small cabal of new advisors he has recruited.

Khan should have seen it coming. On 9 July when the presentation is made to the board about the £845 million write-down, it's Emma Mercer who makes it. Not Khan. Still, Khan leaves with the guarantee of £424,000 in lieu of notice, to be paid over the next 12 months. Cochrane meets with the bankers on Tuesday 5 September. At the end of the formal meeting he convenes a crisis caucus with the bankers and tries to establish the possibility of a £150 million loan to bridge the coming funding gap. He gets the nod. Wheels are set in motion. Just in time.

The announcement of Mercer's promotion and Khan's sacking is made to the Stock Exchange on 11 September. The same notice advises that Lee Watson has been seconded from EY as chief transformation officer. It's also announced that Andy Jones, who was Mercer's chief executive at Carillion Canada, is returning to the UK to work with Mercer as chief operating officer. Cochrane's revolution gathers pace with the notification that, contrary to the previous decisions about his role in the Middle East, Richard Howson is leaving at the end of September. Two other managing directors, Adam Green and Nigel Taylor, will go at the same time. There is an announcement of the impairment of 'goodwill' on the balance sheet of £134 million. A first in Carillion's existence. When the news about the 'morning of the long knives', breaks inside the company, 'Bloody hell' features in a lot of whispered conversations.

Mercer's rise from what was seen in the company as the Canadian outback to the second highest post of chief finance officer is remarkable. Her post as chief finance officer in construction (CFOC) was now vacant. When Zafar Khan worked in Dubai on Carillion's Middle East projects, one of his closest collaborators there was managing director Khalid Nawaz. Nawaz got the call to leave Dubai and come to the UK to replace Mercer as CFOC. The appointment was approved by Cochrane. It was acknowledged that the board had to do something about the Government's perceptions that Carillion's board was 'all male white faces'. So Khalid Nawaz fitted the bill in more ways than one. He departed Dubai, leaving his wife and children there, and took up post at Carillion's headquarters in Wolverhampton. He was ready and more than willing to deliver a turnaround in the finances of Carillion's major construction projects. Unfortunately, he found the charms of the receptionist at Carillion's Crown House headquarters irresistible. Over a few months they had a torrid affair. We can use the tabloid 'torrid' here, because when they broke up the receptionist posted the intimate details of their affair all over her Facebook page. This was shared by practically every Carillion staffer who was on Facebook. Khalid Nawaz had seemed to be a safe pair of hands. His appointment seemed a good idea at the time.

Despite the allegations of 'spooking' the board, Zafar Khan's second set of predictions about the current state of affairs came true. The 29 September statement to the Stock Exchange was an update on the half-year figures to June 2017. It wasn't good. Instead of the promise of what might become a future transformation, there was a further £200 million profits write-down. That took the half-year losses to £1.045 billion – the original £845 million estimates with the latest £200 million added. This is catastrophic. What it means is that by the end of September, Carillion's directors have been forced to make a billion-pound confession. It means that the difference between what they thought the business would make to the end of June 2017, and what it was actually making, is more than £1 billion. The £1.045 billion figure wipes out the total declared profits of Carillion for the previous seven years. A further crisis write-down in November of £60 million would take the eventual losses to £1.1 billion.

Worse, the September figures are from the support services side of the business – where two-thirds of the firm's profits came from – and it involves 23 support service contracts that are in trouble. The financial results statement also notes that underlying pre-tax profit would be down by 40%. One of the explanations offered is the 'trading of contracts with half-year provisions at zero margin'.[1] To you and me that's contracts that were making a loss. The contagion of debt, even more borrowings, bidding at a loss, unsustainable rewards including dividends, all shrouded in sham accounting, has now spread all over the business. The tagline on the 2016 annual report is 'Making Tomorrow a Better Place'. That will never happen. Carillion is actually running out of tomorrows.

In the monthly dial-ins he has been holding for senior staff,

Keith Cochrane has been trying to assure everyone that it is possible to get through these tough times. He's on message for the Stock Exchange investors at the September announcement – the results are disappointing, there's no doubt of the challenges ahead, but 'led by a fresh management team with a mandate to drive cultural change I am confident that a strong business can emerge'. *Construction News* carried a gloomy report on its website on the same day: 'Carillion reveals £1.15bn [sic] half year loss as problems spread to support services'. The comment section on the *Construction News* website was headed by 'Anonymous' who posted a one-liner: 'How can you lose that much?'

On the same day as the September post, Keith Cochrane got a message from the Cabinet Office. It was blunt – Carillion had not been 'open about the seriousness of its position in the past'. The Carillion directors should have realised then that this was a funeral notice. But they refused to acknowledge this – they were too big to fail, the Government could not walk away from £1.7 billion of its own contracts. Surely? So what is the update on things after the July and September write-downs? How are the 'fresh management team', 'the interim chief executive', the arrival of hot-shot experts in restructuring from EY and the pledge of the coming of a new Carillion which is much leaner but fitter all really going down? Really and truly? You could have asked one Murdo Murchison.

Murdo Murchison founded his Edinburgh-based investment fund company Kiltearn in 2011. This was after starting his career in fund management with Schroders, and following that up with career-making experience in Singapore and the Bahamas, dealing with global investors. Murchison speaks quietly but carries a verbal stiletto. By 2018 Kiltearn was managing almost £10 billion of its clients' assets. At the time of the Carillion AGM in March 2017, Kiltearn had major investments in Carillion amounting to more than 10% of the company shares. Kiltearn had a long-term position on Carillion, confident that patient investment would see it come good. From Murchison's point of view the 2016 annual report gave absolutely no prior warning of the £845 million provision to come. When it arrived he was 'put out', as they say in middle-class Edinburgh circles. That expression doesn't quite cover it.

A week after the write-down, four of Kiltearn's heavy-hitters – including some of Murchison's founding partners at the business – have a meeting with Cochrane and John Denning, head of Carillion's investor relations. One plausible reason for Murchison's absence is that, given his 'frustration' about the £845 million announcement, the others fear he may stop speaking quietly and use the metaphorical stiletto. The meeting is an unmitigated disaster. The four from Kiltearn want to know about the £845 million, Carillion's balance sheet and what the two taken together mean for the future. The first line of argument from Cochrane and Denning is a return to the safe haven of the 'perfect storm'. They say 'the first indications of issues with four of the large contracts subject to impairment arose around the time of the AGM'.[2] Open brackets – 'No-one could have seen it coming.' Cochrane says it's tricky for him to comment on the long-term debt scenarios because 'I've only been in the job a week'. His short-term memory fails him. He forgets he's been a non-executive director since the middle of 2015. He tells them that the £845 million had factored in £50 million due to be paid towards the pension deficit, about which there were ongoing discussions with the Trustees – good news: the gap may only be £795 million. He concludes the meeting by telling the Kiltearn delegation that he's not interested in becoming Carillion's permanent CEO.

The four are flabbergasted. Later they tell Murchison that Cochrane never said anything meaningful about how Carillion intended to close its funding gap. The £845 million call-out was bad. Now it is going from bad to worse. There are discussions at Kiltearn about what's to be done. The fact that there was no further information from Cochrane and Denning; that the 2016 annual report, and those before it, couldn't now be considered as reliable; and that the other fundamentals of the business were no longer sound began to play in the discussions. On 3 August 2017 Kiltearn told its investors it was selling down its Carillion stock, and that 'it is in your best interests to do so'. By 7 August that holding was well below 10% for the first time in years. Nobody from Carillion phoned to ask what was happening. Maybe there are some excuses – Cochrane is trying to restructure the company to get back to core business, he's pulling out of contracts all over the globe from Canada to Qatar, he's got new people on the management team to organise and a deadline to meet about a restructuring plan being on the Cabinet Secretary's desk in a matter of weeks.

When the £200 million September write-down is announced Kiltearn send only one member of the investment team, Colin Armstrong, to meet with Cochrane and Co. It's two weeks after the £200 million announcement – 13 October 2017. History repeats itself and so does Cochrane. His opener is to tell Armstrong that he won't be taking the Carillion CEO post permanently. He tells Armstrong Carillion's target for disposals is now £300 million instead of £125 million as stated originally; that it is only when the receipts for that are in that they can get towards the targets for debt reduction. He says that there's no chance of a share issue to swap debt for equity in the current circumstances. At no stage in the meeting does Cochrane raise questions about Kiltearn's 'sell' position. Armstrong tells Murchison later that Cochrane's answers were 'limited and vague' responses to what were fundamental questions about Carillion's future. 'Limited and vague' didn't cut it.

In the following weeks the Kiltearn managers concluded that if the CEO couldn't step up to the plate it was imperative to continue to sell out its clients' position on Carillion. By early December 2017, Kiltearn's significant holding in Carillion is down below 5% and a month later it's all gone. Due to the initial size of the holding, the disposal has taken five months. The crash which comes on 15 January 2018 vindicates the position taken by Murchison, back in July, that Carillion was no longer a viable investment. It is tempting to say that circumstances dictated that nothing Carillion could say or do could have averted the Kiltearn disinvestment. It is also tempting to say that saying or doing nothing guaranteed that. After the £200 million profits warning the death throes are approaching. It is only a matter of time. Yet events are still to unfold which take the Carillion story towards the realm of the surreal. Carillion's directors are locked in a battle for the future, desperate to turn the Government away from a course of abandoning them; the restructuring plan to convince the politicians to take those steps is floundering and the debt mountain is growing inexorably. But still, life goes on. The buses still run. So too the trains. And Carillion's Remuneration Committee still meets to award the executives more money.

There were still matters arising from the board meeting of 9 July 2018, which had to be taken at the RemCo meeting on 23 October. The haste with which Keith Cochrane was ushered in, and Richard Howson was ushered out, means that the fine print on Cochrane's CEO contract and on Howson's redundancy had still to be sorted. The original July offer remained broadly the same but, in both cases, there were significant caveats added. These had been agreed at two RemCo meetings in September, and the RemCo of 23 October would make the final approvals. So less than three months from Carillion's Armageddon, board members were pre-occupied with executive pay and pension problems. Cochrane's base salary was agreed at £750,000 annually. The uncertainties over the length of tenure were resolved. If he stayed in post for up to three months, it was agreed he would be paid for six months. If he remained in post any time beyond three months, he would be entitled to the full annual salary. It was agreed that there would be no bonus for 2017, but that should Cochrane meet his targets for 2018, he could earn bonuses up to 100% of his £750,000 salary.

Then there was Cochrane's accommodation in London. At the time of the RemCo he was staying in a hotel which, excluding VAT, was costing almost £400 per night. It was agreed that he would be paid a relocation allowance of up to £75,000 for a move to more permanent accommodation. The figures Cochrane proposed for that were precise – £2,538 per week, or £10,218 per month. Cochrane turned out to be better with figures than Zafar Khan. These terms were approved by the RemCo. So what does that add up to for his six months as the interim chief executive, to the point of insolvency in January 2018? It is not possible to be exact, because of the flexibility in some of the terms, but it is likely that Cochrane would, before tax, have been paid between £240,000 and £245,000 for his six months as interim CEO.

Howson's dispute was more about how his long-term share options could be cashed in and whether his notice pay would be

paid in a lump sum or 12 monthly instalments, given his entitlement to a year's salary in lieu of notice. The RemCo of 23 October
agreed that from October 2017 his pay in lieu of notice would be
£660,000, paid in 12 monthly instalments of £55,000. In addition
– somewhat differently to what happened to the rest of the Carillion
pensioners – he would have £19,300 paid into his pension pot
every month.[3] There is a dispute about these payments. Howson
says Cochrane cut him out before any payments were made. If that
was not the case, then between October and December 2017, the
RemCo offer entitled him to around £220,000 when the pension
money is included. A substantial price for failure.

The Deloitte auditors who served as advisors to the Carillion
RemCo solved the difficulties with Howson's share options. They
recommended the setting up of a secret account which didn't have
to be declared to the shareholders – an escrow account. That
meant that Howson had to agree any payment with the RemCo
on what would be paid when Howson's share options matured.
Deloitte told the RemCo that if the deal became public they could
say secrecy was the price to be paid for the setting up of the escrow
account. The upside was that it controlled what Howson could
be paid in share options down the line. Clean as a whistle. Any
idea that this is much ado about nothing, in Carillion's wonderful
world of Monopoly money, is wrong. On 7 April 2016 Howson's
LEAP award (Leadership Equity Award Plan) – shares for performance and long-term commitment to the company paid with
cash-in dates some years in the future – is 319,024 shares. At this
time they are valued at £915,280. Of course, when those shares
vested, or matured, the share price at that point would determine
their value.

Still, there is no doubting the significance of LEAP awards as
a loads-a-money incentive. The share awards for Howson which
matured in 2016 paid out £345,881. The financial secretary
Richard Adam's vesting of previous awards for his last year at
Carillion paid £277,939.[4] That's more than a third of a million
pounds for Howson and more than a quarter of a million pounds
for Adam. The figures explain why Howson was so exercised
about the pay-out system when he was sacked. In the Carillion

directors' Never-Never Land of looting the company, Howson gets sacked in the same year as his share bonuses cash in for almost £350,000 and, other things being equal, his redundancy pay, in lieu of notice, could have been £660,000.

Cochrane made communication with senior staff an important element of his leadership. He arranged conference calls every month with the senior staff. The issues raised there were often developed for all Carillion staff in monthly videos posted on the company's internal communications system for Cochrane. Through August, September and October there were common themes. Most importantly were assurances that he believed that the Cabinet Office was confident about the developing restructuring plan and would support it. There were also reminders about getting cash in and cutting costs. One of his favourite cost-cutters was to remind the staff that colour photocopies were banned. People remember the October show. First, the assurances that they would get through the tough times, and then the reminder about costs. Finally there was an appeal: 'Please, please search your soul and ask yourself, are you doing enough?'

Some inconvenient facts conflicted with Cochrane's eternal optimism about Carillion's future and his attempts to convince the staff that there was indeed light at the end of the tunnel which was not an on-coming train. In August 2017 Carillion approached the trustee of the Carillion pension funds, Richard Ellison. He was told there were problems with the cash flow and Carillion was involved in discussions with its banks. Accordingly, the board asked Ellison if he would agree to a deferment of pension payments for a period to help with cash flow and access to other lending. By the end of September the entreaties became threats – if there was no payment, deferment the banks wouldn't put up any new money and Carillion would be insolvent. Ellison agreed to a deal to defer some £25 million of payments due from Carillion between September 2017 and April 2018. The deal was signed off at the end of October 2017. Carillion said it allowed them access to additional bank borrowings of £140 million.

In the first chapter it was suggested that the Carillion board's management of the company pension scheme, and their abject failure to make substantial payments to repair the huge deficits that were growing on all the pension schemes, amounted to criminal negligence. According to The Pensions Regulator, at this point in time, the average recovery plan for pension schemes in deficit – that is the time taken to clear arrears off the pension books – took seven years. By comparison, Carillion's recovery plans were 16 years, even in circumstances where the rules recommend that any recovery plan should not go beyond ten years. Carillion's directors were in the UK's bottom 5% for paying up on pension debts. This refusal to meet their legal obligations resulted in a pension deficit of £990 million on the eve of the collapse. However the final figure, if the liabilities of the debts have to be bought out, is much greater – a deficit of £2.6 billion at the point of insolvency. The end result for every Carillion worker is that whatever pension they were due at the end of their working days will be reduced by 10% in value.

If any of the Carillion directors are confronted by the facts of their own negligence they dissemble. When one of the House of Commons Joint Inquiry team, Chris Stephens MP, asked Cochrane about the pension deficits, Cochrane replied: 'From our perspective it was something the board did discuss; we took our pension obligations very seriously . . . we continued to support the pension fund in an appropriate manner . . . the pension fund was a very important stakeholder for the board and for the group.'

When the chair, Rachel Reeves MP, pushed further on Stephens' question, saying that since Carillion paid out more in dividends to its shareholders than it did into the pension fund, it obviously had a priority towards dividends, Cochrane replied: 'I would not agree with that from my perspective.'[5] Chris Stephens MP, who played a prominent role on the inquiry on the pension deficit, recalls that when he heard that, he thought: 'In the name of fuck.' Cochrane was not a member of the Carillion pension scheme. In fact most of the Carillion board were not members of the Carillion scheme. They had their own arrangements, including Richard and Richard – that is Richard Howson and Richard Adam, the Carillion chief executives – who made sure they were 'alright Jack'. They had their own personal pension schemes paid up, year in year out, by the company. Five years and not a single payment missed – there were no deficits in their schemes. There was always money for the directors' pensions, down to the last £231,000.

In 2016, that's what was paid into Howson's pension pot as part of his total remuneration from the company. For Richard Adam – 'pensions are a waste of money' – that figure was £163,000. That's touching £400k for their last full year with the company. Why would they need to concern themselves about selling out the Carillion workers when their own eye-watering pensions were guaranteed forever? In the five years that Howson was chief executive, together with Adam as the chief finance officer, Carillion paid £1.89 million into their two pension pots.[6] Howson's take on that was just over £1 million and Adam's £818,000.

The desperate need to cut spending and repair cash flows had been brought to a head by the July and September write-downs. The pension deferment turned out to be only a short-term reprieve. It only lasted a matter of weeks, because by the middle of November the cash crisis dictated the necessity of another profits write-down – this time for a further £60 million – and the warning that Carillion was likely to 'breach its covenants'. That's accountant-speak for a warning that Carillion might no longer be able to pay its debts. Running up to this, one of the City's hot-shot share advisors, G. A. Chester, who pens the investment website the Motley Fool, declared that he wouldn't touch Carillion plc stock 'with a barge-pole'. All this time Emma Mercer, as the promoted chief finance officer, and Andy Jones, the new chief operations officer, are the advance guard for Carillion. They make weekly reports to the Cabinet Office, hoping to convince them that Carillion has a future. Cochrane is involved with Cabinet Office meetings also. By this time EY's Lee Watson has been joined by the former Glasgow Rangers FC director, Donald Muir, in the restructuring team, as head of business improvement. Muir was on Rangers' board when it went into administration. He was seemingly brought in by Cochrane to assist in the transformation of Carillion, which included a £100 million costs-reduction programme. The new Group Business Plan would be critical for developing that model, essential to demonstrate to Government that Carillion had a stage-by-stage plan to guarantee salvation. This had to be delivered by 17 January – so time was tight, especially when there was also an endless round of meetings with the banks and investors.

On 22 December the Carillion chiefs meet with their bankers and other financial creditors. Cash is still haemorrhaging from the business. They have to tell creditors that their cash-flow forecast shows that Carillion will have less than £20 million in the bank by March 2018. There and then the assembled financiers decide that without the agreement of all the lenders involved, Carillion cannot draw down what remains of the £140 million of new loans agreed in October. After the Christmas break they toughen that up – no more credit from us unless you make an approach to the Government for funding support as well. Full stop.

Cochrane writes the letter to the Cabinet Office on 31 December 2017. It is the first of what will become a series of modified appeals for support – on 8, 12, 13 and 14 January 2018. However, the 31 December letter is the only one where there is a request for immunity from any fines or other penalties. That includes any investigations into Carillion prior to July 2017. And it encompasses all investigations – the regulators, the Serious Fraud Office, the police, you name it. The Cochrane letter called on the Government and Carillion to 'explore what, if any assistance, could be provided that any investigations that were or may be carried out in relation to the actions of Carillion prior to July 2017 would not, when finalised, lead to the relevant regulator or enforcement agency seeking to take steps to impose fines or other penalties on Carillion'.[7]

Ever since, Philip Green has defended the plea for immunity on two counts. In the first place, he says it was the lenders who insisted Carillion make the plea to cover future circumstances. Secondly, he argues that the request related to immunity from fines and other penalties for the company. Just the company. He insists that this was not a request seeking personal immunity from fines and penalties for the directors or any other individual.

On 4 January 2018, Cochrane meets the Cabinet Office officials. They tell him there is no way there can be any agreement to the immunity pleadings. As a result, despite the 'insistence of the company's lenders', the immunity request vanishes without trace. It disappears in all future letters asking for funding support. As does any copy of the actual original letter. Just like that. One Carillion source says, 'They knew what they'd done. They knew where the bodies were buried. Right. So they were trying to get their hands on a "Get out of jail free" card. My God, if the staff had known about this . . .'

Beyond the immunity appeal the Cochrane letter is equally audacious in its other demands. These are in two parts. In the short term there is £223 million of 'bridging' support to get Carillion through from January to April 2018. This includes a request to the Cabinet Office for £160 million of Government support and a £63 million deferral of tax liabilities; the taxes are already owed to HMRC for 2017, but would now be postponed until the end of 2018. The £160 million would be paid out in a series of instalments as the 'bridging' progressed, including two 'immediate' £10 million Government loans for the weeks beginning 15 and 22 January.

The second element, over the long term, requires the Government to underwrite the complete restructuring of the company. The list for that includes calls for the Government to:

- settle the HM Prisons and Probation Service contracts, including claims and liabilities
- persuade the Pension Protection Fund to accept a restructuring of its pension schemes to cancel the standing £2.6 billion liabilities
- fund the completion of the Midland Metropolitan Hospital in exchange for an equity stake
- buy out Carillion's equity in the Aberdeen Bypass road project and pay the existing claims owed to Transport Scotland
- help to negotiate an exit from the loss-making contracts in the UK and Middle East
- commit to giving Carillion its 'fair share' of future Government contracts
- agree to the possibility of longer-term financial support to add to loans from commercial lenders

and, as already noted:

- guarantee protection from the imposition of fines and penalties from the regulatory agencies.[8]

These demands were varied in the subsequent letters sent to the Cabinet Office. But not by much. The demands for immunity and for an agreement on longer-term financial support were dropped. The other changes were only variations in the estimates of costs. David Lidington, the Secretary to the Cabinet Office, would later say that not only did Carillion want the Government to guarantee its future but also guarantee the bridge to the future.

In the battle taking place over the first two weeks of January 2018, with the benefit of hindsight, you could say that in Carillion's favour were Cochrane, the chairman, Green, Mercer, Jones and the work being done by EY for the restructuring and the production of a viable Group Business Plan. Ranged against were Manzoni and the Cabinet Office, the accountants PwC, and the lenders and their consultants, FTI. In all the various Parliamentary Inquiry interviews, the impression is conveyed that there was no 'for and against' battle. Rather the impression is given that all were locked together in a desperate battle to save the company. However, we know that, despite any so-called eleventh-hour efforts, the Cabinet Office, PwC and, *inter alia*, the Government, had been planning for the company's demise for months. One sentence from the National Audit Office report gives the game away: 'Following Carillion's request for urgent short-term support, the Cabinet Office organised meetings with Carillion and its creditors, and made more detailed preparations for Carillion's insolvency.'[9]

The Cabinet Office met the creditors on Friday, 5 January 2018. The lenders told the Cabinet officials that they were concerned by the rate that Carillion was continuing to consume cash and also by the delay in getting its rescue plans published. FTI, the lenders' consultants, produced a business review which was ferociously critical of Carillion's prospects – their biggest hit was that they predicted by August 2019 Carillion would need £495 million of Government money to keep it afloat.

On Monday 8 January Carillion presents its draft business plan to the Cabinet Office. The draft is an impressive document of 100 pages in which every element of the business is analysed and detailed future forecasts explained. The priorities are a restructuring of the debt, the transformation of all levels of management of the business, cost savings of £100 million, an extensive disposal of assets worth £300 million and a return to 'core' business only. The plan declares: 'We will deliver a recovery plan with strong growth in profit, margins, and cash.' It cuts no ice. It is too late. The numbers don't add up. The Cabinet Office options report, produced in conjunction with PwC, is ready about the same time. Its two cheapest options are the break-up of Carillion and sale of its assets or a short-term investment programme. Both are rejected. The first, ostensibly because there isn't enough time to implement it; the second because the Cabinet Office doesn't have confidence in Carillion's business plan.

A 'trading liquidation' becomes the favoured option. On Thursday 11 January 2018 Manzoni meets David Lidington and the Chancellor of the Exchequer, Philip Hammond. They approve the 'trading liquidation' option. The Prime Minister, Theresa May, agrees the next day. The Cabinet Office sets up a crisis management centre to handle communications for the liquidation. So the execution is agreed by Government three days before the 'financial guillotine' is dropped.

On Saturday 13 January 2018, Philip Green writes again to Manzoni at the Cabinet Office. According to Cochrane the letter is delivered at seven in the evening, so there must have been exchanges between Green, Cochrane and the Cabinet Office during the day to seek a way out. It may seem strange, but at this point Green has not had a face-to-face meeting with Manzoni or Rhys Williams. He tells one of the parliamentary inquiries that he left all the direct meetings to 'the chief executive'.

Among ex-Carillion staff there is a strong suspicion that Green was not hands-on because he spent a large part of the Christmas holidays in South Africa, in his house outside Cape Town. It has not been possible to verify this, as Green and the other former Carillion directors have made no reply to any requests for interviews or even for an exchange of email questions. In 2017, Carillion's year of crisis, its chairman had two informal meetings with Government ministers at some point; neither was 'to discuss a rescue plan for Carillion'. In his letter, Green bluntly identifies two options that are now facing Carillion – either provision of short-term funding from the Government or insolvency. The detailed demands that were outlined in the first letter of 31 December 2017 are referred to in the note, but this missive is much more pointed about the need for immediate financial rescue. He refers to the total funding proposal of around £220 million between January and April, drawn from support from the commercial banks and the Government. However, the deadline money is more pressing – two tranches of £10 million each on 15 and 22 January. If the Government agrees, that money will be matched by the banks. Green notes: 'Our goal is to enter into a commercially sensible arrangement which adjusts and creates greater certainty around future cash flows. Accordingly, if Carillion successfully restructures itself it will be at extremely modest cost to HM Government. It will not be a bail-out and there can be no basis for saying that Carillion . . . is being rewarded for failure or past mistakes.'[10]

Green used to move in high Tory circles and so did Cochrane. So are the terms stated in this manner because they both think that the Government is going to step in with a bail-out, or whatever business euphemism Green would use, for their skins being saved? In any event, Carillion goes bust just over a day after the letter is delivered to the Cabinet Office. It has £29 million in cash in the bank and liabilities of £6.9 billion, which include enormous pension and bank debts. Is this bravado from Green derived from the fact he does not know the figures? Or that he knows Carillion is 'too big to fail'? For Project Ray, restructuring work carried out between July 2017 and January 2018, Carillion paid EY £10.8 million. Apparently despite such lavish fees – £60,000 a day – EY's advice to Green concerning where Carillion stood with the Government was way off the mark. In his letter Green warns the Government about the approaching catastrophe if Carillion is not saved: 'We are not advised that there is any contingency plan, and certainly not one that has been tested with advisers or management in terms of its operational viability. The strong advice we have received from senior insolvency practitioners at EY is that no contingency plan fit for purpose in fact exists or could have been created in the time available.'[11]

Green threatens Manzoni that if the Government does not support Carillion the consequences will come 'with enormous cost to HM Government'. He signs off with the reminder that the group has 'very limited runway' before it ceases to have the funding required to operate. 'We therefore cannot wait indefinitely' are the last words on the ransom note.

However, even by Carillion standards, the day before Green dispatches the Manzoni letter there is another lurch towards the surreal. On Friday 12 January 2018, on what turns out to be Carillion's last day of trading, Carillion pays its accountants, advisors and City law firms £6.4 million – presumably all signed off by the company secretary, Richard Tapp, with his usual grasp of the legalities of company business. The very next day, Saturday the 13th, Green writes to the Government begging for £10 million to keep Carillion afloat. In the Friday proceedings, EY get the top rank. Part of their restructuring recommendations was deferring tax owed to HMRC and extending standard Carillion payment terms to 126 days; but on the last day Carillion was in business, EY got a cheque for £2.5 million. EY didn't have to wait for its money. Next, step forward Slaughter and May – they got paid £1.2 million. Then the consultants FTI another £1.02 million. Lazards, the bankers, who along with Slaughter and May might have had to advise Carillion that they were still a going concern, on the very day of the pay-out, got paid £551,000. PwC, £276,000.

In the story so far we have had 'the chaps regulating the chaps'; we've also become accustomed to the 'chaps giving out contracts to the chaps', so is this now stage three – 'the chaps squaring up the chaps' before the money runs out? If it walks like a duck and quacks like a duck, it must be a duck. Within Carillion there are those who think differently. They say that Green and Cochrane think the Government is still going to blink first, that the bail-out is inevitable. So the pay-offs are made because the accountants, the advisors and the lawyers 'would need to be kept sweet because they would be needed on the other side of the bail-out'.

The GMB's Gary Smith is a Scotsman. You might say he 'calls a spade a shovel'. When the £6.4 million payoffs were raised, in one of the book interviews, Smith offered his opinion that they were only one instance in 'a litany of potential treachery' involving Carillion. He exclaimed, 'This isn't just about paying your mates off in the millions. It's about watching the workers' pension plans go to the wall while pouring millions into your own pot. It's about misleading Parliament and cooking the books in an illegal Ponzi scheme; it's about the whole bloody scandal. And so far we haven't got to the bottom of it.' And he says the only way that can happen is with a statutory public inquiry where those appearing give evidence under oath. 'How else are the real lessons to be learned?' he asked.

After Green's letter is delivered to Manzoni at the Cabinet Office, on the evening of Saturday 13 January 2018, it is not possible to determine precisely how events then unfold. What we do know is that early on Sunday morning, Rhys Williams, the Cabinet Office's chief commercial officer, delivers a report to Manzoni which justifies the *coup de grace*. As if there was any doubt. The Rhys Williams report carries nine deadly, bullet-point warnings about a Carillion rescue. Predominant among them is the argument that the Cabinet Office cannot trust the Carillion board or the banks to deliver. The logic runs that if the banks walk away the Government would be left holding the baby:

> The government would be carrying excessive risk in the short term, and this could lead to an open-ended funding commitment even if the company survived, as it would have given the company and lenders no incentive to repay the government.[12]

On Sunday 14 January 2018, the Rhys Williams review is considered and the Cabinet Office officials take the decision to refuse support for any rescue. They inform Green and Cochrane, although it is not exactly clear when in the day that is done. Green and Cochrane are totally taken aback by the plug being pulled, and try to mount a rearguard action. The first stage of that is a meeting with Manzoni – the first time Green has met him. It is all too little, too late. Apart from the risks about the money, the Rhys Williams report also raises concerns about the poor quality of the Carillion restructuring plan and a general lack of confidence in the company forecasts.

Manzoni doesn't budge. Green tries frantically to persuade him to set up a meeting with the Prime Minister, Theresa May. Meantime, the Cabinet Office has also informed Carillion's bankers that the Government is not supporting any rescue. That leads to an endgame double-whammy for Green and Cochrane. The lenders write to Carillion to tell them that in the light of the Government decision they 'too would not offer further support.' It is now getting late in more ways than one. Cochrane is spitting tacks when he finds out about the bankers' letter.

Theresa May refuses to meet with Cochrane and Green and instead they have to make their final pleas to May's deputy, David Lidington. That meeting takes place sometime on the Sunday evening. It might be around 9.30 pm. It's said that Lidington tells them that PwC officials have been actively preparing the details of the liquidation for more than a week. Lidington says they are on hand to help Cochrane prepare for the declaration of 'compulsory liquidation' under the terms of the Insolvency Act at the High Courts of Justice the next morning. And for the statement of liquidation before the opening of trading on the Stock Exchange. Lidington probably doesn't tell them then that the option for a 'trading liquidation' had been decided upon some time before; nor that the contingency plans for it had been 'stress-tested' in the previous weeks to make sure that public services could continue to be provided.

Cochrane organises a teleconference call for the most senior staff at around eleven o'clock in the evening from the Maddox Street headquarters. He tells the staff that the attempts to persuade the Government to back the rescue plan have failed, and when the Government said no the lenders 'folded'. He qualifies that by saying that it was actually RBS which folded first after the news from the Government, and the rest of the banks followed. This opinion will influence his witness statement presented to the Insolvency Court the next morning. RBS, Santander UK and Lloyds claim they took the decision to pull out together.

On Monday 15 January 2018, a special hearing is called at the Companies Court of the Royal Courts of Justice in the prestigious Rolls Building, in Fetter Lane, off the Strand in London. The extraordinary circumstances mean that it is 6 am when the hearing starts to process the liquidation. This has to be completed before the Stock Exchange opens an hour later. Mr Justice Morgan is presiding. Cochrane, with others, has been up half the night preparing the written statement, which is now before the court. Cochrane is not in court. He makes the supporting verbal statement, on behalf of the Carillion directors, by a phone link into the court. He launches into a bitter attack on RBS. He says that, without notice, RBS had overnight changed the terms of its loans, which has seriously jeopardised Carillion's planned cash flow. He says that RBS had taken 'unilateral action which in the Company's view undermined the Group's efforts to conserve cash'. His next target was Santander, for altering the terms of its support for Carillion's Early Payment Facility, in mid-December, without notice.[13]

However, the written statement goes beyond accusations made against the banks. Cochrane tells the court that on 9 January, Carillion had begged HMRC to defer some of its tax liabilities, to no avail. Referring to the written document before Mr Justice Morgan, he goes further, saying in effect that Carillion had been betrayed by those who could have come to its rescue. He quotes from the statement that in the last two months Carillion had suffered 'because bonding providers withdrew facilities, credit insurers reduced or eliminated coverage, and certain long-standing customers informed the Company that they would not place new work until its balance sheet issues were resolved'. There was to be no 'Regrets, I've had a few', because it was 'everyone but me' who had to carry the blame.

The court hears that Carillion has so little funding available that it has been unable to identify insolvency practitioners willing to act as administrators. When the consultants EY and PwC were approached, both refused because they were afraid they would not be paid. EY had fee earnings for its six-month advisory role to Carillion of more than £11 million. PwC also passed on the offer. They were concerned about getting paid as well, but perhaps they also had eyes on a possible bigger prize – an engagement as 'special managers' to assist in the delivery of the insolvency.

Thus Cochrane delivers the petition for a compulsory liquidation. Mr Justice Morgan makes the winding-up order, in accordance with the Insolvency Act 1986. The Official Receiver is appointed as liquidator. In due course, 'special managers' from PwC were appointed by the Official Receiver to assist him in his winding-up duties. PwC's gamble paid out. From 15 January 2018 to 31 March PwC were paid £22.9 million. That makes the average rate for each of its one hundred-plus 'special managers' around £360 per hour.[14] 1 April to the end of July fetched an additional £9.9 million, making the half-year total £32.8 million.[15] By the time of the first-year anniversary of Carillion's crash, in January 2019, PwC had been paid £44.2 million with the prediction those fees would be over the £50 million mark before the end of the insolvency process. Frank Field MP, chair of the Commons Work and Pensions Committee, noted when the figures first became known that Carillion had been 'ably assisted by a merry little band of advisors and auditors, conflicted at every turn, and with every incentive to milk the cash-cow dry'.[16]

In his statement to the Stock Exchange on 15 January, Philip Green said: 'This is a very sad day for Carillion, for our colleagues, suppliers and customers that we have been proud to serve over many years. Over recent months huge efforts have been made to restructure Carillion to deliver its sustainable future . . . In recent days, however, we have been unable to secure the funding to support our business plan and it is therefore with the deepest regret that we have arrived at this decision.'

He was sorry. Cochrane was sorry. Howson was sorry. Khan was sorry. Morgan was sorry. Adam was sorry. Horner was sorry. Mercer was sorry. They were all sorry. The BEIS and Work and Pensions Joint Committee Inquiry interviewed the Carillion directors on 7 February 2018. Rachel Reeves MP remembers that at the end of the session with Howson, Green, Adam and Horner, her 'blood beginning to boil' about them all being 'so sorry'. So she decides she will ask all four if they think they should give their bonuses back to help with the pension deficit: 'All of you are sitting here with multi-millions of pounds worth of payment from the company over the years and you say how sad and disappointed you are, but what actions do you take to show that? They are just words are they not? "I am saddened. I am disappointed" . . . but the money is in the bank. It is not in the bank for the subcontractors, is it? It is not in the bank for the people who are coming up to retirement. Instead of words, why do you not do something? Why do you not give some money back . . . and try to put right some of the wrong?' Richard Adam says he is 'genuinely shocked and saddened' by the events since he left. He says he is happy to engage with the company to 'understand what the position is'. Whatever that means. Nobody else says a word. Frank Field asks: 'Why should we believe that you feel so sad about all of this, when it does not extend to your chequebook?'

Her Majesty the Queen unveiled the plaque at the front of the Rolls Building to mark its official opening on 7 December 2011. The very same building where Carillion declared its insolvency. When it was opened by Her Majesty, the declared aim of the £300 million project was to make London the world's top legal centre in the same way as the City had promoted itself as an international financial centre. The chairman of the Bar Council at the time, Michael Todd QC, said the Rolls Building would make British courts the gold standard for resolving international legal disputes. The Rolls Building houses 31 courtrooms, 55 consultation rooms and 11 hearing rooms within its 16,000 square metres of glass and Portland stone. It was built by Carillion.

CHAPTER 8

A Gigantic Racket

'Carillion was unsustainable. The mystery is not that it collapsed, but that it lasted so long.'

House of Commons BEIS and Work and Pensions
Committees, 'Carillion', HC769, 16 May 2018

On Friday 29 April 2016, at the High Court of Justice off the Strand in London, Lord Justice Supperstone ordered eight multi-national construction companies to pay £5.4 million to 116 GMB union members. Their lives had been vindictively blighted after being blacklisted by the construction companies' cartel. The GMB had been the first union to take the construction giants to the High Court to seek compensation for the lives that had been ruined; in the court action they also demanded an apology for decades of the secret, organised abuse of construction workers' human rights through the operation of the secret blacklist. If your name went down on the blacklist, organised by the employers' clandestine Consulting Association, you could be banned from getting work in the construction industry for life.

The GMB legal action ended up breaching the wall. UCATT and Unite followed the GMB into court. Thus, ten days after the GMB settlement, the deals for other unions and other legal claims were announced: in total 771 blacklisted workers had won a reported £75 million in damages and legal costs, and an apology from the oligarchs at the top of the UK's eight biggest blacklisters. On 9 May 2016 *The Times* effectively named and shamed them. The newspaper recorded that 'A long campaign to obtain compensation for construction workers who were blacklisted for union activities has ended . . . Balfour Beatty, Carillion, Costain, Kier, Laing O'Rourke, Sir Robert McAlpine, Skanska UK and Vinci have issued an "unreserved apology" for barring hundreds of workers from building sites.' The construction bosses became known collectively throughout the legal dispute as 'the MacFarlanes defendants', after the legal practice which represented them. The apology made in court by the defendants' legal counsel was unqualified: 'The Defendants are here today, to offer, through me, their sincere and unreserved apologies to the Claimants for any damage caused. The Defendants apologise as providers of any information, and for the loss of employment suffered as a result of the communication of information during the operation of the Consulting Association. They also apologise for the anxiety and hurt to feelings caused as a result. The MacFarlanes Defendants, as a whole, agree and endorse that apology.'[1]

Carillion's collaboration and culpability in the blacklisting affair is an indelible stain on its history. It also provides vital clues to how the whole Carillion scandal developed. The ruthlessness involved in the blacklisting, its secrecy, its seemingly untouchable power and its moral bankruptcy, combined with the way Carillion created a panoply of denial about the extent of its blacklisting activities, are critical to any understanding of the real motivations of those who were at the top of the company for years. They said one thing and did another – preaching sermons about openness, honesty and transparency whilst blacklisting hundreds of workers in the real world. Towards the end of 2018, I meet the GMB's national officer, Justin Bowden, at the modest headquarters offices of the GMB, next door to Euston station in London. When I ask him about blacklisting, his burning sense of injustice ignites there and then. He says that historically Carillion was one of the worst offenders. Right away he refers to the union's blacklisting report, published in 2014: 'Over one five-year stretch the figures show Carillion paid the Consulting Association more than £32,000. That accounts for searches against almost 15,000 workers who had applied for a job with Carillion. Fifteen thousand blacklisting checks. They were up to their necks in it.'[2]

At one stage when the building firm Sir Robert McAlpine was facing legal action, they produced documents from the Information Commissioner's original evidence about blacklisting. It backed up the McAlpine plea in mitigation that they were not the only black-listers. The McAlpine evidence recorded that Carillion had paid around £91,000 to the Consulting Association over a long period of time. So there's no denying Carillion were prolific blacklisters, but Justin Bowden says there's more than just proof of 'blood on their hands'. 'If it wasn't for Carillion dealing out the worst treat-ment I've ever seen to a group of Asian workers at a hospital in Swindon – and let me tell you I've seen some scallywags in my time – the whole shooting match would never have happened. No High Court. No millions in compensation. No shaming of the blacklisters. Nothing, if a group of about 100-odd migrant work-ers, mostly women, mostly from Goa in India, hadn't decided to tell Carillion "Enough is enough".'

The back story needs to come first before that tale. Ian Kerr was a schoolteacher in the West Midlands in the late 1960s. He needed to save up to get married. He gets a job as a training officer for an outfit called the Economic League. It doubles his wages. In 1969 that took them to £1600 p.a.

The Economic League operated as a right-wing propaganda think-tank for hardline big business. One of its main sponsors was the construction company Sir Robert McAlpine. In the summer of 1972, building workers across the UK went on strike for better wages and conditions. The strike lasted three months. It grew exponen-tially as the weeks went by, especially after rank-and-file building workers deployed flying pickets to close down major building sites across the land. One of the most famous was a flying picket of 200-plus workers, travelling in six coaches from Chester and North Wales to shut down every building site in the town of Shrewsbury. They became known in trade union history as 'the Shrewsbury pickets'.[3]

In the end, the construction bosses capitulated and the building workers won their biggest-ever wage rise, which almost matched the central demand of the strike of £35 for a 35-hour week. The retribution from the construction bosses came in the form of an organised conspiracy which involved them, the police, MI5 and sections of the media. It resulted in the leaders of the Shrewsbury pickets – notably Des Warren and Ricky Tomlinson – being jailed in 1973 with hefty sentences on trumped-up 'conspiracy' charges. The construction bosses also decided that 'trade union militants' would never 'hold them to ransom' again. They created a black-list system to block any union activist getting work ever again in the construction industry. As a result, Ian Kerr moved from his training position in the Economic League to create the blacklist through what was called the Service Group, which operated within the League. Over the years, names went on the blacklist and the word was passed.

When the League folded, the chair of Sir Robert McAlpine paid out £10,000 to help with wind-up costs and, in 1993, Ian Kerr took his lists with him to what would become the Consulting Association (TCA). The blacklist would mushroom from now on. The system was based on a very simple axis – construction com-panies paid an annual subscription of £2,500–3,000 to the TCA. That allowed them access to the Consulting Association black-list. It was a two-way structure; not only could you get names from Kerr's blacklist to block key activists getting on to your sites, as the new generation of militants came forward you could also add them to the list so that everyone knew who was who and who shouldn't ever get a start. The use of the then ubiquitous fax machine made the sending of lists faster and more secure than ever before. Every company had a code and a 'main contact' identified only by their initials. Therefore, the whole process was secret and from the outside extremely difficult to penetrate.

In 2012 Ian Kerr appeared before the House of Commons Scottish Affairs Committee when it was investigating blacklisting. Simon Reevell MP asked him about how it worked:

> *Q1079 Simon Reevell MP*: I've got a list of people I'm thinking of employing, and either myself, at a senior HR level, or one or two people I trust, have got your fax num-ber and, if there are names on the list that we want to check, we send you a fax with the name, you receive the

fax, you go to your book of information, you look up the name and you then send back a copy of the information that you hold. Is that the mechanics of it?

Ian Kerr: They didn't send information through of people they were concerned about. They would send a whole list through. They could put an advert in their local paper for electricians, bricklayers and what have you – a mixture of people. The whole list would come through. Most of the time we would go back, by telephone, identify the list and say to the HR department girl or man, 'All clear.' If there was a name that we had information on, we would say to them, 'All clear, except a certain name', and that would be the end of the conversation. I would then speak to the main contact.

This polite exchange details the mechanics but doesn't expose the scale of abuse that was perpetrated against construction workers – almost all of whom did not know what was going on. They wandered from one job application rejection to another, often for years, oblivious to the fact that they didn't get the job because TCA had passed on the black spot to a prospective employer. This could label them as a 'troublemaker' or 'TM' for short, a 'militant', a 'health and safety rep' and so on, or further, 'ran safety strike at xxx'. There was also the frequently dispatched 'Do Not Touch', along with the frenzied 'UNDER NO CIRCUMSTANCES WHATSOEVER'. The GMB's Justin Bowden offers a caveat. He says it's important to mark that a whole generation of trade union activists were taken out of the construction industry by black-listing, but he also says it's important to acknowledge that many ordinary workers who were not activists, and might not have even been union members, got caught in the poisonous web. He told me, 'Look, there were thousands blacklisted who were ordinary Joes. They just happened to be in the wrong place at the wrong time and their names went down. Or maybe the site manager took a dislike to them and that was that – name down, no job for life. Collateral damage, the employers called it.'

He also says there were cases of mistaken identity or the mis-spelling of names that meant that people went on the list who had nothing to do with the unions. 'After we got the list we found this Irish worker who had been blacklisted for being part of a pro-test about work conditions on the Jubilee line. He'd never worked in London. They spelled some other guy's surname wrong and this other bloke went on the list and couldn't get a start for years. It's unbelievable what went on.'

Between 2004 and March 2009, TCA's accounts show that almost £480,000 went through the books. Any claims made by the construction oligarchs that TCA did not really operate as a blacklist and that companies only occasionally sought information on recruitment fall at this point. Ian Kerr's final salary in 2009 was £50,000, with benefits including a BUPA subscription and a Mercedes company car.

TCA's offices were in Droitwich, on the edge of rural Worcester-shire, down the M5 about 25 miles south of Birmingham. Early in February 2009, after a tip-off, the Information Commissioner's Office (ICO) raided the offices. Former police officer David Clancy was searching for files that would establish the existence of a secret blacklist. He seized what he needed for that purpose from the card indexes, folders and filing cabinets in Ian Kerr's office.

In due course it would emerge that Clancy had, for some reason, only seized about 10% of Kerr's files. Iain McKenzie MP would later describe that as strange, likening it to a police drugs raid on a dealer's house where after the first pill is found the raid is called off, with the exclamation 'Right, that's enough. Let's go.' However, this aside, the documents that were seized turned out to be dynamite in exposing the blacklisting conspiracy. There was also in addition to the blacklist a 'greenlist' put together of envi-ronmental activists who'd been protestors at one demo or another. The construction employers didn't make any distinction about who got the black spot. They were not going to have their sites infiltrated by troublemakers of any stripe – the famous 'Swampy' and any of his friends included. This added a new dimension, because it linked blacklisting with the security services' infiltration of the Green activist movement. In retrospect, Carillion was guilty then of having links with undercover cops, a number of whom as part of their infiltration operations were moving in with women in the Green movement, under totally false pretences, and even having children with them in some instances.

When the evidence became public, more than 40 companies, Carillion included, were indicted for operating a blacklist which had more than 3,200 construction workers' names on it. After the existence of the blacklist became established following the ICO raid, some Labour MPs raised demands for legislation in Parliament. In 2010 amendments were then made to employment law to make legal challenges to blacklisting possible. Justin Bowden said, 'It was good, but it was really only a bit of a slap on the wrist.' At this point the blacklisting campaign goes into limbo. The only group who made application to the ICO for their own details were the people who already suspected they had been blacklisted. They were mainly trade union activists; they form the Blacklist Support Group, but there are fewer than 100 of them. The rest of the 3,200 victims don't know they have been blacklisted. And the ICO is refusing to deal with the unions because of what they describe as 'data protection issues'.

Dave Smith, one of the workers who did know he had been blacklisted, applied personally to get his details from the ICO. When he got his file it had more than 30 pages of information about him stretching from 1992 to 2005. His employment tribunal started in January 2012. In submissions to the tribunal Carillion accepted it blacklisted him.[4] Eventually he lost the case on a technicality. The blacklisting by Carillion was publicised in a number of newspapers.

So, back to the migrant workers from Goa. By the time Smith's case goes public, in January 2012, the porters and cleaners at Great Western Hospital – built and run by Carillion – have taken rolling strike action over more than ten days of action. In the end their strikes would go to more than 22 days of action in total. In particular they want Carillion to agree to a rota system that allows them to take their total annual leave consolidated together, so that when they return to Goa to see family they can do so for a number of weeks at a time. Historically, Carillion had always officially blocked these requests, and consequently, over the years, a 'shakedown' system had evolved.

The 'shakedown' system meant that if you wanted a longer holiday, you had to pay to get the nod. These 'payments' were made in the form of gold, jewellery, cigarettes, alcohol and even cash, given in exchange for all manner of 'favours' like the length of holiday leave, overtime or jobs for relatives. By late 2011, enough was enough, and the GMB members embarked on the strike action. They not only wanted the holiday rota system totally altered, but were now also demanding an end to the 'bullying intimidation and racist behaviour of Carillion managers'. Justin Bowden is sent from GMB headquarters to Swindon to try and get a deal for the workers. Carillion's head of HR, Liz Keates, arrives from the Carillion Wolverhampton headquarters for a meeting with Bowden and other union officials. There's no negotiation. Although much later Carillion will have to accept that there was 'gift-giving' and 'inappropriate racist behaviour', at the time she denies anything is going wrong. She tells Bowden, referring to the Asian workforce, 'It's all exaggerated, it's cultural.'

At the same time this is happening, one of Bowden's union colleagues notices in the *Observer* newspaper that Dave Smith has been blacklisted by Carillion. He knows the Swindon dispute also involves Carillion. He gets in touch with Dave Smith. Smith agrees to a meeting with the GMB organiser for the Swindon dispute. When they meet, Liz Keates' name comes up in conversation. Smith drops the bombshell that she was the one who blacklisted him. Bowden tells me: 'Bingo! We were away. We now knew Carillion was a blacklister and that the HR manager who had blacklisted people was also involved in the Swindon dispute. It was open season on Carillion. No quarter was given.' Before long, the campaign is unearthing the names of other Carillion managers who've been involved, and suddenly there's new life in the entire union campaign.

Bowden and Maria Ludkin, who was then the GMB's head of legal, go to see Shami Chakrabarti, who is then the director of the civil rights charity Liberty. In these days she can strike fear in the hearts of those who come up against Liberty when it is in full fighting-for-justice mode. 'I hear you may have something we can go on for a judicial review,' she tells Bowden and Ludkin, when they meet in Liberty's offices off Victoria Street in London. They decide to go for a joint judicial review on the decision of the Information Commissioner's Office to refuse to release the names on the blacklist to the GMB. The ICO folds when confronted with the threat of a joint GMB/Liberty legal review, and the union gets the names. You could almost say the rest is history – the High Court awaits.

The list put together by the GMB throws up a host of names from Scotland. The House of Commons Scottish Affairs Committee (SAC) was chaired by the Labour MP Ian Davidson, who stood for a Glasgow constituency at the time. Davidson was one of the GMB's sponsored MPs. They approach him about the blacklisting campaign. Davidson manages to get cross-party support on the SAC to set up an inquiry. It actually starts as an inquiry into health and safety across Scottish industry, but it soon morphs into a blacklisting investigation.

It started in May 2012 and lasted well into 2013. TCA's Ian Kerr gave evidence. He felt he had been betrayed by the construction bosses who had 'thrown him to the wolves'. When the ICO first seized the lists, the construction bosses told Kerr to shut up shop and get rid of all the files that had not been taken. After almost 20 years' service to their cause he got a few weeks wages as a goodbye. So now it was his turn. Names, dates, money, who, when and where followed when he was questioned by the MPs on the SAC. Kerr died from a heart complaint not long after giving evidence. Not one of the bosses who had collaborated with him on the blacklist went to his funeral. Bowden says, 'Kerr blew the lid off what the construction companies like Carillion, Sir Robert McAlpine and Balfour Beatty had tried so hard, for so long, to keep the lid on. After Kerr spilled the beans their secret reign of terror against ordinary workers couldn't be denied any longer.'

It could by Carillion. In its written submission to the Scottish Affairs Committee of September 2012 Carillion states categorically that: 'Carillion plc was not involved with the CA [the Consulting Association]. Senior management was not aware of any use of the

CA's database . . . Carillion categorically denies the assertion that it made use of CA blacklists until the date of the ICO raid in 2009 . . . The assertion that Carillion was at the centre of a blacklisting conspiracy and that it was responsible for significant amount of blacklisting activity is wholly untrue.' Justin Bowden says it may be accurate that Carillion never actually used the blacklist after 2004. However, he insists that on Ian Kerr's lists there was documentary evidence that Carillion's head of HR, Liz Keates, was in touch with Kerr right up to the end. He says 'We've said they were still involved long after 2004 and they've never sued. In any case, what they did before 2004 was prolific.' At the height of the GMB blacklisting campaign, twelve senior managers in Carillion were named on the union website as blacklisters.

Moreover, there is a concrete reference from a set of Carillion's own accounts which seems to contradict the outraged assertions made in the written evidence to the Scottish Affairs Committee. The half-year trading update made to the Stock Exchange to 30 June 2016 – signed off by the Carillion finance director, Richard Adam, and published on 24 August 2016 – shows an underlying profit of £121.3 million. However, there is a footnote which states that this figure is 'before non-recurring operating items of £10.5m'. True to the byzantine traditions of Carillion accounts, that further refers to a note 3 on page 27 of the accounts. This reads:

Non-recurring operating items

The non-recurring operating charge of £10.5 million in 2016 represents the amount expected to be paid, together with associated costs, under The Construction Workers Compensation Scheme set up by eight UK companies to compensate workers who have been impacted by use of the database vetting system operated by The Consulting Association.[5]

So in 2016 – 12 years after the supposed end of Carillion's blacklisting – Carillion is preparing to pay out more than £10 million for its blacklisting crimes. In May of that year, it was also one of the eight construction companies which finally agreed on compensation payments, at the High Court in London, to avoid going to trial.

It is difficult to comprehend the way blacklisting can destroy lives, especially when you can't get work for years and you don't know why. The Smith and Chamberlain book *Blacklisted* contains one heartbreaking story after another. John Breen, a labourer from North Ayrshire in Scotland, told the 2016 GMB conference: 'My blacklisting hit my family hard financially. We couldn't buy anything and had to live day to day and scrimp and save. It was too expensive just to go out and do things. We only made ends meet by relying on my wife's earnings. I would sit awake at night and wonder what went wrong and how I ended up in this situation.'[6] Then there's oil worker Jake Macleod, whose marriage broke up after he was blacklisted and could not get work for years: 'I tried to explain and it was alright for a wee while, but when it goes on and on, one Christmas after another, it becomes very tiring and you begin to argue in the house . . . I was only an ordinary bear but at the end of the day I fully appreciated that my missus could not take anymore.'[7]

In the ICO raid on the TCA offices it is on record that only 5 to 10% of the files held by Ian Kerr were taken. In the panic of being caught red-handed, Kerr was told to get rid of all the evidence. His brother-in-law arrived at the TCA offices and they loaded up his horse-box with all the papers that David Clancy and Co. had left behind. They took it all to the brother-in-law's house and burned the lot. Justin Bowden told me, 'Kerr's wife, Mary, said at one time on Radio 4 that the bonfire lasted for three days.' The point is that the historical numbers identified, including Carillion's actual blacklisting of 224 workers, are likely to be only a fraction of the real total. Justin Bowden says Carillion's history of blacklisting and the way the Goan workers were humiliated at the Great Western Hospital in Swindon tells us a lot about what was to be. 'When you can blacklist and bully for years, without as much as a second thought, turning to robbing the public purse is easy street.'

Carillion was formed out of a demerger from the construction and aggregates business, Tarmac. That was in 1999. Somehow there was a feeling among the Tarmac executives that the construction side of the business wasn't quite making its way. So best to cut it adrift and start counting the serious money to be made from quarrying stone and laying tarmac on roads. This analysis would prove to be mistaken. It is Carillion which became a colossus in construction and outsourced services, and Tarmac which was taken over by the mining giant, Anglo American.

The chief executive of Tarmac, Sir Neville Simms, was born in Glasgow and was a hard-nosed engineer who knew the building business. He chaired the first meeting of senior staff at the Birmingham Conference Centre in the summer of 1999 to mark the beginning of the new venture. Carillion was listed on the Stock Exchange on 30 July 1999. Simms tells the conference that he could see 'a lot of Tarmac ties' among the staff sitting at the tables in front of him. He tells them it is time to 'envisage a world without Tarmac. Time for a new dawn'. Then he explains the new name – Carillion. It comes from the French *carillon* meaning 'a peal of bells'. But, for some reason, with an 'i' added. He says again that this is a new start, a break with the past. The name has been chosen to mark the need for the new venture to grow by everyone working together. Simms says the choice of Carillion is significant for the future of the company: 'To get a proper peal of bells everyone has to be in harmony – each bell-ringer pulling the ropes of their bell at the exact right time.'

As the chief executive of Tarmac, Simms had been given a handsome pay-off to leave to take up the chief executive post at Carillion. He was given a golden goodbye in cash and shares worth £1.37 million. Nothing seems to happen in the history of Carillion without somebody somewhere getting a million pounds for something. This particular award was to help him make up his mind about taking on the new job, but also to compensate him for a £150,000 drop in salary. At Tarmac, Simms was paid £490,000 a year, and the salary at the new, smaller Carillion was £340,000. So right from the very beginnings of Carillion there was controversy about money.

Both staff and shareholders were dismayed about the grandiose excess doled out to Simms at the start. After Sir Neville's introductions at the Birmingham get-together there is a Q and A session. One of the workers asks Simms how he can possibly justify the new salary and the £1.37 million lump-sum bonus. The worker says that this is taking more than a million pounds out of the start-up money for the new business. Simms replies that it is the going rate – 'That's the market rate for a plc company chief executive,' he says. One worker who was at the Birmingham meeting says, 'We should have recognised it was going to be about share price from then on in.'

Sir Neville didn't falter on that front. Along with the other founding directors and managers of Carillion, he created a new incentive-based shares scheme which would reward them all handsomely if the share price reached 276p in three years' time. If the share price did hit that target the incentive scheme would pay out £17 million, with Simms getting some £3 million of that. Alas for them, the shares bombed to 160p due to market uncertainties about Carillion's public-sector earnings. That was in the month before the vesting date and everyone missed out on the possible bonanza. However, Sir Neville had started as he meant to go on. In fact, the creation of the Simms shares scheme was a fitting harbinger of the plunder of Carillion, by its directors, that never stopped.

In its final full set of accounts to 31 December 2016, Carillion's revenue was £5.2 billion for the year. Notwithstanding the recognition that Carillion's accounts had substantial question marks about their veracity – how can we explain the conquest of such dizzying financial heights? First of all, a sense of proportion is necessary. When Carillion was established in the demerger from Tarmac, it was already nearly a £2 billion business. The elements which made that up would prove to be the foundations on which the business was built in the next 20 years. In other words Carillion had a good start in life – the first full year accounts for 2000 record a turnover of £1.9 billion. Within that, commercial building projects – construction – are the largest element, worth £619 million in the accounts; foreign capital projects total £511 million. Among the other sectors it is notable that the two essentials for the future growth of the business – support services and public sector privatisation – are, as yet, relatively underdeveloped. Services, including facilities management, are worth £307 million and PFI (Private Finance Initiative) projects £249 million. The last full accounts before the crash show, for 2016, that support services had grown in value to £2,713 million and PPPs (Public Private Partnerships), which replaced the original PFI outsourcing, reached £313 million. These figures may not be strictly comparable, but they serve as reliable indicators of the most important vectors in Carillion's development. Wikipedia has produced a comprehensive list of the major projects delivered by Carillion before its demise (the whole list is included in the Appendix).

From 2000 to 2017 the major project total is 57. Thirty-six of these were built in the UK. They include projects which are immediately recognisable, including the Royal Opera House, Tate Modern, Heathrow Terminal 5, the Birmingham Library, the Queen Elizabeth University Hospital in Glasgow, and Liverpool FC's Anfield redevelopment. The total list includes 12 projects in the Middle East and six in Canada. Significantly, 47 out of the 57 total are public-sector contracts of one type or another, which have been outsourced to be built and very often also serviced by Carillion.

Over time the public/private outsourcing under the PFI initiative was replaced by PPPs in the UK. Carillion developed the PFI/PPP strategy to win work in the British public sector. That experience was then applied to capture a host of similar contracts for roads, hospitals and schools as successive Canadian governments took to the privatisation road. The Canadian shift was repeated elsewhere, in the Caribbean and other parts of Europe. So the ruthless exploitation of the market created by the outsourcing of major public sector projects and services, in the UK and internationally, is a key element to understanding how Carillion reached its £5 billion zenith. In 2001 the arrival of John McDonough as Carillion's chief executive becomes the personification of the turn the company makes towards service provision and facilities management – school meals and running hospitals and prisons become much more important than building roads and delivering huge construction projects like the Tate Modern. McDonough is the first CEO to recognise the potential in services and facilities management, not least in the rates of return.

From 2003 to 2007, the profit rate in Carillion's construction services crawls forward, year after year, on 1% or just above that. In contrast, over the same five years, the rate of profit in support services averages 4.7%. The differences play out much more clearly in money. By 2007 support services and PPP account for more than double the profits of construction – £99.3 million compared to £41.4 million respectively.[8] 2007 is the first year that the total revenues from support services and PPP projects almost match that from construction.

The move away from construction towards support services doesn't happen overnight. The figures from as late as 2007 – six years into McDonough's term as CEO – demonstrate that. Revenues from construction at £1,660 million are still ahead of support services, if only just, at £1,570 million. The shift begins in the early years of the decade where construction projects are combined with maintenance and service agreements. This involves Carillion delivering support services after the construction phase of a project is completed. For example, with Carillion building hospitals but also then providing non-clinical facilities management – cleaning, laundry, transport and so forth – in what were signed off as 25 to 30-year services contracts. Among the first 'build and manage' contracts in the NHS were the Great Western Hospital in Swindon (2002), the John Radcliffe Hospital in Oxford (2006) and two similar projects in Toronto and Ottawa in Canada around the same time.

Before that happens, in 2001, Sir Neville Simms has to be forced into a sideways shift from chief executive to chairman, and John McDonough, fresh from a decade in facilities management with a multinational American concern, takes over as the CEO. An article in *Building* magazine remarked on the Carillion shift, which by this time, was being pursued by all major construction services companies. 'Such was the relentless switch to focus on support services at the time, it was impossible not to think that here was a firm treating cleaning toilets as though it was the answer to all contractors' troubles. They used to be a builder, didn't they?'[9]

The real explosion in PFI took place under the Tony Blair/ Gordon Brown Labour governments between 1997 and 2010. The financing of PFI projects was done by private backers, so you could get new hospitals, new schools and new roads built without the bottom line going anywhere near government-spending totals. Here was a Labour government that could build you hospitals and schools, but was also able to claim that it prudently watched the balance sheet of government spending. One senior political advisor to the Blair government once told the author: 'It's jam today. Labour builds you a new local hospital. Now you know and I know that the taxpayer will have to pay for it for 30 years, but they'll forget that bit. They'll remember they've got a new hospital from the Labour government'. In 2006 the Labour government signed off PFI projects worth more than £7 billion.[10] The arrival of the Cameron/Osborne government heralds the shift from PFI to PPP, where the drive to privatise services is relentlessly developed but the new private vehicle involves a partnership – with the public-sector partner linking up with a private provider, like Carillion. This shift will be followed later by another – the direct outsourcing of services to private companies.

In order to demonstrate this shift away from construction in the McDonough era, it might be useful to consider where Carillion had got to by this direction of travel at the time it went bust in 2018. At that point some of the support services contracts in the business involved:

- Defence – 10 contracts including the Services Families housing contracts and construction and maintenance services on military sites – worth an estimated £510 million
- Prisons – facilities management services for half the prisons in England and Wales
- NHS – 25 contracts, including support services for 13 NHS Hospital Trusts and the building of two NHS hospitals, both taken together worth £287 million
- Schools – 312 contracts for support services like cleaning, school meals, and building projects, worth an estimated £79 million

- Transport – 22 contracts with Network Rail involving HS2 and rail maintenance projects, worth an estimated £372 million
- Canada – the final contract signed there on 7 December 2016 was worth an estimated £120 million for power line construction and transmission for the state of Manitoba.[11]

Carillion's march towards this development of support services started with winning contracts for rail maintenance and its take-over of Citex in 2002. Citex was then providing repair and security services for local authority housing across the UK. It specialised in boarding up empty council houses. After Citex came three major takeovers – Mowlem (2006), Sir Alfred McAlpine (2008) and Eaga (2011). These takeovers, which were ground-breaking for Carillion's support services development, were also, in the longer term, fundamental to the creation of its unsustainable debt burden.

The combined takeovers cost Carillion well over £1 billion – Mowlem £350 million, Sir Alfred McAlpine £565 million, and Eaga £302 million. On top of that, the purchases included Carillion taking on responsibility for the collective pension deficits of each company. By the time of the Eaga purchase in 2011, the collective pension deficit in the Mowlem and McAlpine schemes had grown to £424 million. There could be trouble ahead. But this was in the era where Carillion's board, led by McDonough, believed that Carillion could capture a monopoly stake in the new support services market through the takeover of its key market competitors. That could guarantee the future. Private provision of support services was growing at breakneck speed as PFI and other outsourcing took hold across the entire British public sector.

As far as the Carillion board was concerned, besides the identifiable risks of costs and burgeoning pension dues, there was one huge payback which made taking the takeovers worthwhile. They allowed loading up Carillion's balance sheet with a mountain of goodwill 'intangible assets'. In all three acquisitions, the estimates of goodwill recorded on the assets side of the Carillion balance sheet were considerably more than the purchase price for each adventure: goodwill for the Mowlem purchase was £431 million,

McAlpine £615 million, and Eaga £329 million. That is compared to the respective purchase prices of £350 million, £565 million and £302 million. As explained in Chapter One, 'goodwill' can be defined as the difference between the price paid for the takeover of a company and the actual value of its tangible assets. It can also be seen as a 'hope quotient' – an estimate of the profits which will flow in later years from the takeover venture. The main thing to grasp is that the costs of the takeovers on the liabilities side of the books was offset by exaggerated estimates of goodwill on the asset side of the balance sheet. The goodwill total for Mowlem, McAlpines and Eaga of £1,375 million, added to the balance sheet, accounted for 88% of the 'intangible assets' then recorded in the accounts for 2011. It has already been noted that the Carillion accounts showed very little impairment of goodwill year on year. From the time of the Mowlem takeover in 2006, there is not a single year where the net assets in the accounts are greater than the goodwill 'intangibles'. In truth, without the goodwill added in the books, following each takeover Carillion would have been insolvent.

Carillion is typical of most mega-services and construction companies in this regard. On the other hand, it has also already been established that such sharp practices, whilst legal, were crucial to Carillion becoming 'an unsustainable corporate time bomb'. There is a further caveat to note. It concerns the 'follow the money' trail. Goodwill helps to maintain the balance sheet. Good profits mean sizeable dividends can be paid out. In turn, that links to what the company executives can be paid. One year after the Mowlem takeover, McDonough offered his opinion: 'It was better than we thought. It was the Koh-i-Noor diamond.' This was a reference to the takeover resulting in the capture of the then biggest-ever PFI contract, worth £12 billion. It was for services and construction projects on the Allenby and Connaught army bases for the Ministry of Defence. This was the 'diamond contract', but that is not the only reason McDonough had fought tooth and nail for the takeover.

You see, Mowlem was ahead of Carillion in the diversification away from construction, and had a pipeline of long-term service contracts worth £2.4 billion at the time. As a result, Carillion went toe to toe with Balfour Beatty in a battle for Mowlem. Corners were cut in the due diligence to get the deal over the line. McDonough was prepared to pay the price. In the run-up to the bid he had agreed to a write-down on Mowlem's books of £45 million. It emerged after the takeover that the forecasts of two major Mowlem contracts were out by £90 million – so that was another hefty write-down which put the buying price up to £440 million – £90 million on top of the original bid of £350 million. One senior City figure said at the time, 'Millions of pounds of write-downs and they don't seem to have been punished. They got away with it.'[12] They wouldn't always.

It took a year for the Mowlem problems to be sorted and the takeover to be integrated into Carillion's new structure. It's not that all the Mowlem interests were subsumed into Carillion. Rather, that they become integrated as part of the Carillion Group plc.

The next stop for the takeover train was 2008. This time the target was the construction and services giant Sir Alfred McAlpine. In February 2008, the deal was done for £565 million. Again the buyout was not determined by the attraction of taking over McAlpine's construction services, but by the scale of its support services. The takeover raised revenues for the new combined Carillion by 32% to £5.2 billion, in the year to end December 2008. But support services revenues went from £1,569 million to £2,227 million – an increase of 37%. There were swirling rumours in the City that Carillion had again botched the due diligence on the deal and was facing a £183 million impairment on goodwill to cover that. It didn't show up anywhere in the books. The dream had come true for McDonough – the new Carillion was now the biggest support services company in the UK. This after embarking on the quest only seven years before. What could possibly go wrong?

The purchase of Eaga, the green-energy products and renewals company, is the answer. It was the third of the 'Big Three' acquisitions. The takeover was complete by early April 2011. Eaga was renamed Carillion Energy Services (CES) when it became the energy services offer for Carillion. The annual report of 2011 was fulsome in its praise of the Eaga takeover and the future prospects that the takeover would bring, in the usual gobbledegook of company annual reports:

> The acquisition of CES in April 2011 was an important strategic development, driven primarily by the need to extend our support services offering to include energy efficiency services, given that these services are an increasingly important part of the integrated facilities management and maintenance solutions required by our customers. The acquisition has also taken the Group into new markets with good prospects for growth.[13]

Unfortunately Carillion's due diligence and analysis were fundamentally flawed. A matter of months after the takeover was signed off, the Conservative government cut the subsidies that homeowners got for installing energy-saving solar panels. Solar panels were a big part of Eaga's business. In the first post-takeover year the subsidies cut resulted in a 20% slump in sales and a £113 million loss. The Carillion board had underestimated the degree to which Eaga's revenues were dependent on government funding; further, they had miscalculated hugely on the Cameron/Osborne government's commitment to continue to fund its much-hyped, so-called 'Green revolution'.

In 2010–11 the Government was spending £345 million on its 'Warm Front' fuel poverty programme, which was run at that time by Eaga. In the year that followed, 2011–12, when CES took over the programme, government funding fell to £100 million. By 2014 the 'Warm Front' programme was no more[14] – fallen victim to George Osborne's savage austerity programmes. In 2011, Carillion had predicted that the proposals in Government's 'Green Deal' programme on home energy improvements would kick-start a £14 billion investment boom in energy efficiency assets which would last for ten years. The 'Green Deal' programme was launched in 2013 and was scrapped two years later due to lack of take up. There was no green investment boom.

When the takeover went through, Eaga's turnover was £663 million. Five years later, by 2016, turnover had slumped disastrously to £43 million. CES was effectively bust by then. Carillion's cumulative losses for the Eaga catastrophe totalled £370 million.[15] In 2016 that was just over half the value of the net assets of the whole group – £729 million. McDonough had been at the helm when Carillion's ship had embarked on the Eaga adventure and there is no doubt it took the shine off what many saw as his golden era.

People respected McDonough – 'If John McDonough told you to paint the boardroom pink, you made sure you painted the boardroom pink,' as one senior manager who wanted to remain anonymous told me. Yet it was not long into the Eaga saga that questions were being asked – 'Has he lost his touch?' There was also the growing crisis of the yawning pension deficit; he might have wanted to avoid that blemish on his business reputation by getting out early. These factors may have been influential in McDonough's somewhat unexpected announcement, in August 2011, that he was stepping down at the end of the year as the chief executive. At the time he told the *Financial Times*, 'I have a house down in South Africa so I'm going to relax down there, hopefully lose a bit of weight, get fitter. Mrs McDonough thinks it's all a jolly good idea . . . I want to take a break and think about life.' Given the way in which McDonough had struggled in his 11 years as CEO to turn the Carillion tanker round in a new direction, if he had, in fact, been told by the board that it was time to go, you just might feel some sympathy for him. But that would be before you had acquainted yourself with all the facts buried in the Carillion accounts. If Sir Neville Simms started the plunder of Carillion, McDonough never missed his chances either.

His top-line pay in the last two years alone may have made his mind up about wanting to feel more of the Cape Town sun on his back. In 2010 two sets of loyalty shares, rewards for sticking with the company, matured. That was worth £1.84 million. His salary and benefits that year are £1.02m; 2011's take is bigger and better at £1.5 million. So, in the two years before leaving Carillion, McDonough takes £4.36 million out of the company. In 2006, McDonough broke the one million pound salary barrier at Carillion. After that he never looked back. His total remuneration for his 11 years at Carillion is £10.65 million. Then, in 2012, he collected his performance bonuses for 2011 – £632,400. That broke the £11 million 'sound barrier', at £11.33 million.

In effect, McDonough is a British oligarch because, in his time, most of the wealth created by Carillion was drawn from lucrative contracts provided by the state. In that sense his £11 million plus rewards can be described as looting the state. Welcome to the club. In fairness we should say he was not alone. Richard Howson took up where McDonough left off. He gathered in £5.62 million over five years as McDonough's successor. Each of them, at one time or another, may have been seen as potentially capable of saving Carillion from the abyss. In reality they were its gravediggers. And it was McDonough and his fellow executives who set Carillion on the path to ruin. That path was built by fiddling the books with goodwill fantasy figures, by ignoring the calamity of the growing pension deficit, by creating a mountain of debt through a reckless takeover strategy that would never pay, while forever concealing the creation of the world's largest-ever Ponzi scheme behind a farrago of lies and deceit.

In Carillion's 2016 balance sheet the £1,669 million entry for 'intangible assets', comprising mostly of 'goodwill' assessments, was actually fictitious capital. It could not pay for anything or reduce debts because it was not real money. When this fog of goodwill on the books was dissipated by the cold wind of a cash crisis – that is, running out of money – there was nowhere left to turn, except to pray for a Government bail-out. The cold wind left Carillion with £29 million in the bank, facing debts and liabilities of almost £7 billion. Their day in court, at the Rolls Building, in the High Courts of Justice, then beckoned.

In a similar way, Carillion's introduction of its Early Payment Facility (EPF) in 2013 represents another historic tipping point which exemplifies what is going on. For years Carillion had been notorious as a deliberate late payer. Rumour has it that invoices presented to their accounts department were sent back because there were spelling mistakes or commas in the wrong place. All to delay payment. That keeps money in their accounts and on their balance sheet. The introduction of the EPF is concrete proof that circumstances are getting desperate. The Ponzi scheme is running out of new deposits. Carillion extends its payment terms to 120 days for all its suppliers. The subcontractors can reduce that to 45 days if they utilise the EPF at one of the named banks which are organising it.

The way that works is that Carillion has to approve the subcontractor invoice, with a discount taken off for the privilege of 45 days' settlement. The bank pays and Carillion settles with the bank at 90 days after their presentation. It is not difficult to see, with 30,000 subcontractors lining up to be paid, how this financial jiggery-pokery keeps hundreds of millions in Carillion's accounts that should not be there. The EPF could also be seen as desperate straits writ large. Carillion didn't classify what it then owed the banks as 'borrowings'. Instead that was kept off the balance sheet under the heading 'other creditors'. After the collapse, the major credit agencies said that £498 million of debts had been misclassified through this scam.

Carillion's indebtedness eventually results in underbidding to win contracts at all costs – to keep the cash rolling in. This has become known as 'suicide bidding'. At worst, when contracts are won by such undercutting bids they at least preserve a place in the market place for the company, in the hope of better days to come; they also provide a certain cash flow, especially if an early cash advance can be negotiated, even if the outcome will be an eventual loss. At best, on some contracts, the bidder can secure a contract on 'land and expand'. That is, it can make a suicide bid on loss-making terms with the aim of trying to bump up the price by securing extra payments for delays, changes in the specification and other contract variations. In its later years suicide bidding was custom and practice for Carillion. In fact, much of its international expansion was established by such bidding.

In June 2018 it emerged that Carillion had won a bid for servicing almost half the prison estate in England and Wales – 52 prisons, almost all in the south-east of the UK. Carillion had undercut the tender guidelines by £15 million. Rory Stewart MP was Minister for Prisons then. He told the Justice Committee in Parliament that the Carillion bid offered to do the prison maintenance for £15 million less than it would cost Her Majesty's Prison Service (HMP). Stewart told the committee that the Prison Service could not wait to sign the deal, such was the offer. In retrospect he says maybe more time should have been given to exploring the question 'What on earth is Carillion proposing here? They're basically proposing to do this and lose £15 million a year. Is that really sustainable, or are we going to end up in the situation where we are paying for it?'

Here endeth the lesson? Not quite. The PACAC (Public Affairs and Constitutional Affairs Committee) Inquiry Report into Carillion includes a savage indictment of how the Tory government, since it came to power in 2010, made lowest price the determinant of the outsourcing of Government contracts. It described the Government's preoccupation with price as 'a matter of grave concern'; adding further that 'The Government's failure to assess the quality of services as well as their cost is lamentable'.[16] PACAC called for a complete re-appraisal of the current outsourcing practice where price has become the only factor to be considered in procurement. This leads to the conclusion that if the directors of Carillion are to be indicted for the criminal negligence of their duties under the Companies Act, they should be accompanied in the dock by a platoon of government ministers.

Late in 2018, when I met Rudi Klein, the head of the Specialist Engineering Contractors' Group representing thousands of engineering companies, I asked him about Carillion's downfall. He repeated a quote he had made at the time: 'The most shocking revelation is that a £5 billion global company was run by a bunch of incompetents.' He qualified that opinion by noting that the Carillion directors were not incompetent at drawing down their salaries, ensuring their pensions were paid up and cashing in their share options. During the history of Carillion the company directors looted the business for £46,627,000. They counted their money as some of the best engineers and craftsmen the world has known left the company before they were drowned in a sea of maintaining American military bases across the UK, serving up thousands of school dinners, organising the laundry at hundreds of hospitals, or making sure that the cookers and fridges worked in the houses where soldiers and their families lived. The history of Carillion is a story of how a construction company, once capable of creating some of the engineering wonders of the world, was reduced to a gigantic racket.

On 15 January 2018, the GMB's National Management Team met at the GMB offices in London. An alert buzzed on one of the union members' mobile phones. Right away he blurted out, 'Bloody hell, Carillion's gone into liquidation.' Gary Smith, GMB Scotland's general secretary, remembers thinking when he heard this that 'Thousands of jobs will go. The subbies [subcontractors] will get slaughtered. The taxpayers will have to cough up and the top people will walk away, not a hair on their heads out of place.' Steve Paul remembers very clearly how he found out about the Carillion collapse. At the time he was running his plastering and flooring business in the West Midlands. His company, SDP Plastering, had contracts with Carillion for building floors on the Midland Metropolitan Hospital project in Birmingham. What had started out as a half-million-pound contract had turned into potential returns reaching four times that. 'It had the look of a real good earner,' he tells me when we meet.

Also on 15 January 2018, Steve got a call from one of his supervisors on the Met project at about eight in the morning. 'He told me the gates were locked and the men couldn't get on site. Everything was padlocked. There were security guards. All our materials and plant for the floors were inside the gates. We had to wait for weeks to get them out,' he says. Steve never really saw it coming. Carillion's payments had become awkward before Christmas. As usual they were disputing what they owed. Steve puts that down to the usual obstructions and evasions of payment negotiations in the construction business. He tells me, 'That was the same with Carillion every Christmas. They had a reputation in the trade for shutting down for Christmas – then they could go to 90-day payments in the New Year and that could mean not paying their suppliers between December and March. People took that as normal. So when they only paid out a fraction of what we were owed in December I didn't think much of it. That was how it worked.' He makes his point and then shrugs his shoulders with a kind of 'What can you do?' air. You can tell he's got a weariness in his bones about it.

When Steve's company took on the Carillion Midland Metropolitan contract it was worth, as he says, around half a million pounds for laying floors. Then, just as the job was starting, the surveyors told him that the design for the main frame of the building had been botched, and as a result the columns across the entire building were not strong enough to carry the load that would be in a conventional concrete floor. Steve says that meant they had to invest in a special product for the construction of much lighter floors – 'That cost a lot of money, but the contract with the lightweight flooring became potentially worth millions for us. Millions. Because we had the special flooring we were getting much more for each floor and were signed up for a much bigger share of the total flooring because we found the right product to make the lightweight floors.'

At the time of the Carillion crash Steve recalls that his firm had some 20 men working on the Midland hospital contract. He says he had 300 men working on 20 different sites, on different jobs across the West Midlands. Carillion's collapse meant they were left out of pocket for more than £700,000. Along with payment problems with another major contractor, that provoked a cash flow crisis in the business. Here's how he describes the way the cut-throat payment system goes round and round. Early in 2017 – in other words long before Carillion went down – there was another contractor who owed Steve's company more than £400,000. The contractor knows Steve has a lot on with Carillion and they are taking 120 days to pay. He offers to pay Steve an initial £40,000. 'What are you going to do, Steve?' the contractor asks him. Then he follows up with a threat: 'We are going to dig our heels in. I've got a team of lawyers working in London on this stuff. It'll cost you fifty grand just to go to court and you don't have the money. Better to accept this offer.' Steve says, 'Outside of the construction industry it would be called organised crime.' He got the down payment and then some, but nowhere near the whole amount. So before the Carillion collapse there was little in the bank to help out when the crisis came.

Steve told me, 'We couldn't pay the men, we couldn't pay suppliers and we couldn't pay for the plant. The dominoes came tumbling down. We had to let 100 people go in the January. Right away. I've taken some hits in business in my time but Carillion put me over the edge. It broke me. I couldn't take it anymore.' Steve had a nervous breakdown. His wife Steph says that in all the struggles they've had in business she had never seen him in such a state. She says, 'He couldn't get out of bed. It seemed to last for weeks and weeks. He couldn't speak. But every morning I had to get out of bed and go to work, to keep the business going. What else could I do? Quite frankly, every day I wondered what I was going to walk into when I came home.' Steve is much better now, but Steph says the whole thing is still raw. 'He can break down any time talking about what happened.'

Not every business in Carillion's supply chain has suffered as much as Steve and Steph's company. Nonetheless, the scale of personal tragedy should be exposed. Carillion's collapse left 30,000 small businesses owed £2 billion according to official reports. Steve and Steph would both agree that the building industry has given them a decent life, not least because in the good times they made good money – in fact the good times put money in the bank which allowed them to ride out more than one crisis. It is different when every penny has to be counted. While the business was at its very best Steve and Steph had hundreds of employees on the books and an annual turnover reaching more than £13 million. He can remember, though, that even in those times of plenty there were payment problems that overnight could plunge them suddenly towards financial disaster. He talks about the precarious economics: 'The wage bill was £450,000 a fortnight for squads making up more than 300 on the wage bill. That is a £900,000 pay-out in wages before your first monthly invoice is submitted. Now if the big contractor takes 30 days to pay, if you get lucky, the business is still out £2 million before there's a penny put in the bank from the work! Sometimes I wonder how we managed it.'

Steve believes that the construction industry is now so corrupt that when the big companies know you are in trouble with one contract they'll put the squeeze on you. And if that puts the subcontractor out of business then the main contractor can then walk, paying much less than they actually owe. 'I've been told that the big companies have training schools for their survey- ors on "how to screw the subbies". I don't doubt it,' Steve says. Steve has worked in construction since he left school and got a job as a plasterer. Early on in the trade he was already thinking that he had to build his own business, because he recognised the physical demands of the job would be too much by the time he was in his 50s. His first big break came in the mid-1980s was when he got a four-month contract with Walsall Council. By the mid-1990s he had built up the business, largely on contracts from Wolverhampton Council, to 60 staff. He says it's been 'a proper rollercoaster' ever since.

If you ask him about the rollercoaster he talks about surviving the Crash which followed the 2008 banking crisis. He says he remem- bers the dread he felt when the letterbox rattled. Every day there were letters from another set of accountants or lawyers telling him that another of his customers had gone bust. Steve and Steph think the 2008 crash cost the business between £700,000 and £750,000. They survived that miraculously without even having an overdraft in the bank and rebuilt the business. That was possible because they had money in the bank from a previous long-term bonanza in building when the contracts just kept coming and everyone in the supply chain was happy to pay. They didn't survive Carillion because they had no capital in the bank to bail themselves out. He doesn't say that was because the contractor who owed him £400,000 didn't pay up in full, but you get that impression.

I interviewed Steve and Steph at their house outside Lichfield in the Midlands. That was in mid-October 2018, nine months after the Carillion collapse. Steph and I talked whilst we were waiting for Steve to get back home. She has been steadfast in trying to save the business – she and Steve were the two shareholders. She told me they had sold out a month before. The new owner took on more than a million pounds in debts and paid them £1 each for their shares. That was it. When Steve got to that point in his part of the story he had to take a breath to compose himself. He employed six family members in the business and feels as if he has left everyone down. Steve and Steph are going to have to sell the house because they took personal guarantees to raise money for the business. 'We can't afford to keep it up,' Steve sighs.

Steph tells me she had been to the Job Centre the day before. 'First time I'm my life. I've worked for 40 years, always worked. Even when I had the kids I worked part-time in the local shops or something. We've never been in this situation. I asked the woman at the Job Centre "How do you sign on – is that what they call it now?" She asked me if I was willing to accept the minimum wage – £10 an hour. I said "Yes, of course." Then she asked if I was willing to take a job that could take me a one-and-a-half-hour commute to work?'

CHAPTER 9

'Money from Heaven' and the Crash

'There is one and only one social responsibility of business – to use its resources and engage in activities designed to increase its profits . . . anything else is unadulterated socialism.'

> Milton Friedman, *New York Times Magazine*, 1970.

'In there we were all in one place, a generation lost in space, with no time left to start again.'

> Don McLean, 'American Pie', October 1971

How did we get here? If Carillion is being considered as an exemplar of the state we are in, then the answer to the question obviously has to go well beyond Carillion. To this end, some of the contributors to *Foreign Affairs* – the in-house journal of the American establishment – argue therefore that today's crises merit a return to some of the sweeping theoretical conceptions first developed by Karl Marx. A 2018 essay by Robin Varghese, the leading economist and academic, noted: 'He [Marx] predicted that capitalism's internal logic would over time lead to rising inequality, chronic unemployment and underemployment, stagnant wages, the dominance of large, powerful firms, and the creation of an entrenched elite whose power would act as a barrier to social progress . . . As a result, Marxism, far from being outdated, is crucial for making sense of the world today.'[1] For good measure, Varghese commented further: 'The rich are getting richer, the masses are getting screwed and the system is finally going into crisis. What did you expect from capitalism?'[2]

Marx's theory of historical materialism argued that it was the movement of the great economic forces of society which was the determining factor in the evolution of history. So he argued that 'the development of the means of production' was the key to understanding the social structure of society. Economics was the base on which the superstructure of social relations was built.

Marx also wrote that the struggle of the classes – the working class and the capitalist class – would be a permanent feature of capitalism, based on the development of capitalism being predicated upon periods of huge growth in the means of production being contradicted by the inevitability of periods of crisis. The closest the modern idiom gets to those ideas is the concept of 'boom and bust'. Many academics and politicians spent much of the 1990s explaining that this Marxist theory was now totally discredited by the way capitalism's enormous economic forces were cancelling out the inevitability of crisis. Capitalism was now 'self-stabilising' and thus had gone beyond periodic crises. The Crash of 2008 put paid to that argument.

In modern history, the 2008 banking crisis and the Crash which followed stand out as decisive events in which, as predicted by Marx and Engels, slow quantitative changes resulted in eventual qualitative change – the collapse of the world's financial system. At the time, Ben Bernanke, chairman of America's central bank, the Federal Reserve, called it 'the worst financial crisis in history'. The Crash also had significance for how the later crisis at Carillion developed.

So how should this analysis of 'How did we get here?' proceed? Firstly, we have to consider a number of significant economic variables. These include the shift from stakeholder to shareholder capitalism; the deregulation of the banks and the rise and rise of financial capitalism, collectively recognised as 'financialisation'; the explosion of what became known as 'credit derivatives' and their effect on global capitalism; and how all these variables played out in real life. These variables are interconnected in time. They develop, they meet, overlap and then create a new economic synthesis, but it is possibly easier to analyse them separately, 'other things being equal', as the economists like to put it. They are important for an understanding of how we got to the Crash of 2008 and what followed.

Enter Professor Milton Friedman, chief evangelist of the group which became known as the 'Chicago Boys' – those who first preached the economic ideology which became known as monetarism. Friedman and the 'Chicago Boys', from the University of Chicago, eventually became advisors to President Ronald Reagan, Prime Minister Margaret Thatcher and Chilean military dictator Augusto Pinochet. In the inflation-haunted 1970s they extolled the economic virtues of controlling the money supply, letting the free market rip and reducing the state as near to ground zero as was practically possible. Friedman argued that it was big government spending that was ruining the delivery of profits at the sharp end of corporate capitalism. He once admitted that in the 1970s and '80s he was considered a crank. By the 1990s his ideas had become the new mainstream of economic ideology.

In 1970 Friedman wrote an article for the *New York Times* in which he argued for a boardroom revolution to make the promotion of shareholder value the new economic science of corporate capital. It was time to shift 'stakeholder' capitalism to a much more functional 'shareholder' capitalism, if the market was to be free and profits maximised. Just like his monetarist theories it took time for this new theory to become universally exalted. But by the early 1990s the omnipotence of the share price and rates of profit was the new irrefutable doctrine of capital. Maximising shareholder value or MSV was going to sweep all before it. The dividend obsession of the Carillion directors cannot be understood without first examining MSV.

The concept of MSV was based on the emergence of the 'agency theory'. This proposed that when companies were run by managers or agents who were at a remove from the investors or shareholders, they would inevitably serve additional interests beyond the maximisation of profit. They would become part of a waged bureaucracy, spending too much time and money on employees, customers and the community at large. Friedman, and the others who followed, argued for this 'managerial capitalism' to be junked in favour of maximising shareholder value. That outcome would be forged by the creation of a new executive class dedicated only to the maximisation of profit at the expense of all else. In her book *The Value of Everything*, Professor Mariana Mazzucato compares two mission statements from two IBM presidents. In 1968 Tom Watson Jr extolled IBM's three core priorities: 1, respect for individual employees; 2, a commitment to customer service; and 3, achieving excellence. How times changed. By 2000 the IBM president, Samuel Palmisano, had dumped the managerial flim-flam – IBM's main aim, he insisted, was 'to double earnings per share over the next five years'.[3] It could not be clearer.

So how was the managerial bureaucrat to be transformed into a corporate capitalist, obsessed with share price and dividends? The answer was simple – a substantial proportion of the senior executives' salaries and bonuses would be tied to the company share price and performance. That would deliver an army of corporate executives determined to promote the company share price. Those certainly became the watchwords for Richard Adam and the other directors at Carillion. If share options are then loaded up on top of these rewards, we reach the end game. MSV becomes the key motivation in every boardroom, share price is sacrosanct and the corporate bosses of the world think they are entitled to percentage deals in millions of dollars, or their equivalent, if company assets grow. And in many cases, even if they don't grow. This is the road that led to Enron's fraudster chief executive, Jeff Skilling, taking home hundreds of millions of dollars for decades before his downfall and the jailing that followed; it led to Lehman's chief executive, Richard Fuld, owning six private jets and too many fast cars to count on his earnings of $485 million between 2000 and 2008, before Lehman's debt mountain engulfed him; it led to the initial £45 billion tax-payer bail-out of RBS and its chief executive, Fred Goodwin, with him demanding he walk away with an annual pension of more than £700,000; and it led to Richard Adam retiring from Carillion with a £1.1 million pay off and share options which he cashed in months later worth more than three-quarters of a million pounds.

Grace Blakeley is a research fellow with the Institute for Public Policy Research (IPPR) which in 2018 produced what could described as a future prospectus for Britain in the final report of its Commission for Economic Justice (CEJ). Blakeley produced a discussion paper for the CEJ entitled 'On Borrowed Time – Finance and the UK's Current Account Deficit'. We met in a Pret a Manger coffee shop near the Old Street tube station in London. 'On Borrowed Time' is high-end economics, but Blakeley seems to have a precious ability to explain in plain English the complexities that often have to accompany PhD-style academic papers. We started talking about maximising shareholder value. I asked her why it had become so all-powerful in the world's corporate boardrooms, and why did she think the chief executives of today – like the Royal Mail's CEO Rico Back lifting a £6.6 million 'golden hello' – could get away with it. She replied: 'Under today's capitalism, if you are a corporate boss you are going to do whatever you can to make money. Then more on top of that. That's the name of the game. They do it because they can. Only the power of government and, on the other hand, organised labour, can stop that scale of greed.'

She added that, starting with Thatcher, Conservative governments have actively encouraged the creation of a Britain fit for billionaires. She argued that the political justification for this was the ideology of trickle-down. The old assertion that a rising tide raises all boats in the harbour. 'Nobody argues that anymore. Austerity has seen to that. Some trickle!' she scoffed. Blakeley believes that a class hatred of the rich is now growing in the UK because of the gargantuan scale of wealth the corporate oligarchs are appropriating for themselves. As we have seen, Frank Field MP once described the motives of the Carillion directors as 'greed on stilts'. Grace Blakeley believes that this conspicuous greed factor, which is omnipresent within the British corporate class, is undermining social support for capitalism. She adds, 'How do they get away with it? Well, the decisive decline of the trade unions figures in that in a big way.'

She insists that in today's Britain there is no substantial countervailing force challenging corporate power because of the relative weakness of the unions. 'In the private sector, in effect, there is hardly any collective bargaining to speak of. So you have this one force in corporate Britain, one force maximising shareholder value, and you don't have the unions on the other side saying "No, no, no".' In the Pret a Manger she describes financialisation as the way in which the stock market, the banks and other financial institutions have come to control almost every single other process in our economy. In her paper 'On Borrowed Time' there's more:

> Over the last 30 years the financial sector has grown as a proportion of the UK economy. It is now a major contributor to jobs, tax receipts and value-added in the UK economy. But these benefits have come at a cost. Financialisation – defined as the increasing role of financial motives, financial markets, financial actors and financial institutions in the economy – makes the UK prone to financial crises, by increasing the volume of lending to businesses and consumers in the upswing of a financial cycle, and the withdrawal of such credit as the bubble bursts, leading to periods of . . . deeper and longer recessions than might occur otherwise.[4]

She says that financialisation means that the people at the top of the *Sunday Times* Rich List most likely don't make anything. 'They'll be rich through hedge funds, banking, real estate, insurance; they don't create wealth, they don't create jobs, they're into wealth transfer from one section of the economy to another.'

When asked to explain further she uses the million-pound man as an illustration. She argues that if an entrepreneur had come into a million pounds in the 1950s and wanted his money to grow, he might have bought a factory, or factories, to make things which are needed and could be sold at a profit to increase the value of the investment. So there's a post-war housing shortage and the entrepreneur builds a brick factory. The factory would create bricks for sale on the market, which in the good old days would deliver a profit; there would be more people in steady reasonably-paid jobs; they would be paying taxes to the government as well as corporate tax coming in from the company; a process of real wealth creation is how she described it. Then she talked about what you would do with the equivalent sum of a million pounds today – obviously much more than a million pounds in today's prices – if you wanted your money to grow. 'Today, if you had say a billion pounds and you were in London, you'd put the money into real estate and wait for the price of the real estate – the office block, the housing or whatever – to go up. Then you'd sell it off and put the money through your shell company in the Cayman Islands to avoid tax.' She went on to quote some Marxist economics. Marx's old theory of value is based on the equation M-C-M. Money creates a commodity which is sold for a greater amount of money after it is produced, which creates profits. 'Today that equation has been totally undermined by the monopoly of financial capital. The equation from the London property deal is now M-M. Money goes to more money, and there's no real wealth created. One piece of paper becomes another piece of paper,' she told me.

She might have been talking about the Celtic Tiger in Ireland, because what happened there turned out to be the embodiment of the Crash. It was also the embodiment of a moral poverty which in the years leading to the Crash gripped the world's business elites. The Celtic Tiger brought undreamed wealth to those able to exploit the economic boom signalled by its roar. Beyond doubt, the Tiger was fed on the fruits of financialisation and its precursor, deregulation, which developed an 'anything goes' ethos in Ireland's financial world; in turn that became the driving force behind the emergence of the Celtic Tiger's own *nouveau riche* Irish oligarchy.

Above all, the glory years of the Tiger boom were based on a banking boom made out of banknotes piling up on bank balance sheets with billion-euro totals. The watchwords still echo down history – Lend, lend, lend! Spend, spend, spend! Then, when the Tiger roared no more, brought down by the laws of the capitalist jungle which took the very skin off its back, who was to pay the price? Not the new banking oligarchs and their awestruck admirers in the Irish government, but the poor who had never really fed on the bounty of the hunt at any point. It was they who would redeem the Tiger's paper promissory notes in the form of a decade of savage government budget cuts and austerity that followed the Crash. Thus the Celtic Tiger, and the politicians and bankers who worshipped on their knees before its miraculous economic achievements, ended in the imposition of a mass financial penance dictated by the forlorn economic panacea of reducing government debt to 'balance the books'. The Celtic Tiger's greed, skyscraper lies and corrupt swindles were also triple-A grade typical of how the global Crash reached us. Here were Irish banks and other international shadow financial concerns lending money they did not really have to borrowers who ultimately could not pay for the loans they received. The road to this ruination started a long time ago.

In 1985, there was a meeting of businessmen at the Shelbourne Hotel in the centre of Dublin. It had been called to consider new ideas for building the Irish economy. Dermot Desmond, an Irish investment broker, wasn't from the old money of Irish stockbroking but had built his own company and his own fortune on a host of big money deals, including shorting on the Russian rouble. At the meeting he suggested, to those willing to listen, that they should consider the setting up of an international finance centre in Dublin, in the light of the 'Big Bang' of financial deregulation coming their way.

It might have been Desmond, now the major shareholder and benefactor of Celtic Football Club in Glasgow, who first raised the flag, but it was the Irish political Godfather, Charles Haughey, who carried the standard for an Irish finance revolution into political battle. Two years later Haughey had the proposal for an Irish offshore-style financial centre emblazoned on his Fianna Fáil party's election manifesto. In March 1987 Haughey was elected Taoiseach – prime minister – at the head of his Fianna Fáil party. Later that year the Irish parliament passed the 1987 Finance Act. That made way for the creation of what became the International Finance Services Centre (IFSC). Nicholas Shaxson, in his masterly book on financialisation, *The Financial Curse: How Global Finance Is Making Us All Poorer*, notes: 'The IFSC explicitly targeted global money managers, dealers in foreign currencies, futures, options, bonds, equities, insurance, clearing, information storage and miscellaneous trading . . . which marked it down as an all-guns-blazing tax haven model.'[5] Luxembourg on the Liffey was about to march into the pages of Irish history.

By 2003 half of the world's biggest banks, the twenty largest insurance companies, and more than 1,000 shadow banking derivatives all had a base in the IFSC. Mutual funds, then worth $125 billion were lodged in the IFSC, more than in the Cayman Islands; by 2004 hedge-fund managers had invested $200 billion and Dublin's investment funds industry, worth almost $500 billion[6] was trading blows with London to be the world's biggest.[7] The point here is that this is actually the Irish sub-prime moment.

By 2008 the value of total foreign investment in Ireland was $2,000 billion. Investment in the IFSC accounted for more than 70% of that amount, at that time 11 times the size of Ireland's GDP.[8] The trick was in the Catch-22 of Irish regulation of the movements of foreign capital – the 'light-touch' regulatory regime. Whenever challenged, the Irish government regulators explained that they could only regulate banks and finance houses which had their headquarters in Ireland, so it was the duty of others elsewhere to levy corporation taxes on the banks and businesses in the IFSC which did not have their headquarters in Ireland. Whenever the financial institutions and multinationals piling up billions of their profits in Irish banks or other financial agencies received tax demands at home, they would explain that all their money was actually tied up in their companies incorporated in Ireland.

In 2017 the EU took legal action against Apple and the Irish state for non-payment of taxes. The fine was €13 billion. Apple subsequently lodged the money, but the fine is still subject to appeal and is now being contested in the European courts. Brussels had previously accused Apple of avoiding taxes for more than 20 years on almost all profits in Europe, by allocating profits to a 'head office' in Ireland which had no employees and existed 'only on paper'. On the day of the latest hearing, in September 2019, Tim Cook, the chief executive of Apple, said 'The claim has no basis in fact or law'.[9] Apple Operations International, which owns most of Apple's offshore subsidiaries, had an estimated $215 billion stored offshore by the end of 2017.[10]

According to the Irish commentator Fintan O'Toole, what the Irish government called its 'light-touch' regulation meant that the financial sector in Ireland developed an all-pervading business ethos where 'right and wrong were strange and elusive concepts'.[11] For example, it meant leverage ratios rose and rose to another place in a faraway galaxy of recklessness. When Bear Sterns Ireland collapsed in 2008 it had equity ratios of 119:1 – for every dollar of actual equity it had $119 in posted loans and other financial bonds. That meant a 1% fall in the value of the assets would do for it. It did. Of course, for a period all this 'funny money' sloshing around in the Irish economy had to go somewhere, and for a time investments in property and construction, in particular, created an economic boom. But even in the early years of this awe-inspiring 'economic miracle', there were clouds no bigger than a man's hand warning of the storms to come.

In *Ship of Fools*, Fintan O'Toole describes the bubble in private credit which was destined to go bust. By 2004 private credit had reached €190 billion. This private credit is beyond big bank commercial loans – in the main, it's personal loans and small business loans. So, in 2004 these loans had reached €190 billion – almost one and a half times the size of Ireland's GDP. By 2008 those figures had climbed to two and a half times the size of the Irish GDP, reaching €400 billion. How could this go on forever? O'Toole explains that in 1994 the average price of a three-bedroom house in Dublin, in a desirable area, was €73,000. By 2007, on the eve of the bubble bursting, if the market value had grown in line with the rise in the consumer price index it would have been worth €109,000; if the value had grown in line with average earnings it would have reached €124,000. The actual average price for that year was €323,000.[12] In 2008 the housing bubble burst and house prices slumped. That triggered the collapse. The Crash followed.

On 29 September 2008 the three predominant Irish banks – the Anglo Irish Bank, the Bank of Ireland and the Allied Irish Bank were the first to head for the financial abyss. That would prove to be a stark warning for what was coming when the contagion spread globally. When the Big Three crashed, their balance sheet assets amounted to more than 700% of Ireland's GDP. Nicholas

Shaxson, in *The Financial Curse*, details the eventual scale of the shattering of the Irish 'shadow-banking' dream: 'The European Commission's 2012 official investigation into the global financial crisis, known as the Liikanen Report, shows how much state aid each country provided to its banking system during the crisis. Eight member states gave no support. France provided the equivalent of 4% of its gross domestic product, while Germany provided 10%, and the UK nearly 20%. For Ireland the figure was 269%.'[13]

The point here is that Ireland, and the collapse of the Celtic Tiger, is a paradigm for what happened across the globe. All the money washing around in the Irish financial system created a frenzy of lending for housing and property development. Fintan O'Toole called it a 'demented property cult' based on 'the economics of idiocy'. When the economy went into meltdown, the Irish government had to borrow more than €50 billion immediately from the European Central Bank to recapitalise its banks. To you and me that's banking-speak for bailing out their losses. By the end of the bail-out debacle that total was at least €90 billion. Probably much, much more.

So step forward Sean Fitzpatrick, the one-time chair of Ireland's biggest bank, Anglo Irish. Seven days before Christmas 2008, 'Seanie', as he is known in Irish banking circles, resigned as Anglo's chair. It had become public knowledge that he had personal loans outstanding to his own bank of €84 million. One chief executive. One bank. One loan standing at €84 million. Mind you, Fitzpatrick was not alone. When the trail of Anglo's lending to its own executives unravelled, the total of outstanding loans owed by the bank's senior executives was €225 million. They were borrowing from their own bank to make personal investments in housing, property and in buying Anglo shares in the boom.

There had to be some financial engineering to cover what was going on and make sure that the bank's accounts did not harm its share price. Even when the books are being cooked the maximisation of shareholder value remains paramount. Every September, just before the Anglo Irish accounts had to be published, Fitzpatrick borrowed tens of millions from the Irish Nationwide Building Society to cover his loans and put the money into Anglo's accounts.

Depending on when Anglo's accounts were being published in that particular year, the loans were usually taken out from Nationwide around 26 September and then paid back four or five days later. This went on for eight years and amassed a total of back-to-back loans of €228 million. Money came in on 26 September for the audit, and out again on 30 September after the accounts had been approved. Strangely, the auditors, Ernst and Young, never noticed a pattern – maybe because their auditors' eyes were watering every time they looked at the books. If that was the case it lasted for all eight years that this was done. At one point Ireland's Financial Regulator blustered in public that 'these loans were not appropriate'. There was no further action taken thereafter.

As the hole the Anglo directors were digging got deeper and deeper, so the financial crookery got greater and greater, eventually overshadowing even Fitzpatrick's own Nationwide carousel. A year before Anglo's demise, in a new scam the executives took €450 million out of Anglo's accounts. They shared it out among trusted associates of the bank who then deposited it back into Anglo accounts or used it to purchase Anglo shares: 'Everything's fine – can't you see Anglo's just taken in €450 million' might well have been the word in the halls of the Irish Stock Exchange before the collapse. For what was defined as 'the most lurid chapter in the sordid saga of Irish banking's dodgy deals',[14] Anglo's chief executive, David Drumm, was jailed for six years. That sentence was handed down in June 2018 because Drumm did a runner to America and had to be extradited from there to stand trial. In 2016, in a separate trial, on the same carousel and fraud charges, two other senior bankers at Anglo, Willie McAteer and John Bowe, were jailed for three and a half years and two years respectively. Denis Casey, the former chief executive of Irish Life and Permanent, was sentenced to two years and nine months. They were unlucky; they got caught. In 2014 and 2018, two trials, where similar charges were made against Seanie Fitzpatrick, collapsed.

So in this Irish story there is a forewarning of what was to come on a global scale. Here was fictitious capital in billions of euros flooding the markets; here were bankers signing off loans to borrowers they knew could never pay them back; here were bankers in their thousands, Irish and international, who bribed, cheated and lied to save their own skins when the days of being on the make ended. Here was the utter corruption of Irish banking. Bar none. The Irish crisis would prove to be a harbinger. For America and Europe read Ireland multiplied by billions. One of the causes of the Irish debacle was a decline of decency in business – a culture, both in banking and bank regulation, in which right and wrong became, in Fintan O'Toole's already quoted words, 'strange and elusive concepts'.

A former British investment banker told me the same thing during an interview about the British banking crash. Ian Blackford MP is the leader of the SNP MPs in the House of Commons. Before he got into politics he spent a large part of his working life in the high echelons of investment banking in the City, in London. He told me, 'When I joined the Stock Exchange its motto was "Dictum meum pactum" – my word is my bond. Those were the days when serving the client came first, above all else. Then the Big Bang arrived and I'm afraid things changed – all that went by the board.'[15]

The Big Bang is so called because it lifted the most restrictive banking regulations in the UK; the new *laissez faire* rules were introduced by the Thatcher government in the mid-1980s. Among other things, exchange controls and limits on the flow of international capital were abandoned, asset/liabilities ratios relaxed, and the division between retail and investment banking became decidedly opaque. Thatcher's aim was to promote the power of financial capital at the expense of industrial capital. From her point of view that had the advantage of reducing the power of the trades unions in manufacturing industry. The resultant reduction in Britain's GDP was to be taken up by a massive expansion of the City and the financial sector. Part of the plan involved welcoming corporate America to our shores – in this case America's bankers, who led the way to million-pound banker bonuses.

It may have been called the Big Bang appropriately, because after that 'Things went bang!' according to Ian Blackford. For a number of years he ran Deutsche Bank's investment interests for the UK and the Netherlands and watched from that viewpoint as

City banking changed. He recalls how the current banking structures were brought into question, following the relaxation of the rules. 'Suddenly, executives in old school-tie banking were asking why we were paying these clever advisors loads of money to advise our clients how they can make money, and not taking the advice ourselves? Why don't we use all that intellectual capital on our own books as well?' That simple last question captures the shift that took place. Before that, the 'old school tie' banking was not so far away from the perhaps apocryphal description of banking as being governed by the '3–6–3' rule. Bankers borrowed money from their depositors at 3% interest, lent to their borrowers at 6% and were on the golf course by 3 o'clock. However, now every retail banker could be an investment banker. For the sake of simplicity you could say that the banks then used two loan books – one for the 'old school-tie' customers and another book for their own investments and trading, borrowing from other banks and institutions to play the international money markets. One way or another, old school-tie banking was on its way to the casino.

Ian Blackford told me: 'With the benefit of hindsight, of course, that was the root of the whole problem – the ethos of the firm, any firm, became about what you could make on your own book – what you could make for your own bank, in playing the markets, never mind the customers. That's the nub of it, to be brutally honest.'

Time would tell that there wasn't a senior executive of a major bank anywhere in Europe who could resist the lure of the lights of the casino. Adam Tooze developed these issues in his analysis of the Crash: 'Beginning in the 1980s, however, banks across the world increasingly moved toward "wholesale" banking, funding their operations through large, shorter loans from other financial institutions, such as other banks and money market funds. The motive for this shift was profit and competitive survival. Wholesale funding gave banks the ability to borrow much larger sums of money than they could in the retail market, allowing them to become more leveraged – and thus more exposed to risk – than ever before.'[16]

This establishes that the road to the Crash has deregulation of the international banking system as its point of departure. 'More exposed to risks than ever before' as Tooze warned. In the film *Inside Job* the billionaire investor George Soros uses the analogy of an oil supertanker to describe the perils of deregulation. He points out that all supertankers are made with separate divided compartments in the hull. This prevents huge shifts of the entire load moving all at once in rough seas, which could be catastrophic. Soros likens the compartments to regulation of the financial markets – once they were taken away, who knows what might happen in 'rough weather'. In addition he says that the removal of the compartments brought with it the temptation for 'captains of the ship' to take more and more on board, irrespective of the risks that brought. More dangerous cargoes meant more money, didn't they? In its own way, the analogy describes the journey from the deregulation of international banking to the galaxy of financial cyberspace which delivered the sub-prime catastrophe. Sub-prime lending created a global banking boom like never before. The Crash was its bust.

Before we reach the banking galaxy of lending defined by asset-backed securities (ABSs), mortgage-backed securities (MBSs), collateralised debt obligations (CDOs), credit debt swaps (CDSs) and asset-backed commercial papers (ABCPs), it is necessary to establish what is fundamental. What happened is that a classic banking crisis grew because a huge amount of money was lent to a huge amount of people who couldn't pay it back. That didn't happen because the world's bankers suddenly went mad, although there is a case about that to be answered, as Ireland shows. No, what happened is the evolution of 'the banking equivalent of space travel', as Gillian Tett, the *Financial Times* journalist described it, that had convinced the world's banking oligarchs they had found a way to make lending money risk-free because someone else would pay the price of any defaults.

This involves the financial engineering that generated the US sub-prime boom. It is a story of what became known as the 'securitisation' of loans and bonds meeting the new spellbinding 'credit derivatives'. When the Crash came, as credit ran out internationally, it was all the more spectacular because of the super-concentration of capital across the globe – what Adam Tooze calls 'a tight-knit oligarchy of around 25 global banks' which controlled the world's financial systems.[17] By then, the types of people sitting in front of computer terminals on trading floors had been transformed by the millions to be made and the skills needed to do so. The time when the world's best physicists were vying for jobs with NASA or trying to develop a cure for cancer was long gone. They had been sending their CVs to the 'kings of Wall Street' for years. In the end it was these 'quants' – quantitative derivatives experts – who took over the trading floors with their new cyberspace financial instruments. In time, algorithms in hand, they took the globe. In *Fool's Gold*, Gillian Tett described the journey that had been travelled: 'As the pace of innovation heated up, credit products were spinning off into a multi-layered cyber world that eventually even the financiers struggled to understand. These complex products could not be analysed with just a pen and a piece of paper, or even a hand-held computer. The debt was being sliced and diced so many times that the risk could only be calculated with complex computer models.'[18] It's worth remarking that *Fool's Gold* is the title of her book. That was journey's end. It might be said its beginnings were in the US housing market in the 1970s, when securitisation came to town.

Seventy-six million Americans were born between 1946 and 1964. So how could the American dream of home ownership, based on the traditional model of single-household mortgages, ever deliver enough money to satisfy the demand for loans to buy houses for these new generations? The answer was that new capital had to be sourced, on a scale never seen before, which would be way beyond that found in the traditional housing markets. Capitalism would again prove to be the most creative and innovative economic force in history. There was no challenge blocking the way to riches which could not be met by market innovation to overcome it. Even if that ended in tears.

Lewis Ranieri, a mortgage bond trader with the Wall Street brokers Salomon Brothers, gets the historic credit for creating a new mortgage market based on what became known as 'securitisation'. Securitisation was a complicated pooling of different bundles of debt to make the bundles attractive to investors on the

Stock Exchange. Somehow. That involved pooling tens of thousands of mortgages together into one single bond or security and then selling it, at attractive rates, to Wall Street investors. The pooling or bundling of thousands, then hundreds of thousands of mortgages, reduced the risk for the lender. The mortgages were sold on to investors as multi-million dollar bonds. Thus the sale of bonds created income for the lenders, and for the investors in the stream of money coming from the payments of the still standing mortgage-holders, once the bonds were purchased. There was seemingly something in it for everyone. In time, this would totally transform the US housing market, creating access to capital markets way beyond the traditional banks' lending out 30-year mortgages for house buying. The US government agencies dominated the development of the new mortgage products for a long time. From a standing start in the early 1970s, by 1983 Fannie Mae (the Federal National Mortgage Association) and other government-backed bodies had issued $230 billion in such securities and the private sector $10 billion.[19] Mortgage backed securities (MBSs) were born.

When Wall Street started to take up MBSs as a market mechanism that could deliver big fees and big profits, it became clear that the potential in this market could be grown only if the bonds on offer could be graded for quality in the same way as the big rating agencies did for Treasury or corporate bonds. If MBSs could be graded in that way, then a 'triple-A' grading would make them able to compete with the return guarantees offered in US Treasury bonds; 'double-B' where the risks and the returns were higher could attract a different type of investor. Not only that, if Treasury bond returns dropped, going into the MBS market would suddenly become an attractive investment proposition. Thus 'tranching' of these mortgage-backed securities arrived. So the pooling of original mortgages resulted in the creation of huge mortgage bonds which could be mixed and 'sliced and diced' according to their grading by the agencies like Standard and Poor, Fitch & Fitch and the like. But in turn, that made the growing financial cybernet of bond buying and selling look all the more reliable. What could possibly go wrong?

So how do these mortgage-backed securities meet derivatives and their financial synthesis – credit derivatives? In *Fool's Gold*, Tett offers a working definition of derivatives: 'A derivative is, on the most basic level, nothing more than a contract whose value derives from some other asset – a bond, a stock, a quantity of gold. Key to derivatives is that those who buy and sell them are each making a bet on the future value of that asset. Derivatives provide a way for investors to either protect themselves . . . against a possible negative future price swing, or to make high-stake bets on price swings for what might be huge payoffs. At the heart of the business is a dance with time.'[20]

The critical word here is 'bet'. In the modern financial world the derivatives markets emerged with traders making 'bets' on the future value of commodities and currencies. The wheat farmer is an often-quoted example. The farmer wants to get some assurance for the price he can be paid for his crop when it is harvested. In most cases this would be a contract to hedge against a bumper wheat crop which would drastically reduce the price he can get for his wheat at the market. So he sets up a contract with a derivatives trader on an agreed price per bushel of wheat. Let's say that is $7 a bushel. When the wheat crop is harvested and the market price is stabilised as $6 a bushel, the farmer has made a successful derivative trade and reduced his risk of a lower than average price. If on the other hand the market price emerges as $9 a bushel, it's the trader who makes the killing. He can buy the farmer's wheat at $7 a bushel and sell it on the markets for $9 a bushel. The Chicago Board of Trade was established in 1849 for the buying and selling of options on agricultural commodities. Today the commodities market covers everything from copper to soya beans.

In the 1990s world of financial engineering the big question suddenly emerged: 'Why not create a derivative that enabled banks to place bets on whether a loan or bond might default in the future? Defaults are the biggest source of risk in commercial lending, so banks might well be interested in placing bets with derivatives that would allow them to cover for possible losses, providing a form of insurance against defaults.'[21] The logic of the question takes us to the new world of 'credit derivatives' and their most significant manifestation, 'credit default swaps' or CDSs. In 1991, Blythe Masters, a British Cambridge economics graduate, joined the J.P. Morgan investment bank. In due course she emerged as one of the bank's leading innovators in the quest for credit derivatives.

By 1997 J.P. Morgan had signed a deal which could probably be described as the game-changer in the emergence of these derivatives which would, figuratively, take lending to another planet. Masters was the 'mover and shaker' on the deal. The oil multinational Exxon asked J. P. Morgan bank to underwrite a $5 billion loan in case their fine for the *Exxon Valdez* disaster turned out to be of that magnitude. Masters persuaded the European Bank of Reconstruction and Development (EBRD) to swap the liabilities. J.P. Morgan offered to pay a huge annual fee to EBRD for essentially underwriting J.P. Morgan for the eventuality of a $5 billion drawdown from Exxon. The essentials were not that different from the derivatives trader taking a bet with the wheat farmer on the future wheat price after the wheat harvest. But this deal was not in commodities, but mega-finance. The bank had taken on insurance against the 'default' of Exxon and would pay EBRD handsomely for the privilege. J.P. Morgan still retained ownership of the bond for Exxon, but liability had been 'swapped' to EBRD. The first credit derivative had arrived. It would, in time, create history.

The next big question was, how could such derivative deals on a loan-by-loan basis break into a mass market where the real money could be made? The answer would be our old friend 'securitisation'. The evolution of the mortgage-backed asset (MBA) market had seen the further securitisation of MBAs into greater and greater bundles of loans, which became known as CDOs – collateralised debt obligations. When CDOs were further bundled and transformed into credit debt swaps it seemed that the creation of risk-free billion-dollar banking had truly arrived. If all that I am lending is being backed against default by other buyers buying my original loans, how can I lose? By the end of 1997, American banks had some $100 billion of such deals on their books. Scarcely six months later that had boomed to $148 billion and the world total was $300 billion. At this time Blythe Masters told Wall Street that 'Five years hence commentators will look back to the birth of the credit derivatives market as a watershed development . . . credit derivatives will fundamentally change the way banks price, manage, originate, distribute and account for risk'.[22] In 1999, the Clinton administration repealed the last provisions of the Glass–Steagall Act and, in the following year, Congress ruled that the derivatives market should not be subject to banking regulations.

The original credit derivatives were mainly based on corporate and private debt – business mortgages. credit card debt, car loans and the like. The final part in the credit derivatives jigsaw was when the scientific end of the business of these debt swaps developed new algorithms that allowed financial engineering to create mega-loan bundles in the US housing market. Credit derivatives then took the residential mortgage bond market from here to infinity – credit debt swaps for housing mortgages, in trillions of bundles. The conventional wisdom until then was that credit derivatives had eliminated the dangers of default in key sectors of the banking system. Now, in the new physics of finance, lending banks could make loans in the gargantuan US housing market, where seemingly they could be free of the risk of default because that was covered in the structure of the credit derivatives. All the instruments for getting 'money from heaven' were in place. And these new derivatives for the housing market would also not be subject to regulation. As one banker said at the time, 'It was off to the races.'

This was Ireland's policy of 'Lend, lend, lend, spend, spend, spend' now riding on a global tidal wave. Eventually, the supply of reliable borrowers with reliable properties dried up. Everyone was covered. But since the credit derivatives system couldn't fail, it was time to lend the riskiest money to the riskiest people in the mortgage markets. These high-risk mortgages were originally described as 'non-conforming' mortgages, which were parcelled in their tens of thousands to create 'non-conforming' mortgage bonds. In 2000 there was about $80 billion locked into these bonds in the US markets. Five years later that had risen tenfold to $800 billion. By this time 'non-conforming' had become 'sub-prime' mortgages. The 2006 sales were $1000 billion ($1 trillion) – ten times the size of the market five years before. In 2006 sub-prime mortgages made up 70% of the entire US mortgage market sales. So millions of people were borrowing money to buy houses that they couldn't afford to pay for. Essentially that meant that the borrowed money was on borrowed time.

By 2008 the International Swaps and Derivatives Association estimated that the total size of the world market had reached $54 trillion/$54,000 billion.[23] That was almost the same as the entire GDP of the world. Financialisation had gone mad. But when the boom was seemingly never-ending, the amount of money the major global banks were worth rose on an exponential curve. In one year, between 2003 and 2004, their market capitalisation grew by $900 billion to $5.4 trillion – an all-time record high.[24]

The billions and trillions of international finance discussed in these paragraphs may need some perspective. It might be useful to adopt a technique from John Lanchester's book *Whoops* to quantify what is going on. One million seconds amounts to just under 12 days. One billion seconds takes us to just under 32 years. A trillion seconds amounts to just under 32,000 years. On that scale 54 trillion seconds is 1.75 million years.

No-one could resist going to the financial party of all time. Hell hath no fury like a banker on the make. The European banks borrowed on the American money markets so that they could buy into the US boom. They borrowed dollars to lend dollars. Like a new corporate Mafia coming to town, they muscled in on the mega-mortgage bundles for sale in America. In the markets this was dubbed, somewhat quaintly, as 'round tripping'. By the time of the Crash, European banks, including RBS and HBOS, owned more than one third of the dodgy mortgage bonds in the US markets. Some estimates put that figure beyond that, at almost half. Those billions established links in the financial chain that would take the US sub-prime mortgage meltdown across the globe to the UK, Europe and beyond.

Bubbles go pop. Booms go bust. What happened to all the 'happy-ever-afters'. It started in San Francisco, Las Vegas and Miami first; in 2006 house prices started falling there. Then those who couldn't pay didn't pay. And as the default momentum grew, the sub-prime lenders started to collapse suddenly, all over America. Then this tsunami of debt crashed on to the beaches of the banks who had posted the loans to the sub-prime mortgage brokers in the first place. Between 2006 and 2009 sub-prime mortgage defaults in the US reached $738 billion. By 2015, nine million American families had lost their homes to foreclosure – repossession for non-payment of their mortgages. In the US, between late 2008 and mid-2009, 800,000 people were losing their jobs every month.[25]

The trillion-dollar loans had been sliced and diced, mixed and matched, packed and parcelled and offered up as bonds or securities incorporating tens of thousands of individual debts. These were then sold to any investors, anywhere in the world, who wanted to roll the dice, hoping to cash in big style if the gamble paid off. This debt parcelling and re-selling was done in the name of spreading risk. It was hugely effective at delivering that spreading of risk. However, when the risks eventually came home as defaults, their international diversification turned into its opposite – the spread of failure. A programme which was supposed to eliminate risk ended up becoming a pandemic of financial disaster. Credit derivatives had not, after all, created the risk-free loan. Default had returned on a scale that threatened the very existence of the world's financial system. The pay-back would last forever.

In 2001 Trevor and Colleen Pace bought 418 Homeplace Drive, in Stockbridge, Florida for $200,000. 'It was everything we had ever dreamt of,' Mr Pace told the *Financial Times*.[26] For the Paces and their two children, 418 was the first home they had ever owned. They borrowed all of the $200,000 and, two years later, on the back of its value borrowed an additional $14,000. This was in the early years of the US housing boom, which, as the *Financial Times* noted, was created by 'the proliferation of mortgages at unheard-of terms, offered to first-time buyers or people who had previously struggled to get loans'.[27] We can include the Paces in that.

The American Dream for the Paces turned into a nightmare. First, the original mortgage broker sold the loan to Countrywide Financial, an Atlanta-based mortgage broker. Then Countrywide parcelled the Paces' loan with 10,506 others it owned into securitised bonds in the CWABS Trust – the CountryWide Asset Based

Securities Trust. The original broker did not need to worry about the creditworthiness of the borrowers after he sold the loan to Countrywide, and Countrywide didn't need to bother either once their loans had been bundled into a tranche of CDO bonds. What could go wrong? After all, half of the Countrywide bonds had been officially rated triple-A, paying 0.16% over the average bank lending rate. In 2008 the CWABS Trust was one of the first US housing agencies to collapse. The Bank of America bailed it out by buying it for $4 billion and settling debts of $20 billion. The old Countrywide was still responsible for collecting on its mortgages. In August 2008, the Paces' mortgage dues went up by more than 50%, from $1200 a month to $1900 a month. They couldn't pay.

In 2006 the investment bank Goldman Sachs bought mortgage bonds worth $2 billion. This included hundreds of millions of dollars' worth of loans owned by Countrywide. The Paces' loan was among them. Goldman Sachs then packaged them into another 'collaterised debt obligation' called Davis Square VI, which it then offered up for sale on the derivatives markets. Ninety-one per cent of the Davis Square VI bonds were rated triple-A. So there were takers, among them the Landesbank Baden-Württemberg (LWB), in Stuttgart in Germany. After the crash, LBW sued Goldman Sachs for $37 million. Societe Générale, the French bank, hedged against Davis Square VI by buying credit debt swaps from AIG, the insurance company, which, in essence, was a bet that Goldman's Davis Square VI would go down. It did. But so did AIG. After the Crash, when AIG was bailed out by the American government, Societe Générale got compensated to the tune of $11.9 billion.[28]

The Paces filed for bankruptcy in an attempt to hold on to their house. By 2011 their mortgage was $53,000 in arrears on a house then valued at $140,000. In 2013 they lost the house. Their marriage broke up and the Paces separated. In the Crash, in Florida, 960,000 families lost their homes.

There's a scene in the Ryan Gosling film *The Big Short* which paraphrases the entire sub-prime catastrophe. Gosling is a thrusting hedge funder who is trying to persuade a group of investors to short the US housing market – to bet on its collapse. Gosling's potential backers for the hedge scheme visit Florida to see if the sub-prime mortgages there are actually going bust. They visit one development which has become a ghost town. House after house is boarded up, the swimming pools are full of green algae and the postboxes are overflowing with mail which will never be opened. The New York brokers engage with two of the newly rich mortgage boy-brokers in the area. The young banksters tell the New Yorkers they got rich selling NINJA mortgages to their gullible borrowers. NINJA – No Income No Job Applications. One of the young men says, 'I used to be a bartender. Now I own a boat.'

CHAPTER 10

The Bankers, the Crash, Those Who Paid for It and Those Who Didn't

'A report by Hong Kong consultancy group, Quinlan and Associates, estimated that since 2009 US and European regulators have slapped the top fifty global banks with fines to the tune of US $342 billion for misconduct, rigging markets, money laundering, mis-selling financial products, misreporting, misleading investors and trading scandals. That figure will rise to US$ 400 billion by 2020.'

Adele Ferguson, *Banking Bad*, ABC Books, 2019

In his time, P.G. Wodehouse described it as a 'restful temple of food'. Charles Dickens, George Bernard Shaw and Sir Arthur Conan Doyle were also regulars, as were a host of British prime ministers, including Disraeli and Gladstone from the days of Empire. In 1914, when Thomas Davey, the head chef at Simpsons on the Strand, died, *The Times* carried his obituary. It noted that he had commanded a brigade of 100 men who every day toiled ceaselessly to serve table with an average of 1400 lbs of British meat, 300 lbs of turbot and 100 lbs of Scottish salmon, along with two wagon-loads of fresh vegetables. Today the standing of Simpsons on the Strand is not as grandiose as in the days of Empire. Nonetheless, it still remains an icon of fine dining, in the Savoy buildings on the Strand, for the city's great and good. People like Lord Stevenson, the one-time chair of HBOS. Stevenson liked to hold an annual dinner there for the esteemed heads of the best of the bank's clients. It was always a grand affair with fine fare, fine wine and lashings of self-aggrandisement all round.

So it was that on Thursday, 8 May 2008, the BBC's obsequious Royal correspondent, Nicholas Witchell, opened proceedings at Simpsons and introduced Lord Stevenson to make his welcoming remarks. There were four or five tables, each with ten places, under the crystal chandeliers in what Simpsons refer to as 'one of our elegant spaces that can be arranged and dressed to suit your requirements'. There were two HBOS 'top people' hosts on each table. 'Both were determined to convince us of how well HBOS was doing, how things could scarcely have been better,' as one of those who was there described it. At the top of the dining room there was a raised dais. After each course of the meal, Witchell and Stevenson took their positions there, sitting opposite one another. There was then a short Q and A between the two, with Witchell slavishly bowling proverbial soft balls down the wicket along the lines of, 'Lord Stevenson, another year of growth?' 'Are you confident of the bank's performance in the coming year?' and 'What are the new challenges for you and the bank?' Of course questions such as 'How do you explain that the bank's loans to deposits ratio is now touching 150%?' never got a look in.

However, at the end of the meal things got a bit more challenging. The Q and A session was thrown open to the guests. The Panglossian complacency was about to be rudely interrupted. From the dais Witchell called in a relatively young gentleman, of Asian background, who then asked Stevenson, 'Is there a possibility, Lord Stevenson, that the bank is playing in markets that you don't fully understand? In fact, could it be that there much more risk in the bank's portfolio than you realise?' Stevenson pushed back his chair, got up and took a few paces forward to the very front of the dais. Demonstratively pointing at the questioner he raised his voice and said, 'You do not know what you are talking about.' Suddenly, in the embarrassed silence that followed, everyone was looking down at their coffee cups. The businessman who had raised the question stood up and said, 'I've no wish to ruin the harmony of the evening so I'll retire.' He left. Cue Witchell floundering to restore the previous bonhomie of the evening.

At the time of Stevenson's outburst, the 2007 HBOS accounts had contained stark warnings for all those who wished to see them. The bank had a market capitalisation of £40 billion and a tangible book value of £18 billion. This reality would, much later, allow the Parliamentary Commission on Banking Standards to describe HBOS, at that point in time, as 'an accident waiting to happen'. One dinner guest recalled that when the Q and A session started again he excused himself from his table to go outside and call his wife. She was the one in the house who managed their small stocks and shares portfolio. 'Darling,' he said, 'if we have HBOS shares in our portfolio, sell them first thing tomorrow morning. Is this clear, darling, I've had a few? I mean first thing.' So at least one of the guests took heed at Simpsons. The husband's call to his wife would prove to be prescient.

In a matter of weeks, the condescending Stevenson was presiding over an emergency £4 billion rights issue by HBOS in a desperate bid to avert a coming catastrophe. It failed. Only 8% of the offer was taken up, and the underwriters had to take a monumental hit for the rest. By September 2008, four months after Stevenson's rude riposte to his questioner in Simpsons, HBOS shares had lost 96% of their value as downfall loomed. With Lord Stevenson still on the bridge, the ship was going down – saved only from total collapse by a government-inspired and funded £20 billion takeover of HBOS by Lloyds. The HBOS story provides evidence about how the British oligarchs seem destined to repeat the mistakes of history – they learn nothing and forget nothing. It cannot be gainsaid that the HBOS story is one of a crisis of the bankers, by the bankers, for the bankers, who would all escape the blame with the loot spilling out of their pockets.

In March 2008, when the first rumblings of the coming Crash were rattling bankers' windows across America, a British regulator phoned Lord Stevenson. 'How is HBOS doing?' was his inquiry. Stevenson told the regulator that 'We are feeling as robust as it is possible to feel . . . the bottom line is that, without wishing to be the slightest bit complacent, we feel that HBOS, in this particular storm . . . is in as safe a harbour as is possible . . .'[1] If we fast forward from Stevenson's 'robust' statement, the words of Philip

Green, the Carillion chair, repeat history. In 2017, we should remember Green told the Carillion board, on the eve of their declaration of the £845 million hole in the Carillion accounts, that 'work continued towards a positive and upbeat announcement . . . focusing on the strength of the business as a compelling and attractive proposition' (see Chapter 3). For 'robust as is it is possible' read 'compelling and attractive proposition' – two parallel, baseless proclamations separated by nine years. In the affairs of the British oligarchs it seems there is nothing new under the sun, even their delusions.

There's more. In evidence before the Parliamentary Commission and the Treasury Committee, the two chief executives of HBOS, who were in post in the years leading to the collapse, trotted out 'Don't blame me, no-one could have seen this coming' pleas. HBOS's Sir James Crosby denied that the reckless growth plan carried out by HBOS executives 'made the collapse inevitable' and declared that what happened 'was not a foreseeable scenario'. His successor as chief executive, Andy Hornby, described the HBOS collapse as 'unforeseen and unprecedented'. Just like the pleas lodged by the Carillion directors, based on their 'perfect storm' PR stunt. These assertions of Crosby and Hornby are confounded by the commission findings that, over a period of years, including before Crosby's departure, risk management in HBOS was identified as a 'cardinal area of weakness' in the bank. As early as 2004, these fears led to a special inquiry into staff performance in risk management. It found that the risk management processes within the bank 'appeared to work well'. That 2004 investigation was carried out by the accountants, KPMG, who also signed off the 2007 accounts without any qualification. Years hence, KPMG would prove to be equally complicit in the assessment of the affairs of Carillion. When things go wrong the British oligarchs are never to blame and the Big Four auditors never find anything amiss before that anyway.

In July 2006, Crosby resigned as chief executive. After leaving HBOS, he sold off two-thirds of his company shares – some two years before HBOS collapsed. When asked, he explained that his motive for the urgent sell-off was 'balancing my portfolio of assets'.[2] It has never been established how much he made by cashing in. However, the 2006 HBOS annual report justifies an estimate of just under £1 million. In addition, Crosby had long-term incentive shares which matured in 2006, the year he left. 218,000 of these shares vested, which would have delivered a pay-out of £2.15 million. So his shares bonanza as he waved goodbye to HBOS – now 'holed below the waterline' according to the Banking Commission – was £3.13 million. Almost ten years later, Richard Adam, Carillion's finance chief, left early as well. As we have already seen, Adam's 'balancing his share portfolio' by selling his Carillion shares brought in £776,000, and in his last year his long-term incentive shares matured at £278,000 – so his shares goodbye was not as much as Crosby's but still over £1 million. In both these cases, these pay-outs would be for steering the proverial course of two ships that finished by crashing spectacularly on the rocks.

In other words, in British business there is evidence of a consistent practice of monumental cash-ins for failure. This is contrary to the usual media spin saying how deserved chief executive bonuses are because the executives delivered increased millions to the value of the company concerned. Adam was the finance director on a board 'which drove a company off a cliff' at the end of a story of 'recklessness, hubris and greed'. Crosby was the main architect of 'an accident waiting to happen'. So what did Crosby and Adam ever do to justify their scale of reward for failure? The answer is they did not need to do anything. They took the money because they could. They were looting the state. Britain's executives are also fond of saying that their remuneration is justified because 'the buck stops with me'. It doesn't. Most of the time they just walk away and cash in their shares.

One of the HBOS executives, Sir Ronald Garrick, when asked what had gone wrong, declared that HBOS had become the bank 'that could not say no'. This recalls the statement made by the one-time chair of RBS, Sir Philip Hampton, regarding the RBS collapse. When asked, he told the 2013 CBI conference 'We were lending to anyone with a pulse.'[3] As with HBOS, part of RBS's road to ruin was paved by the way in which key bank executives became mesmerised by the lure of the world's credit derivatives market. RBS's first forays into the world of CDOs (collaterised debt obligations) started in the early 2000s. The tipping point in this gargantuan greed-inspired gamble was the takeover of an American mortgage house, Greenwich Capital, based in Birmingham in Michigan. RBS Greenwich Capital, as it became known, was given almost total autonomy within the RBS Group to gamble in the derivative markets with the bank's money – in billions of dollars.

All in all, Ian Fraser, the author of *Shredded: Inside RBS, the Bank that Broke Britain*, estimates that between 2003 and 2007 RBS Greenwich Capital underwrote sub-prime mortgage bonds to the tune of $188 billion. That made them third in the world in sub-prime underwriting between 2005 and 2007, behind only Bear Stearns and Lehman Brothers, according to Fraser. 'That's why the initial fines levied on RBS by the American authorities were so significant. RBS was fined $11 billion for palming off $32 billion of what was toxic waste and selling it on to Fanny Mae and Freddie Mac, owned by the American government, as if it was a good investment,' he told me.[4] In March 2007, RBS chief executive Fred Goodwin told stock market analysts, 'We don't get involved in sub-prime lending.' Later on, at another analysts' conference in August that year, Goodwin qualified the original cover-up statement, saying, 'The short answer is we are one step removed. We have never lent directly to people who are the customers in sub-prime so we stand back from that.'

This isn't true. But it may be that Goodwin had his eye off the ball, because by then he was totally preoccupied with the takeover of the Dutch bank, ABN AMRO, which was to make RBS the biggest bank in the world. Goodwin's crazed obsession with building RBS into the world's biggest bank meant that the ABN AMRO bid had been preceded by a takeover bonanza in which, in a period of little more than seven years, the bank was involved in 28 takeovers. The ABN AMRO adventure would prove to be the last but greatest delusion. However, at the time of the takeover, many media commentators lauded Goodwin's 'masterstroke'. Even the *Financial Times* declared that 'The deal is a triumph for Sir Fred Goodwin, RBS's Chief Executive, who persisted in spite of the turmoil in the credit markets . . .' One London *Times* columnist eulogised Goodwin's achievements, asking in her column headline: 'Is this man the world's greatest banker?'[5] A matter of months would prove that the answer to that question was 'no'.

RBS's breakneck expansion from a regional bank based in Scotland before its NatWest conquest to becoming the world's biggest bank was the prime factor in its demise. That, along with its hat-trick of disaster in the subprime adventure, the ABN AMRO takeover and the liquidity crisis that followed, sealed the bank's fate. Sir Fred Goodwin had delusions of grandeur. His board listened and applauded, demonstrating their own financial bankruptcy. That, in turn, was a powerful symbol of Britain's broken corporate governance. In 2012, because of his role in the RBS crash, Goodwin was stripped of his knighthood. He thus became a member of the same notorious 'annulled' club as Romania's tyrant, Nicolae Ceauşescu and Zimbabwe's Robert Mugabe. Given the public furore over the scale of the RBS bail-out, Goodwin eventually had to agree to take a voluntary cut in his pension from £700,000 to £342,000 a year. Mind you, not before he had taken £2.7 million out of the fund in a lump sum.

When the government bail-out of the banks is considered, most people who follow current affairs would have in mind figures like £45.5 billion for RBS and some £20 billion for Lloyds. These amounts only cover the purchases of shares for the government to take an 83% share and a 41% share in RBS and Lloyds respectively. The National Audit Office (NAO) records that the total bail-out of RBS, involving all measures, amounted to £256 billion. The figure for Lloyds is £277 billion. The nationalisation of Northern Rock (£60 billion) and Bradford and Bingley (£46 billion) cost the taxpayer £106 billion. According to the NAO, by August 2018 the total cost of the rescue of all the banks came to £1.2 trillion (£1,162 billion).[6] If the loss of GDP for the ten years which followed the Crash is counted in, then the total cost figure rises to £2.4 trillion. In September 2008, as the Crash was gaining momentum, government debt was £665 billion. Ten years later it had trebled to £1.8 trillion. This surely suggests that any government debt crisis followed the Crash. It did not cause it.

The boards of the major banks in the UK devised plans to reduce what they owed to the Government for the bail-out and to repair their balance sheets, fractured by their credit derivatives adventures, by systematically seizing the assets owned by a significant section of their clients. This involved finding ways of bankrupting businesses across the UK, repossessing their assets to pay off loans, and where that was not successful, flogging the debts still outstanding to the world's biggest debt-collecting private equity fund. The process was almost identical in most cases. Firstly, a technical breach in contracts would be determined by the bank; the client would then be put in the hands of a special business unit set up for dealing with 'problem accounts'; in turn the unit would use court action to plunder any assets owned by the client to pay off outstanding loans; and the endgame would be the sale of the still outstanding loans to the American vulture fund Cerberus. After the Crash, Britain's bailed-out bankers reduced all customer relations to the cash nexus. Ask John Guidi.

The Guidi family story actually starts on 2 May 1909 with the single toll of the bell in the church on the hill in the village of Montebono. Montebono stood in the hills above the town of Barga in northern Tuscany. Giovanni Giuseppe Guidi was a farmworker, but he'd had enough of standing in the hiring line every day in the village, waiting to see if the manager of the local estate would pick him out of the line-up of labourers for a day's work. The church bell's single toll was a message to the folk in the village that somebody was leaving that day. The local paper, the *Gazzetta di Barga*, had a column announcing the comings and goings of local folk. The day after the bell tolled it recorded 'On 2nd May 1909 Giovanni Giuseppe Guidi left Montebono to go to seek work in Scotland.'

Six years later, when his son Renato was born, Giovanni Guidi had long forsaken the use of a shovel. By that time he and his wife, Emilia, had a small cafe business on the south side of the city of Glasgow, in the west of Scotland. Renato Guidi would develop the business beyond the cafe's lemonade, ice cream, sweets in small paper bags drawn from huge jars and cigarettes behind the counter; Renato's cafe had all of that plus fish and chips. By then the cafe was in the East End of Glasgow. This was the beginning of the future that Giovanni and Emilia had dreamed of for their children and grandchildren. Every day Giovanni would tell his wife that their sacrifices would guarantee that future generations of the family would have lives far removed from the crushing poverty that they had suffered in rural Italy.

It took two generations for the prediction to come good. By the mid-2000s, Giovanni's grandsons, Carlo and John, had both built successful businesses. By then, both businesses had reached well beyond the boundaries of their father's fish-and-chip shop. Today, Carlo Guidi has a substantial Italian restaurant business in Coatbridge, outside Glasgow. By 2005 John Guidi, who was actually baptised Giovanni Giuseppe Guidi after his grandfather, had a property and letting business turning over £800,000 a year, worth not far south of £15 million. He had built the business from scratch. He had been supported every step of the way by his bankers – the Clydesdale. In fact, Guidi was one of the bank's model clients; a regular at the annual dinner for the Clydesdale success stories. He recalls discussing the quality of fine Italian reds at one dinner, when he sat next to the then Clydesdale chairman, Lord Sanderson. That was then. On 17 March 2019 – St Patrick's Day – John Guidi pitched a tent on the doorstep of the Clydesdale Bank in the heart of Glasgow. He was on hunger strike against the bank which had bankrupted his business and ruined him.

John Guidi was desperate. No-one was listening. No-one truly knew what is going on. He had nothing to lose. When his tent was pitched between two trees on the pavement opposite the Clydesdale's headquarters, he stretched out a yellow banner between the trees. In red letters it exclaimed: 'Shame on Clydesdale Bank'. Guidi had help from a couple of journalist friends with his media profile. In his first media release about the hunger strike, Guidi, 63 at this stage, declared: 'I am going on hunger strike because people need to know what the Clydesdale Bank has done to small businesses all over Britain. This is one of the great scandals of our times. It seems to me that right now these people don't have a shred of decency in their bones. They knew they were getting me to sign up for the financial Armageddon of my business. Now they want my house.'

In 2019 St Patrick's Day fell on a Sunday. Guidi had given the *Observer* columnist, Kevin McKenna, an advance interview. McKenna didn't miss his chance. He splashed the story in the Comment section of the paper: 'Few other issues seem to define the essential wickedness at the heart of unrestrained capitalism than the conduct of the banking industry during and after the Crash of 2008. In pursuit of riches beyond the imagination of most people, many senior bankers deliberately ruined the lives of millions by selling financial products that they knew had become poisonous. The trick was to fill their pockets with as many bonuses as possible before the game was a bogey. In this world, you could never have too much money, nothing could be deemed excessive and there was no such thing as human cost. It was the elixir of pure Thatcherism.' There was also sympathetic coverage of Guidi's hunger strike nationally in the *Mail on Sunday*. 'I'll starve myself to the end to shame this bullying bank' is the headline on John Guidi's story. In a matter of days, these beginnings become the media equivalent of throwing a grenade into a machine-gun bunker. Three days into his hunger strike, if you Google 'John Guidi', the drop-down menu takes you to 'John Guidi Clydesdale Bank'.

When the executives of the Clydesdale Bank arrived for work on Monday morning, 18 March, those who didn't follow current affairs might have been slightly bemused at the sight of the 'Shame on Clydesdale Bank' banner stretched out in the street opposite the bank, and a bedraggled 63-year-old sitting on a garden chair in front of a tent. However, the officials responsible for the bank's PR machine were suffering from no such perplexity. They'd been pumping out a clear line to the media from mid-afternoon on the Sunday. It was a Pontius Pilate declaration – the position Mr Guidi finds himself in is unfortunate, has already been discussed exhaustively by the bank, and there is nothing further can be done. Then the pay-off – actually, it's nothing to do with us now. Mr Guidi needs to talk to Cerberus, who hold his loans after they were sold by the National Australia Bank.

The process of bankrupting Guidi started with the Clydesdale

Bank transferring his loans to the National Australia Bank (NAB) who owned the Clydesdale. In turn, NAB sold the loans to the American private equity fund, Cerberus, headquartered in New York. On the second day of his hunger strike Guidi holds a news conference in the street beside his pop-up tent. He states his case to the media pack: 'How can it be that I take out my loans from a bank which is subject to regulation in the UK and I then finish up in the hands of an unaccountable, unregulated, cold-blooded vulture fund based in New York? How can it be? You sign up for the loans with the Clydesdale Bank; "Here for You" is their advertising tag-line, and you end up with a remorseless asset-stripper in America?'

Guidi has been in touch with his local MP, Angela Crawley. Along with other MPs who are members of the All Party Parliamentary Group on Fair Banking, she secures an urgent debate in the House of Commons. On the floor of the House she declares: 'This tragic case brings attention to the vulnerability of UK businesses to abusive treatment by lenders and vulture funds, and the inadequacy of current regulation preventing it. Sadly, John Guidi is not alone. There are hundreds of people across the UK whose tailored business loans were sold by Clydesdale Bank to Cerberus Capital Management ... Since the banking crisis of 2008, we have seen a sorry catalogue of thousands of instances where the banks have forced legitimate borrowers into distress through no fault of their own, and because loans to SMEs [small to medium enterprises] are not regulated properly, the customers have little or no redress. John now finds himself in that category. All he wants is a fair say before he loses his family home.'[7]

This provokes a response in the debate from the Economic Secretary to the Treasury, John Glen MP, which is devastating for the Clydesdale's Pontius Pilate act regarding Guidi. Glen tells the House of Commons: 'The sale of debts to third parties is covered under the standards of lending practice, to which Clydesdale is a signatory. That means that it is committed to ensuring that third parties that buy loans have demonstrated that customers will be treated fairly, and also to allowing customers to complain to the original lender if there is a dispute between the third party and the business that cannot be resolved.'

So this means that the Clydesdale is duty-bound to consider Guidi's case and the Clydesdale response – 'not our problem' – is invalid. Glen also confirms that Andrew Bailey, head of the banking regulator, the Financial Conduct Authority, has spoken to Clydesdale about Guidi's case. So Guidi's campaign is getting traction. On the Wednesday morning, he gets a letter hand-delivered from a Clydesdale PR executive to his tent in Glasgow. It invites him to a meeting in the bank that afternoon to discuss his situation further. He goes along with Ian Lightbody of the CYBG Remediation Group – the support group for those seeking redress from the bank for the mis-selling of loans. The Clydesdale had been taken over by the National Australia Bank (NAB) in 1987. Three years later NAB moved in on the Yorkshire Bank. In 2005 it was merged with the Clydesdale. Eventually this would become the Clydesdale/Yorkshire banking group – hence the CYBG acronym. At the meeting in Glasgow, Guidi and Lightbody are offered a meeting, on the coming Friday, with the Clydesdale chief executive, David Duffy, in the CYBG's offices in the City of London. Thus, after seven years when no-one would listen to him, four years of relentless stripping of his assets combined with silent stonewalling from Cerberus, five days on hunger strike, and his case raised in the House of Commons, Guidi gets a face-to-face with the CYBG chief executive.

So what is John Guidi's backstory to this point? The National Australia Bank (NAB) owns the Clydesdale and Yorkshire Banking Group (CYBG). In the late 1990s NAB developed what were known as tailored business loans (TBLs) to exploit the exponential growth of credit derivatives in the world's money markets – already discussed in the previous chapter. Within the TBL deal there was a credit debt swap element. This was what was introduced to clients as 'an embedded debt swap'. TBLs proved to be very profitable for the bank in Australia, so NAB decided it was time to exploit TBLs in the British market. In 2002, TBLs arrived in NAB's subsidiaries in Clydesdale, Yorkshire and its two Irish banks. NAB's credit swap variation, in the fixed-rate TBLs, offered the bank customer what was a fixed-term, fixed-interest rate deal. That would prove to be an attractive proposition in turbulent financial and economic times, where bank interest rates were fluctuating. That was the hard-sell element in the offer – 'Why not swap all your floating-rate loans for the security of a fixed-rate loan on a fixed term?'

In 2002 John Guidi was persuaded to change almost all his traditional loans into TBLs. Why not? Guidi signed up. After all, he had been advised and assured that this was the best thing to do. How was he to know then, that in 2014 the then chief executive of Clydesdale and Yorkshire Banks, David Thorburn, would repudiate the entire TBL project. He would tell a House of Commons Treasury Committee that the way TBL clients had been treated was 'unforgivable'; that the contracts on offer were so complex that they could not pass a 'plain English test'; and that such was the avalanche of accusation about fraudulent mis-selling facing CYBG that they stopped selling TBLs in 2012.[8]

John Gatt was the Clydesdale's best salesman of TBLs between 2002 and 2012. After he left Clydesdale he became a consultant with the John Taylor Group, advising former Clydesdale and NAB clients who had been ripped off after signing up for TBLs, how to seek redress. Gatt says that initially the sale of these TBL packages was controlled through banking strategic advisors. There had to be advisors because the TBLs were very complex. Your local bank manager could suggest you should shift your loans to TBLs, but he could not deliver the deal because the finances were linked to credit derivatives in world markets. So, that had to be done by an advisor in one of the TBL strategic teams. But as the profits bonanza started to emerge in the deals, that caution soon gave way to indiscriminate 'Sell, sell, sell TBLs'. John Gatt says when that took hold, effectively Clydesdale clients were being sold loans with conditions they didn't understand by staff who couldn't explain them anyway. He says: 'It became the task of every business manager to not only bring on board new lending, but to target every floating-rate loan in their portfolio . . . the erosion of the sales process was down to the huge pressure to sell TBLs driven by the greed of the bank.'

Patrick Walton, a former senior manager of Clydesdale's 'Financial Solutions Centre', in Leeds, was another Strategic Advisor in TBLs,

like John Gatt. Walton told the Treasury Committee inquiry that
the bank developed a culture where there was a 'pressure to sell at
all costs that was driven from the top of the organisation'. Staff who
did not meet targets faced 'disciplinary action'. Walton described
Clydesdale's culture 'to be the most corrosive and threatening [he
had] ever encountered'.[9]

In 2010 John Guidi went to the Clydesdale to pitch for new
loans to develop his business. He had established a new project,
based on the purchase of an apartment building and an adjoining
land site. He needed £1.6 million. After negotiations, the bank
approved the loan. It took a while for the sale of the apartment
building and the land to be completed. On 18 November 2011,
John Guidi drew down the last £1 million of the loans to complete
both deals. In the first week of 2012, that is a mere six weeks
after the £1 million drawdown, Guidi got a call on his hands-
free carphone from someone who introduced himself as 'your new
bank manager'. He was told that the National Australia Bank had
decided to stop lending for commercial and real estate loans in the
UK. 'So the Clydesdale has stopped. This means your loans will
be the subject of a strategic review in this case. And we'll take a
decision on that in the coming months,' the manager said.

The National Australia Bank (NAB) executives had decided
on a retrenchment of the bank's operations. They wanted out
of British banking and to retreat to Australia. They also had to
repair the balance sheet damage caused by the Crash. The NAB
executives had decided to kill two financial birds with the one
stone. If NAB pulled out of commercial and real estate markets,
Clydesdale and Yorkshire would be forced to follow. The assets
which they could then acquire by forcing the indebted SMEs on
their books to pay off their loans would have two results. On
the one hand it would improve the Clydesdale and Yorkshire
balance sheets and make them fit for a stock market flotation;
on the other it would also rid NAB of their twin British balance-
sheet problems.

Some weeks after John Guidi had been informed by his 'new
manager' at the Clydesdale that his loans were on hold, he was
told the loans were to be transferred to the Strategic Business

Services (SBS) unit. Overnight, the model customer with a successful, solvent business was branded a failure with 'non-performing loans'. The SBS was run exclusively by a dedicated corps of some thirty bankers, all newly recruited for that purpose by NAB. They had offices in Glasgow, Leeds and London. In March 2019 the House of Commons All Party Parliamentary Group (APPG) on Fair Business Banking noted: 'Clydesdale engaged in an activity known as "covenant squatting" – actively looking for excuses to call loans in, using small print in the contract. In Guidi's case they managed to find one. They identified a "technical breach" in the rental covenant. This did not affect the health or prospects of the businesses at all, indeed no monthly payment had ever been missed and the company was doing better than ever, but it was enough to start calling the loans in.' [10]

The Clydesdale and Yorkshire banks sold more than 11,000 interest-swap products. 8,372 of them were toxic TBLs. The marketing for them had initially been based on offering to protect clients if interest rates went higher and higher. After the 2008 Crash, base interest rates went in the opposite direction, from around 5% to little more than 0.5% by mid-2009, and stayed that way for years to come. John Guidi was among many caught by the TBL 'break costs'. If you wanted to pay off your loans early, the costs of breaking the contract could be as much as 25–40% of the original loans. That could have run to more than £3 million break costs for John Guidi on his loans of £10 million. So like many other TBL victims he was trapped on the original interest he had signed up for in 2004. Across his loans Guidi was paying 4.75% when the market average was 2.5%. The nature of these break costs levied on customers would become hugely controversial because, as time passed, it would become clear they were also weaponised to bankrupt clients and seize their assets. The process would start with an engineered default, followed by an early termination of contract as a consequence. That would then allow the levying of break costs, since the contract had been broken. In many cases these, added to outstanding loans, made insolvency inevitable.

Professor Michael Dempster of Cambridge University is a recognised expert on the complexities of credit derivatives. His report on the Clydesdale/NAB tailored business loans investigated two client cases. One business had loans worth £433,000 and was charged break costs of £103,000 in circumstances similar to those described above; another had loans amounting to £3.95 million and was charged £713,000 in break costs. These costs are respectively 24% and 18% of the outstanding loans, in the circumstances where the likely expectation of the borrower would be that break costs would be charged at 1% of the outstanding loans at the point of an early termination of a contract.[11]

Dempster concludes that very few clients who signed up for TBLs were made aware of the potential break-costs usury contained within them. John Gatt, the former NAB advisor, says by the time the TBL sell was at its height, there was no way clients could have been getting an accurate assessment of what their potential break costs could be. Because the loans were 'priced off derivatives', local managers did not have the skills necessary to do that. Gatt argues, 'In all my years with NAB I worked with hundreds of excellent business managers all over the country. I never met one who could properly explain how a break cost was calculated.'[12] The Clydesdale chief executive, David Thorburn, went on the record at the Treasury Committee to say no-one could have foreseen the interest rates plunging to such low levels and the break costs on loans which emerged. The 'embedded interest rate hedging' within the TBLs meant that they escaped similar loan regulations. The TBL clients were locked in because they had no redress through the normal regulatory structures. Or they had to pay extortionate fees to get out. Or they went bust when they couldn't pay the monthly fees which fell due. The Treasury Committee on Small Business Lending found that: 'Clydesdale understood that TBLs were unregulated. It created TBLs to avoid requirements imposed by the regulator on the sale of a regulated product . . . The use of TBLs has left regulators powerless to enforce compensation for customers to whom products were mis-sold . . . Clydesdale created a product that retained the risks and complexities of the regulated product, but had none of the safeguards.'[13]

Clydesdale had gone rogue. It was selling products to more than 8,000 businesses that it knew could not be subject to a comeback from those clients. Unless they had the funds to go to court. In September 2015, the NAB Strategic Business Unit told Guidi that all his loans and standing assets had been sold to a 'new lender' – Cerberus. The name Cerberus comes from Greek mythology – it's the three-headed dog which guards Hades, the Underworld. Cerberus prevented anyone from leaving Hades and was also on guard to prevent enemies entering Hades to bring about its downfall. The dog had three heads to ensure one of them was always awake and able to attack all comers at any time of the day or night. Cerberus, the private equity fund, which has its world headquarters in New York, would prove to be aptly named. It would make John Guidi's life a living hell from which there was no escape.

Cerberus Capital Management is the equity fund's holding company with a host of inter-related criss-crossing subsidiaries in every country where it operates. The Cerberus subsidiary which broke John Guidi's business was Cerberus Promontoria. In the first telephone call to Guidi, the Cerberus Promontoria executive told Guidi he had a month to pay all his debts – approaching £10 million by then. In October 2015, Guidi went to the London offices of Cerberus in Savile Row, Mayfair. He offered up the same deal that he had tried to broker with NAB – £6.7 million, with time to pay the rest. He argued this amounted to more than 70p in the pound with a guarantee to raise the rest. The Cerberus executive told him, 'We paid more than that. You'll be hearing from our lawyers.' Strictly speaking, Guidi didn't hear from the Cerberus lawyers. In December 2015, they took action in court, put one of his companies into administration and applied for the appointment of a receiver.

That started a series of legal battles between Guidi, his companies, the receiver and the lawyers for Cerberus Promontoria. The fight cost Guidi tens of thousands, but in the end he lost everything. By the end of 2018 all his properties, worth around £15 million at market prices, and other financial assets had gone. Sold off by the Cerberus vulture fund. Despite his lawyer making enquiries with Cerberus Promontoria, Guidi has never found out who bought his businesses and for how much. In 2017, Cerberus

Promontoria won a sequestration order in court against Guidi – that's the Scottish legal term for bankruptcy.

To get the final £1.6 million loan from Clydesdale, Guidi had signed a personal guarantee for £450,000, based on the value of his family home. By early 2019, the legal proceedings by Cerberus Promontoria to repossess his house were reaching an end point. He says, 'Of course signing up for a personal guarantee was a mistake. But I had plans. I had built a business that was paying Clydesdale £400,000 a year in interest. I thought we had a strong business with a sound relationship with the bank. I never thought they would walk away from that. No chance. Listen, I never missed a payment in 14 years.' When I tell him that numerous people in business would say, 'Hell mend you. So sad, too bad, never mind. You signed,' he hits back. He argues that there was fraudulent misrepresentation in the way the loans were structured, and that the British and Australian parliaments have accepted that. Then he insists, as he would do every time the same issues were raised in the future, 'Besides, the bank shifted the goalposts on the deal. How was I to know they were going to complete my loans by lending me a million in November and demanding all of it back six weeks later? When I signed up, nobody, but nobody, warned me that the hustlers in NAB were planning to drop all their commercial real estate loans. Nobody told me when I signed for the TBLs that there's enough here, in the fine print, to bankrupt your business and sell your loans to whoever we like.' That calamity led Guidi to take the desperate action of going on hunger strike on 17 March 2019.

Now the story moves to the Friday 22 March meeting in London with David Duffy, CYBG's chief executive. The meeting takes place in the CYBG offices in the Leadenhall Building in the City. David Duffy was born in London but brought up in Dublin from the age of two. He calls Ireland his spiritual home. Before CYBG, he was the chief executive of AIB in Dublin. He was appointed there to lead the AIB's recovery from the Crash and gets credit, in banking circles, for its rescue. He joined CYBG late in 2015, after the TBL fiasco forced the previous Clydesdale chief executive, David Thorburn, to fall on his sword. So Duffy wasn't on point duty when the Clydesdale/NAB TBL scam was forced on 8,300 CYBG customers; nor during the years of the bank's own 'Spanish Inquisition', when its executives systematically and remorselessly looted thousands of Clydesdale/ Yorkshire/NAB businesses illegally. That seems from another time and another place when Guidi is sitting listening to Duffy's Irish lilt in the CYBG boardroom. Ian Lightbody, from the CYBG Remediation Group, is there with Guidi. Duffy's opening line surprises him. Duffy says, 'Afternoon, gentlemen, sorry I'm late, just had a grilling from the regulator.'

Duffy tells Guidi he's concerned for Guidi's health if he continues his hunger strike. Duffy tells him that he once did an overnight sleep-out on the streets, in the cold of Edinburgh, as part of a charity event for the homeless. 'I found that very difficult,' he says. So, he adds, given that Guidi has now done five nights, he has to think about his health. Duffy tries to assure both Guidi and Lightbody that the bank wants to engage with them. Genuinely. Sincerely. To try and find solutions for the grievances Guidi and all the others in the remediation group are presenting to the bank. Duffy says he needs time – weeks if not months. He tells Guidi that it's complex, because the bank is going to have to deal with the executives of NAB and find a way of dealing with Cerberus, probably through NAB. Guidi agrees to suspend his hunger strike to allow that. He wonders if the bank, and Duffy, are playing for time.

In the summer of 2018 CYBG took over Richard Branson's Virgin Money in a deal that cost £1.7 billion. By the end of 2019, the uninspiring CYBG acronym was replaced by the new, thrusting, challenger bank name, Virgin Money UK. On 19 June 2019, CYBG chief executive David Duffy told investors at the company's Capital Markets Day at the Stock Exchange that 'The new group combines the ethos of Virgin, with its distinctive and brilliant customer experience, with CYBG's technology, product expertise and knowhow... Achieving our financial targets will create a significantly more efficient and profitable business with strong and sustainable returns for shareholders.'[3]

The January 2019 CYBG annual meeting approved new pay scales for Duffy and Ian Smith, then CYBG's chief finance officer, if all the financial targets for the roll-out of Virgin Money UK were met. One-third of shareholders opposed the proposals, but the majority carried the day which means that Duffy's pay for 2019 might rise to £4.2 million from £1.8 million, and that of the CFO, Ian Smith, might grow from £0.6 million in 2018 to £2.1 million in 2019. In the event, Duffy's total remuneration according to the Virgin Money accounts reached £3.37 million – up 84% on 2018 – while Smith's pay reached £1.4 million – up 53%. Proposals to be put to the Virgin Money AGM could take Duffy's money up to £5.1 million – a 51% hike. You could observe that it's not what people say but what they do that is significant. The old habits of the banking oligarchs die hard.

At the same Capital Markets Stock Exchange meeting for the Virgin Money UK push, Ian Smith told the audience that the majority of the legacy issues around the PPI and TBLs controversies 'are largely behind us'. Thank goodness. That may prove to be wishful thinking if proposed legal action against the Clydesdale goes ahead. According to the CYBG Remediation Group, the Dempster Report, which they commissioned, and its four pillars of accusation, establish an extensive indictment of the bank's mis-selling of TBLs. It is worthwhile detailing them, since they indicate the extent of alleged fraudulent selling of TBLs which the bank to this day has never accepted. The Remediation Group allegations include that the Clydesdale/CYBG tailored business loans:

- were fraudulent because they were sold under false pretences; borrowers were persuaded to take out TBLs as an insurance against interest rates rising, long after the sophisticated forecast systems about interest rates available to the bank, and events, were warning about the coming financial crisis which would bring with it plunging interest rates as a response to economic crisis
- were fraudulent because the bank was committed to a hard sell on TBLs and consequently almost completely failed to warn customers about the huge break costs they would be confronted with in the circumstances of falling interest rates
- were fraudulent because at the height of the sale of TBLs, customers were being sold TBLs which they did not understand,

by bank executives who could not explain them; and the same bank executives certainly could never have worked out the scale of possible break costs, because they did not have the necessary skills to do that

- were fraudulent because the documentation provided to customers for TBLs in most cases did not include clients being given detailed Terms and Conditions notices with their loan sign-offs, but rather were issued with Facility Letters to sign, which contained the assignation that they had seen the Terms and Conditions of the loans

- were fraudulent because the selling of the fixed rate TBLs in almost all cases involved suggestions to customers that their loans contained an 'embedded hedge product' which would give the bank and the client insurance against high interest rate changes and guarantee a steady supply of funds; in actual fact there was no individual hedge contained in individual loans but rather the parent company, NAB, had a partial 'loan book' hedge as cover

- were fraudulent because customers had to pay for the services of these individual hedge products which in reality did not exist in their individual loans; and despite this the break costs charged to customers were calculated on a scale which assumed that these individual loan hedges actually existed

- were fraudulent because, to date there is no single example in the 8,372 TBLs agreed where a bank customer was warned that the small print of their Terms and Conditions meant their loans could be sold to a third party, like the vulture fund Cerberus

- were fraudulent because the Clydesdale Bank operated a system of engineered default to create the conditions where they could call in loans with demands for complete payment, in contrast to the verbal guarantees that borrowers were given about the long-term nature of the loans being available to build their businesses

- were fraudulent because there is clear evidence that the Clydesdale charged customers 'Additional Loan Elements' in 'hidden margins' of which they were not informed; that is the interest rates applied to loans had increased interest rates about which customers were not informed.[14]

On 31 July, John Guidi and Ian Lightbody of the CYBG Support Group went to yet another meeting at the Clydesdale Bank head-quarters in Glasgow. David Duffy, the bank's chief executive, and James Pierson, its head of legal, were there for CYGB. This was now more than four months after Guidi had started his hunger strike on 17 March 2019. Duffy opens the meeting. He says that the bank has reconsidered Guidi's complaints but concluded that it 'can do nothing more' for him. Duffy tells Guidi, 'We do not believe we are responsible for this situation. We are back to square one.' He tells Guidi that he will have to pursue his case further by taking it up now with National Australia Bank and Cerberus Promontoria. Thus it has taken more than four months of alleged investigations for Duffy to deliver a grandiose zero. Guidi accuses Duffy of abdicating all moral responsibility. The bank's original response to Guidi's hunger strike, in March, was almost identical to their July abnegations. This time, face to face, Guidi accuses Duffy of being 'a Pontius Pilate'.

Pierson joins the argument by telling Guidi, 'This is not a matter for us. It has nothing to do with us.' Guidi asks in fury, if that is the case, why are Pierson's signatures all over the documents that Guidi has seen concerning the sale of his loans from NAB to Cerberus. Pierson was one of the bankers given power of attorney by the National Australia Bank regarding the transfer of Guidi's loans. The meeting breaks up in acrimony. The next day Guidi receives a letter from the bank stating its case in full. It is a carbon copy of its original stonewalling from years before. The establishing of Guidi's personal guarantee was done correctly and the issue 'will not be revisited'. The terms of the original TBLs Guidi was sold included the right of the bank to sell his loans to a third party, which in his case they did, to NAB. Since matters rest now with NAB, and subsequently Cerberus, Clydesdale cannot comment further. It concludes that Clydesdale, and NAB, 'treated you fairly at all times'.

John Guidi's case is the epitome of tens of thousands of others who have suffered the same fate as him at the hands of Britain's banking executives, their collaborators in accountancy and audit, and their cohorts in unaccountable, rapacious debt-collecting. Clydesdale/NAB was far from being alone in this fraudulent mis-selling of what became known as IRHPs (interest related hedging products). Between 2001 and 2014 there were 60,000 fixed rate hedged products, like CYBG's TBLs, sold to unsuspecting customers across the UK, most of whom would pay a heavy price for signing up.

When eventually, in 2012, the then regulator, the Financial Services Agency, got round to investigating what was going on, it found that RBS, Lloyds Banking Group, Barclays and HSBC were ahead of Clydesdale in what turned out to be the IRHP roll of extortion. One man's tailored business loan was another man's IRHP swap. The regulator would find that RBS had mis-sold 10,258 swap loans.[15] They were all at it. Behind John Guidi stands a national banking scandal, which is testament to the scale of moral bankruptcy in the UK's business banking community.

RBS's infamous Global Restructuring Group (GRG) is probably number one in that league of infamy. On 18 January 2018, in the House of Commons, the Labour MP Clive Lewis opened the debate on the scandalous operations of the group. He said: 'We know that 16,000 small businesses were put into the GRG from 2008 and the majority were liquidated. That tells us all we need to know. This was meant to be somewhere from which they could try to come back as a viable business, but far from being an intensive care unit, it was more like an abattoir, where they were stripped and taken apart.' He closed his moving of the motion by saying that the costs of this were immeasurable and could run to tens of billions of pounds. 'Let us be clear: that is the potential size of the injustice that has taken place in our country . . . it may be the largest theft anywhere ever.' The largest theft anywhere ever.

On the eve of the GRG debate, the House of Commons Treasury Committee had published a leaked RBS internal memo instructing staff how to systematically take 'defaulting' RBS businesses apart. The memo in question was entitled 'Just Hit Target'. In it, RBS management instructed staff how to give customers 'enough rope to hang themselves'; how to 'whack' customers with 16 different types of fees which would be more credible if they avoided round numbers – £5300 was better than £5000; and how to send 'fresh facility letters' which persuaded customers to sign up for new contracts, allegedly on better terms but which actually allowed the bank to change terms and conditions and terminate loans at a moment's notice.[16]

Initially, the GRG's operations were not made public. The first note in RBS accounts which actually acknowledges the existence of the GRG is in the 2010 Annual Report and Accounts. It notes that one Nathan Bostock joined RBS from Abbey National as head of restructuring and risk, which includes 'responsibility for the Global Restructuring Group'. The first financial entry is in the 2011 accounts. It states that commercial real estate holdings are worth £74.8 billion and that £34.3 billion of that 'is managed within the GRG'. This is telling. It means that, at that point, just under half of the bank's loans in commercial real estate are held in a unit designed for alleged restructuring of companies experiencing financial 'distress'. In reality this means RBS was actually running an operation which was dedicated to the ruthless pursuit of client assets to benefit the bank's bottom line in its accounts – no matter the scale of the ruination of businesses that this produced.

The accounts are not definitive regarding the number of businesses which suffered at the hands of GRG's rapacious operations. The range is between 12,000 and 16,000 client businesses which were subject to 'restructuring'. By 2013, the last reference in the accounts to the GRG, the total commercial real estate portfolio was reduced to £52.6 billion, with £24.7 billion 'managed in the GRG'. In other words, the GRG accounted for almost half the write-downs in RBS real-estate loans in two years. How can this be explained other than as a financial witch-hunt of RBS's own clients? Nine out of ten businesses which went into the GRG never came out. They were bankrupted and their assets seized, or sold off. By the 2014 accounts, published in 2015 when the accusations about the GRG were long established, the GRG was replaced, at least in name, by the RBS Restructuring Group.

Crucial to part of RBS's defence for these nefarious activities was the definition of the GRG as non-profitmaking. If the GRG didn't make profits for the bank, surely that undermined the thrust of the accusations that it was making businesses bankrupt to improve its own bottom line. In June 2014, the two senior executives in charge of the GRG – Derek Sach the head of GRG, and Chris Sullivan, RBS's deputy chief executive – went before the House of Commons Treasury Committee. They told the MPs just that. GRG was not a profit centre. Nineteen times they said it. Then the cock crowed, because in another investigation the bank had admitted that the GRG did bring money in. Substantial amounts of money. Just how much would be finally confirmed in October 2016, when *BuzzFeed News* released a remarkable 11,000-word investigation piece on the GRG. It was based on a massive leak of RBS internal documents covering the period from 2008 to 2013. In the *BuzzFeed* report the '2013 Budget Review for the Global Restructuring Group' revealed it had global assets totalling £68 billion – including £20 billion in Ireland, £14 billion in the UK, £13 billion in Europe, the Middle East and Africa, and £7 billion in the USA. The same report showed that in 2011 the GRG had made £1.2 billion profit in that one year.[17] Proof, if it was needed, of the barefaced lies that RBS bankers have been capable of throughout the whole banking controversy.

The first exposure of what was going on within the RBS's 'Gestapo' came in a report published in November 2013 by a businessman, Lawrence Tomlinson. He had been seconded to the Government's Business Innovation and Skills department (BIS) as part of the programme to build better links between business and government. Tomlinson was the 'entrepreneur in residence' at BIS when, after six months of research, he produced his bombshell report. It found that:

> The experiences of many businesses across the country suggest that, at least within RBS, there are circumstances in which banks are necessarily engineering a default to move the business out of local management and into their turnaround divisions, generating revenue through fees,

increased margins and devalued assets. Much evidence was received about the practices of the RBS' turnaround division, Global Restructuring Group (GRG) which typifies this behaviour.

Once in this part of the bank the business is trapped . . . forced to stand by and watch an otherwise successful business be sunk by the decisions of the bank. The bank extracts maximum revenue from the business, beyond which can be considered reasonable and to such an extent that it is a contributing factor to the business' financial deterioration.[18]

Although the Tomlinson report was only 20 pages long, it produced a storm of protest in the business media and in the corridors of the House of Commons. The victims here were not lacking in voice. They were articulate business people capable of vehemently making their protests about their victimisation by unaccountable bankers. In May 2014 the Financial Conduct Authority (FCA) was forced to set up an independent inquiry. It was to be conducted by the financial consultants Promontory Financial Group and Mazars Accountants. The events which unfold around the controversy then became a touchstone for the abject failures of the main players involved. By 2016 the Promontory report was completed, but the FCA would not release the full report because it feared the findings were so damning that RBS would sue the FCA. Cue a battle between the Treasury Committee, MPs and the regulator about the cover-up on the Promontory findings. The FCA issued a series of redacted reports, but by the time of the parliamentary debate on the GRG, on 18 January 2018, there was still no full publication of the Promontory report. Up to this time the government had said nothing.

Incredibly, on 20 February 2018, the stand-off with the FCA was resolved by the Treasury Committee using parliamentary privilege to publish the entire unredacted Promontory report on its website. The report was an annihilating indictment of the conduct of RBS's GRG executives and of the senior management of the bank, who 'were aware or should have been aware' of these issues. Promontory found that 'There was in certain respects widespread inappropriate treatment of SME customers by RBS'; that this treatment was both 'systematic' and 'endemic'. Further, it found that while RBS 'did not set out to engineer' financial difficulty, staff were nonetheless encouraged to prioritise the boosting of revenue rather than looking after the needs of small firms. 'This was not in our judgement a result of idiosyncratic decisions by local managers but was endemic in the GRG's arrangements in dealing with SMEs' which often placed an 'otherwise viable business on a journey towards administration, receivership, and liquidation.'[19] And we know that these observations had been softened up with several redraftings, one of which was actually supervised by RBS executives.

The *Guardian* reported that the bank's reply to this searing indictment was to say it was 'deeply sorry' that during and after the Crash customers were not treated well by staff in the GRG.[20] Then RBS reached for one of its old stand-by defences – selective interpretation. It said that the Promontory report indicated that the most serious allegation that staff had 'deliberately targeted otherwise viable businesses in order to distress and to asset-strip them for the bank's profit has been shown to be without foundation'.[21] It is extraordinary, given the scale of the excoriating accusations in the Promontory report that, in its final analysis, the bank would still refuse to accept liability for the predations of the GRG.

The RBS chief executive who was in charge for the period from when the GRG machinations were exposed until the publication of the Promontory findings was Ross McEwan. He had taken on the RBS CEO role in October 2013, one month before the Tomlinson report was published. In all that time he never once acknowledged the GRG calamities. In fact, on one occasion he described the claimants as 'chancers' and said later, post-Promontory, that there was no case to answer on the allegations of 'systematic' pursuit of bank clients. Maybe he was obliged to try to protect the share price. He left the bank in October 2019 to take up post as the chief executive of National Australia Bank. By that time, his total earnings for his five years at the helm of RBS were around £18 million. His total remuneration at NAB is reported to be set at A\$9.5 million a year, which in RBS money is around £5.4 million. A £2 million hike in his pay from that at RBS.

At the RBS AGM in April 2019, when McEwan announced his resignation, he was challenged by a businessman who had suffered at the hands of the GRG and accused the bank of being 'evil, greedy and dishonest'. As usual, McEwan replied obliquely. 'The only regret I have is that because of all the conduct litigation and restructuring issues I haven't really done enough on the customer service delivery.'[22] Between 2015 and 2019, on McEwan's watch, RBS closed 414 branches or three out of four of its total branches.[23] In 2018 alone, when RBS made an operating profit of £3.35 billion, McEwan headed up a branch-closure programme across the UK which closed 259 local branches. In RBS's native Scotland, 62 branches were axed, more than one third of all RBS branches in the country. The closures were almost all in rural areas and were railroaded through despite robust community and union campaigns demanding a stay of execution, especially where the closure was of the 'last bank in town'. In this context, it seems passing strange for the CEO's valedictory statement to express the wish that, in his time, customer service should have had greater priority.

As noted in the previous pages, when the Tomlinson report was published late in 2013, such was the furore engendered about the GRG that the banking regulator, the Financial Conduct Authority (FCA) commissioned an independent inquiry by the consultants Promontory. That was in 2014. In October 2017, the FCA published its initial findings on the Promontory report which noted that the regulator's next step would be to focus on whether there was 'any basis for further action within our powers'.[24] That statement would prove to be more significant in the final analysis than might have been first thought. In June of the following year, the FCA agreed with the independent Promontory review that there were 'widespread and systemic' problems at the GRG, but found that no action could be taken as the FCA did not have the powers to do so. Commercial lending remains unregulated in the UK regulatory system, so given this 'regulatory parameter' the FCA concluded that no action was possible. Further, no names were named. The FCA ruled that this would 'not be legally justifiable'. So after more than four years of investigations and much controversy about the 'hush-hush' strategy deployed by the regulator, the end result was precisely zero. The joint chair of the Parliamentary Group on Fair Banking, Kevin Hollinrake MP, condemned the report as 'another complete whitewash and another failure of the regulator to perform its role'.[25]

Andrew Bailey is now the Governor of the Bank of England. His time as the CEO of the FCA remains hugely controversial. Many like Kevin Hollinrake believe he could have exercised the powers of the FCA to allow the investigation of senior managers or even activated its own codes for 'good regulation' but chose not to. The *Guardian*'s Larry Elliot said the so-called City watchdog had proved to be a paper tiger. He concluded that 'The lack of action will merely feed the widely held belief that those who caused the Crash have escaped punishment, while those who were blameless have paid a heavy cost'.[26] Others speak of a cover-up.

CHAPTER 11

It Wasn't about One or Two Bad Apples, It Was about the Whole Barrel

'In Australia the Government set up a Royal Commission. Its report is devastating and the police are now taking action against the bankers and associates involved. In the UK nothing has been done. There would appear to have been a systematic cover-up.'

Anthony Stansfeld, Police Crime Commissioner,
Thames Valley Police, 10 June 2019

In November 2012, Anthony Stansfeld was elected as the Police Crime Commissioner for Thames Valley Police, one of the largest non-Metropolitan forces in England and Wales. Stansfeld comes from a long family line of soldiers. He joined the Royal Green Jackets when he was 17 and rose to officer rank with ease. He is, to give you an indication of the cut of his jib, an esteemed member of the Cavalry and Guards Club in Piccadilly. After a lengthy army career he went into business and was the managing director of a light aircraft manufacturing company for many years, selling and servicing aircraft in more than 120 countries. As a police crime commissioner (PCC), Stansfeld has become one of the most out-spoken critics of what he sees as the greed and corruption now permeating the UK's banking system. That might cause a double-take as he is obviously a son of the Establishment. Stansfeld says, 'I didn't think that, as a PCC, much would shock me. I was wrong. The scale of corruption within the major UK banks, aided and abetted by their legal advisors, auditors and accountants, has been on a massive scale. The round figures will run to £100 billion according to reliable estimates we have.'[1]

Stansfeld makes the point that the evidence of recent years points to systematic fraud, because the same thing happened time and again to thousands of businesses. The magnitude of this takes it beyond circumstantial allegations. Stansfeld says that the processes were established is undeniable. He explained: 'The sole purpose was to make as much money as possible for the bank by liquidating any company on their lists. They would grossly under-estimate the value of the assets, buy them at far less than actual value, recoup the loan, share the profits of the resale at proper value amongst their cohorts and then go for the personal guaran-tees of the company owners. Often this would be done through documentation that had been altered and signatures forged. The bank would regain far more than the original loan and those that assisted made fortunes. The victims lost everything.'[2]

Stansfeld should know. Thames Valley Police is the only force in England and Wales whose investigations have led to the crim-inal conviction of any bankers in the UK since the 2008 Crash. In February 2017, at Southwark Crown Court, six people were found guilty of an array of offences connected to a criminal con-spiracy to defraud customers of the HBOS branch in Reading, in Berkshire – which is within the Thames Valley jurisdiction. The conspiracy included deliberate fraud, corruption and money laun-dering. The six convicted were sentenced to a cumulative total of 47 years in prison – the heaviest prison sentences for fraud ever in the UK. Two of them were HBOS bankers, Lynden Scourfield and Mark Dobson. Scourfield, the ringleader on the HBOS side of the scam, was sentenced to 11 years and Dobson to four and half years. What is interesting here is not just the moral bankruptcy of the bankers and their willingness to lie, cheat and muscle their customers, but how the executives of the bank reacted when they found out about the racket. It might be argued that Scourfield and his gang were proverbial bad apples. What cannot be denied is that HBOS executives responded to the gang's crimes with a stonewalling cover-up which was morally bankrupt and ruined lives. Every senior executive stands charged with failing to do the right thing. Over a long period of time.

Here's what happened in the egregious swindle. Scourfield headed up a division at HBOS which dealt with small companies on the bank's books which had financial problems. The unit was based in the HBOS branch in Reading. The scam took place roughly between 2003 and 2007, before HBOS was taken over by Lloyds in the aftermath of the 2008 Crash. Scourfield set up the pre-planned swindle with David and Alison Mills, who ran a business consultancy, Quayside Corporate Services (QCS). Scourfield and Dobson would advise clients that the only way HBOS could lend them more money was if they signed up for business restructuring with QCS. The Millses then loaded up the businesses that came to them with huge fees and other charges, and the bank then allowed dangerously higher borrowings. In due course, when the business couldn't make the payments on the new debts, they were bankrupted and their assets sold off, at considerable profit. That done, where clients had put up a personal guarantee for the loans in the shape of their homes, the crooks at Reading HBOS pursued repossession mercilessly. Perhaps this gives new meaning to HBOS's slogan of the times, 'By your side'.

Scourfield and his associates got payback from the swindle in the form of high-rolling foreign trips across the world, including to Florida, Mexico, Bangkok, Washington, Las Vegas and Miami; he was also wined and dined at the Mills' expense at some of London's most exclusive restaurants, had an American Express card which they paid for, as well as frequent sex parties with prostitutes. There were financial bribes on top of all this. At the 2017 trial when the six fraudsters – Scourfield and Dobson, David and Alison Mills and two of their associates – were convicted, Scourfield's bank statements showed unaccounted-for income, from between 2004 and 2007, of £348,887. In the end the bank had to write down £245 million as a result of the Reading scam, but an internal report found that the bank had also been swindled out of £100 million on its own accounts. The aggregated costs of the racket across the bank divisions touched £1 billion. In 2013, Thames Valley Police started the second phase of its seven-year,

£7 million-investigation into the Reading scandal. Sally Masterton, who worked for HBOS in its High Risk division, co-operated with the police investigation.

Some time after Masterton had given evidence to the police, she was asked by her then Lloyds boss[3] to produce an internal report on what had become known as 'the Reading Incident'. Masterton's 'Project Lord Turnbull'[4] investigation reached explosive conclusions. It alleged that for years, HBOS directors and senior managers systematically concealed the Reading scandal and failed to record its financial ramifications in the company accounts. It also alleged that the auditors, KPMG, approved a series of those falsified accounts, were complicit in the cover-up and then also in misleading the Financial Conduct Authority regulator. This means that, if the Project Turnbull allegations were true, then back in April 2008, when HBOS produced accounts for a £4 billion rights issue, and in September that year, in a prospectus for its takeover by Lloyds TSB, the figures given to the Stock Exchange were falsified. That is *prima facie* criminal behaviour.

In 2014, when Masterton's report first surfaced, the bank went into full-on denial. It said Masterton's report contained 'many unsubstantiated allegations about individuals, auditors and regulators, as well as HBOS, and the majority are made without any supporting evidence'.[5] They said she had acted on her own volition in producing the report and sacked her. KPMG refuted the allegations, 'which we believe have no basis in fact'.[6] In 2017 the auditors' watchdog, the Financial Reporting Council (FRC) eventually dropped its inquiry into KPMG's audit of the 2007 HBOS accounts, which preceded the 2008 rights issue and the prospectus for the Lloyds takeover late in 2008. It found 'there was nothing to justify further investigation'. Sir Win Bishoff was then the chair of the FRC. He was appointed on 1 April 2014. Before that, between 2009 and 2014, he was the chair of Lloyds Bank.

Throughout the Reading controversy, HBOS maintained a stonewalling position of 'there is no evidence of criminality at the Reading branch'; it used that to justify not paying financial compensation for the HBOS/QCS victims for 10 years. More than that, a 2017 *Financial Times* investigation proved that an internal

HBOS inquiry in 2007 actually exonerated Scourfield *et al*. Despite stark evidence to the contrary, it stated: 'In conclusion there is a lack of evidence that Lynden Scourfield's actions were for personal gain or of a fraudulent nature, and the HBOS Corporate Financial Crime Prevention case was therefore closed on 13 August 2007.'[7] Although the actual offences took place a long time ago, the story has present-day significance as it demonstrates the preparedness of banking executives to dissemble, delay, deny and, if they think it is necessary, to lie to defend their corrupt dealings.

The current Lloyds chief executive, António Horta-Osório, joined Lloyds in 2011. So he, and others whom he recruited, got caught in the web of HBOS's 'no evidence of criminality' denial. In March 2012, two years after the then regulator had found 'a number of serious irregularities and suspicious transactions' at HBOS Reading, and two years after the arrests of Scourfield and his crew, Juan Colombas, chief risk officer at Lloyds, wrote to one of the Reading fraud victims: 'You will appreciate that until this matter has been determined by a court, it is not clear that a criminal offence has taken place and/or that financial losses (if any) suffered by any party are a direct consequence of that criminal activity.'[8]

Thus it seems that five years after a £1 billion fraud had been perpetrated at HBOS that the head of risk, and by implication his boss, the chief executive, have perhaps not yet noticed anything untoward? Either it's gross negligence or complicity in non-disclosure. The Project Lord Turnbull Report indicts 14 senior directors and managers by name, along with the auditors KPMG, as being culpable for non-disclosure. After the 2017 Reading verdicts, Lloyds appointed a retired High Court judge, Dame Linda Dobbs, to consider the Reading events and to find out 'whether these issues were investigated and appropriately reported to the authorities'. The FCA's then chief executive, Andrew Bailey, seemingly approved her appointment as an appropriate next step in the HBOS/Lloyds controversy. She is expected to report late in 2020 at the earliest. This is a second-time around inquiry, since Lloyd's first so-called independent investigation was so widely dismissed as yet another banking whitewash that the bank had to set another one up.

Eventually, in 2018, more than a year after the Reading verdicts, HBOS had to admit it told lies about Sally Masterton and her Project Turnbull report. It admitted that she had been requested to write a report about her concerns by the bank and had not acted alone. Also that she had acted with 'integrity and good faith'. As a result, Lloyds had to pay her additional compensation on top of an original settlement reached when she won her case for unfair dismissal for her 2014 sacking. No-one has been disciplined at the bank for this litany of misconduct and dishonour. Anthony Stansfeld believes the continuing cover-up goes right up to Cabinet level in government. And to the top of the City. He says, 'Lloyds lied consistently about the fraud at HBOS – the whole thing was covered up by the bank directors and the accountants; and, in the face of damning evidence, for years the regulatory authorities did nothing.'

Finally, however, the regulator had to act. Fifteen years after the first complaints from Reading customers surfaced at the bank, twelve years after Lynden Scourfield left the bank under a cloud of suspicion, nine years after the first regulator's report found 'serious irregularities' at the Reading branch, and two years after the guilty verdicts at the Southwark Crown Court, the Financial Conduct Authority fined the Bank of Scotland for failure to report the Reading fraud. The FCA report of 21 June 2019 announced: 'The Financial Conduct Authority (FCA) has today fined Bank of Scotland (BOS) £45,500,000 for failures to disclose information about its suspicions that fraud may have occurred at the Reading-based Impaired Assets (IAR) team of Halifax Bank of Scotland.'

These pusillanimous conclusions were accompanied by an explanation that the £45.5 million fine had been reduced from £65 million – a 30% discount – because the bank had co-operated with the FCA investigation. Anthony Stansfeld told me that the fine should have had at least another zero added on to it. But he was also adamant that the FCA should be going much further to investigate the criminal concealment and false representations of certain directors and senior managers at HBOS/Lloyds. He told me: 'The board of HBOS issued a rights issue for billions without informing potential investors about the Reading fraud and the fact that there was a £38 billion hole in the HBOS accounts. Considering all the regulators – the FCA, the FRC, the CMA, the Bank of England and the PRA[9] – it's ridiculous; all they do is pass the parcel to each other, pass the inquiries around among themselves and in the end after all the rigmaroles no-one is brought to court.' He pointed out that the FCA '£45 million' findings make no mention of the Project Lord Turnbull report. Incredibly.

Stansfeld emphasises that the enormous wealth of the banks – much of it a direct result of their multi-billion bailouts from the taxpayer – means that they can always afford to sit out legal challenges as a tactic to avoid being called to account. He says that for many police forces the lessons learned from the Reading investigation is that it cost £7 million. That makes taking on such potential prosecutions financially punitive for any force involved. This may explain why there have been so few such police investigations like the Reading one. When the FCA imposed the £45 million fine on HBOS, the Lloyds chief executive, António Horta-Osório, apologised for what he called 'the dark period in HBOS's history'. He has always maintained he never had any detailed knowledge of the Reading events.

Anthony Stansfeld believes it is now time for drastic change. 'There's a great paradox here. The taxpayer bails out the banks in billions and they can use that money to defend themselves in court when they face utterly justifiable claims for redress. Sitting it out, funded by the taxpayer.' He believes it is time to follow the Australian example of a Royal Commission into the historic and current misconduct of the banks in Britain. 'In Australia the Government set up a Royal Commission. Its report was devastating and the police are now taking action against the bankers and associates involved. In the UK nothing has been done. There would appear to have been a systematic cover-up.'[10]

Noel Stevens, from Shellharbour in New South Wales, Australia, might be seen as the man whose legal pursuit of the Commonwealth Bank of Australia became the tipping point which precipitated the setting up of the 2018/19 Australian Royal Commission into the historical misconduct of the banks there. That reckoning would eventually expose the industrial scale of fraud, forgery, bribery, cover-ups and theft which, by then, had saturated Australia's banking system. Shellharbour is a beach town of around 5,000 people, about two hours' drive south of Sydney. People holiday there for the surfing, the scuba-diving and the exploration of the coastal rainforest inland from Shellharbour's golden beaches. Noel Stevens ran his small scaffolding business in Shellharbour. One day, in 2010, he got a call on his mobile from his local bank manager. 'Why don't you come in and see us sometime about your finances? Maybe we can help you out,' was the invitation.

So, the next day, Noel went to the Commonwealth Bank of Australia (CBA) in Shellharbour Square in the centre of town. He only had A$8,000 in the business account so nothing doing there. However, he did have a substantial life insurance policy, with the Australian mega-insurers Westpac. The advisor at the bank said they could offer a better deal if he swapped to a CBA life insurance policy. Noel did. A year later he was diagnosed with pancreatic cancer. When he lodged a claim with his CBA life insurance, he was told he wasn't covered. He spent the last six months of his life, with his daughter, Teagan Couper, fighting CBA in a legal battle for compensation. It emerged in court that the teller at CBA who advised Noel Stevens to switch policies got an incentive kick-back payment for that, and the financial planner who sold him the new policy got a bumper commission on the sale.

On 3 July 2012, Noel Stevens won his case. He died three days later. He had given evidence by video link to the court, in his pyjamas, from his hospital bed. As his daughter, Teagan, was making preparations for her father's funeral, she was served with legal papers from the bank's lawyers intimating that they were going to appeal on the case. The family eventually won the appeal case also. At that point, the CBA stated that 'Noel Stevens – We respect the decision of the Court of Appeal, and wish to express our sympathy for the tragic circumstances of the customer and their family. We acknowledge that the most appropriate action in this case would have been for the customer to have remained with their existing policy.'[11] This was two years after CBA had dragged a dying man through the Australian courts and then his surviving family through the Appeal courts.

Adele Ferguson is one of Australia's leading investigative journalists. She featured the Noel Stevens story in her 'Four Corners' TV programme and in her newspaper columns. She says that the CBA's rapacious dealings with Noel Stevens sparked public outrage. In turn, that gave significant impetus to the calls in the Australian Senate for an Australian Royal Commission on Misconduct in Banking to be set up. After just over a year of deliberations, the initial findings, published in September 2018, castigated Australia's top four banks: 'Too often the answer seems to be greed – the pursuit of short-term profit at the expense of basic standards of honesty. How else is charging fees to the dead to be explained?' the commission declared.

Some four months later, in February 2019, the commission's final report was published. Eight CEOs and eight chairs of major financial institutions in Australia were forced to resign as a consequence of the findings. Among them were Andrew Thorburn, the chief executive of National Australia Bank, and its chairman, Ken Henry. The commission singled out Henry and Thorburn, who presided when NAB was selling John Guidi's loans to Cerberus, for special comment. It stated that the commission inquiry heard how NAB, Australia's fourth largest bank, charged almost A\$100 million (US\$71 million) in fees to customers without providing them with any service. Some of the billings were charged to clients who had died. It also heard evidence of how NAB counter staff, in parts of Sydney, accepted cash bribes to facilitate loans, based on fake documents, to hit sales targets.[12] Adele Ferguson published a book about the downfall of the Australian banks entitled *Banking Bad*. She says that the Royal Commission exposed as a sham the banks' claim that the accusations facing the Australian financial system were a result of 'one or two bad apples'. Ferguson says 'Clearly it wasn't about one or two bad apples. It was about the whole barrel.'

There is growing pressure in the UK for Britain to follow the Australian lead and hold a Royal Commission on misconduct in banking in the UK. Anthony Stansfeld of Thames Valley Police is already on the record about this. He rejects the arguments of those who say it would take too long to report and so cost too much. 'We could put a time limit on it like the Australian one,' he says. 'Besides, what is the cost of not having a commission and nothing being done about the injustices suffered by so many people, so many families, at the hands of the bankers?' he asks. The joint chair of the All Party Parliamentary watchdog on Fair Business Banking is Kevin Hollinrake MP. He is equally unequivocal about the UK following the Australian example with a Royal Commission. He makes the point that the Australian Royal Commission was completed in 15 months and cost £40 million. He echoes the 'whole barrel' of bad apples view expressed by Adele Ferguson. Hollinrake says the commission's 'damning findings' exposed both the disgraceful misconduct of the financial sector in Australia, but also the serious failings of the regulators there. There's more. He believes a British Royal Commission would establish that what has gone on here would eclipse the scale of the Australian scandal. He told me: 'We need exactly the same process here, but my feeling is that the revelations of culture, behaviour, misconduct and regulatory failures will be even worse than the Australian report.'

The GMB union echoes that. Its Acting General Secretary, John Phillips, who took over after the previous leader, Tim Roache, resigned, concurred with 'the whole barrel is rotten' sentiment. Phillips measures his words carefully. Always. He told me: 'In our view you could say it's the whole orchard that needs cleaning out. There are very few signs that the bankers and the others, left to themselves, will change. Day after day *The Financial Times* has headlines where scams seem like an everyday occurrence. I remember last year, just for example, there was the scandal of HSBC having to pay a $192 million fine in a US tax evasion case, where they had hidden $1 billion from the tax authorities. A $1 billion scam, just like that. We need a Royal Commission on the banks, the City and the whole finance industry. The lot. It's long, long overdue.'

Professor Prem Sikka of Sheffield University argues that any UK Royal Commission must have a broader remit than just banking. He suggests that many private equity funds have proved to be powerful partners with the Big Four banks in financial fraud and asset-stripping. Sikka believes that just as the banks had a structured, systematic approach to bankrupting their own clients to improve their own bank balance sheets, so too private equity has a structured model of operation. That has developed as a consequence of decades of banking deregulation and the resultant financialisation. Complicated financial engineering, using loan-loading to set up new profits in interest payments and management fees in the so-called rescue of companies in crisis, is the result. Ultimately, the model ends with massive returns in the coffers of private equity, accrued from the sell-off of assets when the grim reaper of insolvency arrives. Offshore registration of these funds, more often than not, puts them beyond regulation. And tax, of course. Private equity cannot be exempt from any review of misconduct in the finance system in the UK. Take Greybull Capital.

In 2016 the private equity fund Greybull Capital took over one of Britain's last two steelworks at Scunthorpe, in Lincolnshire. Greybull bought British Steel – as the Scunthorpe business was known – for £1 from the Indian conglomerate Tata. In 2007, when Tata bailed out the original British Steel, it was hailed as a saviour. So too was Greybull when it arrived following the failure of the Tata 'redeemers'. More attention should have been paid to the fine print in the Greybull offer. By May 2019, the Scunthorpe plant was insolvent. Greybull was set up by two rich French brothers, Marc and Nathaniel Meyohas, with Daniel Goldstein, a former Lehman Brothers trader. By the time of the Scunthorpe debacle, Marc Mayohas and Goldstein were the company's movers and shakers. Greybull has the complex company structures of financialisation. British Steel was owned by a holding company, British Steel Holdings Limited, which in turn was owned by another Greybull entity, Olympus Steel 2 Ltd, based in the tax haven of Jersey.[13]

At the time of the Greybull takeover it was Olympus Steel which made a £154 million short-term loan to British Steel, at the hefty rate of 9.6%. This allowed Greybull/Olympus to levy £33.8 million in loan interest charges over the three years based on the £154 million loan lodged after its takeover. This also gained corporate tax relief for British Steel as an offset for the costs of the same interest charges. In addition, 'management fees' were £6 million

to the end of 2018. In May 2019 the *Guardian* headlined on the
Scunthorpe collapse: 'British Steel's owners charging firm £20 million a year in fees and interest.'[14]

Greybull has form on this sort of business. In recent years it has
attempted the financial rescue of the electrical retailer, Comet, the
Riley snooker halls and sports bars enterprise, the M convenience
store chain and, notably, Monarch Airlines. All of which went
down, but seem to have made Greybull substantial earnings before
their demise.

Prem Sikka says that putting private equity in charge of business
turnaround is like surrendering the keys of the town bloodbank
to Dracula. He would also insist that financial behemoths, like
the 'vulture fund' Cerberus, are worthy of inclusion in any indictment citing those called to appear before a Royal Commission
on the finance industry. Today, Cerberus is the embodiment of
unregulated, unaccountable, unapproachable, untouchable private equity. Cerberus was founded in 1992 by an ex-US marine,
Steve Feinberg, allegedly one of Donald Trump's former personal
advisors. The Cerberus headquarters is in New York. Its biggest
operations beyond the USA are across Europe. In the early years
the business was built on a model of takeover and turnaround,
big on cars and guns. At one time it owned Alamo Car Rental,
National Car Rental, a sizeable chunk of Chrysler and large interests in the American bus industry. Then there was Remington.
Cerberus was an enthusiastic investor in firearms and used to
own the Remington Group – one of the USA's major gunsmiths at
the time. That particular part of the business went belly up when
a Remington rifle was used in the Sandy Hook primary school
slaughter in Connecticut. In December 2012, six teachers and
20 school children died in the attack there.

However, by then, Cerberus had long been transformed from
a takeover and turnaround asset-stripper into a major property
player, specialising in real-estate purchase and vulture-fund debt
collection. The debt collection element is now almost totally tied
to default real estate loans – non-performing loans or NPLs as they
are known. Cerberus is now the world's biggest debt collector. The
2008 Crash was groundbreaking in the building of the Cerberus

colossus. The Crash resulted in financial institutions across the globe having bad debts pile up on their balance sheets, literally in trillions of dollars. Step forward Cerberus to make a pitch to take mass loan books filled with NPLs out of the European banking system, which was then submerged in a liquidity crisis. Britain was high on those lists.

With an ever-watchful eye on moves to improve their balance sheets, and hence their everlasting bonuses, the British bankers were only too keen to oblige. Between 2013 and 2014, major British banks sold off loan books touching at least £11 billion to Cerberus holdings. Cerberus bought loans from RBS worth £6.7 billion, from Lloyds worth £2.7 billion, and from NAB for CYBG loans worth £1.8 billion. That was done on the usual usury terms. For example, in December 2014, Cerberus bought loan books from RBS held by its Irish subsidiaries. They paid £1.1 billion for loans that were worth almost £5 billion.

Between 2010 and the end of 2018, in Europe alone, Cerberus completed real-estate deals worth just over €52 billion (£46.7 billion). The acquisition of huge NPL loan books of outstanding debt accounted for a large share of this. There's gold in them thar bills. The biggest of these debt transfers involved the Spanish bank, BBVA. Cerberus bought loans on 78,000 properties from BBVA for €5 billion. Their face value was €13 billion. That's what makes the debt collection carousel go round. Buy at considerably less than value, sweat the monthly payments inexorably and then flog assets to raise real returns; these days returns are counted in billions of pounds, euros or US dollars. These figures are also a totem of financialisation. Eight of the deals Cerberus closed in Europe in 2018 were worth £5.7 billion. That matches the value of total investment in the British car industry in the four years from 2015 to 2018.[15] According to Cerberus, this is the sort of resource from which investment returns of 17-20% are delivered. These returns are also a foreshadowing of bloodcurdling court papers summoning the owners of small businesses to attend court, on the noted date, so they can be present when all they own will be stripped from them to pay for the preordained banking debt traps which have consumed them.

From day one Cerberus has been mired in controversy about its 'ruthless and unjust' debt collection practices, its ruination of thousands upon thousands of family businesses and its structured tax-avoidance schemes. Cerberus has been scathingly criticised in a number of parliamentary debates, so much so that it is now frequently referred to as a 'vulture fund'. Kevin Hollinrake MP, of the parliamentary banking watchdog, goes further. He told me: 'So-called vulture funds, like Cerberus, would be better described as vampire funds, as many of their customers would be able to manage their finances if their lifeblood wasn't being sucked out of them by these entities. It is quite extraordinary that we allow these funds to operate outside the perimeter of regulation and also allow UK lenders who are regulated to evade their regulatory obligations by selling their lending books to them.' That is an accurate description of the financial crisis that has engulfed thousands of British businesses. Like John Guidi's, we may recall. Here is a debt-collecting symbiosis – the banks bankrupt you with changed loan terms through planned default and then sell your debts to a vulture fund like Cerberus. And when you are screaming for help, your bank turns its back saying it's nothing to do with them, since the loans are with Cerberus. Then the regulators wash their hands like a banking Pontius Pilate, saying they would love to help but they can't because private equity funds, like Cerberus, are unregulated – beyond the 'regulatory perimeter', you understand. And you face ruin.

Cerberus disputes any accusations about the ruthlessness of its debt collection services. Ron Rawald, Cerberus' head of international real estate, claims that 85% of the deals done with NPL debtors are 'consensual'. He says, 'We sit down with the borrower and come up with a solution that the borrower and ourselves are happy with.' Lee Millstein, the global head of real estate for Cerberus, concurs. 'What we don't like to do is to have to go through enforcement and foreclosure – it takes time, money and is not a positive experience for anybody.'[16] Problem? What problem?

In February 2017, in one of the House of Commons debates on Cerberus, the then SNP MP George Kerevan raised the issue of deliberate tax evasion: 'Cerberus manages distressed debt bought in the UK and Europe through a multiplicity of shell companies based largely in the Irish Republic. Those entities usually have the word "Promontoria" in their titles.[17] They are, in turn, subsidiaries of other Cerberus Group companies registered in the Netherlands. Essentially, the Dutch companies lend money to their Irish subsidiaries at high interest rates to effect the asset purchases. That ensures that most of the cash generated from the purchased loans, or from liquidating distressed assets, flows back to the Netherlands in the form of transfer payments. According to an investigation by the *Irish Times*, six key Cerberus Promontoria holding companies in Ireland collectively paid a miserly €15,500 in tax in 2015.'[18] These practices still stand today, as does the Cerberus denial that the company organises its businesses with reducing its tax liabilities as a priority.

In 2015 the British Chancellor of the Exchequer dealt with Cerberus. Not to punish the debt collector for its iniquitous plundering but to join the queue of private bankers who had already stood in supplication before Cerberus executives, beseeching them to take over their troublesome bad debts. The bankers sold the loans. And their souls. Because they knew that when the furore grew about the rapacious pursuit of these debts by the three-headed hound of Cerberus they could wash their hands of the matter. Not us. Not Guilty. No case to answer. See Cerberus. Just like David Duffy at CYBG in the John Guidi case.

Northern Rock and Bradford and Bingley went bust in the Crash. In 2015 George Osborne sold their 200,000 mortgages to Cerberus. Between 120,000 and 150,000 of these mortgage holders have been trapped by that deal on the interest rates they were paying when they took out the mortgages. Cerberus refuses to reduce the rates to today's averages. So these 'mortgage prisoners' trapped on higher rates, have been paying Cerberus monthly mortgages well over the going rate. That is entirely legal. Cerberus paid £5.5 billion for the Northern Rock and Bradford and Bingley loan books. Their real asset value was £13 billion. George Osborne said it was a good deal for the taxpayer. Kevin Hollinrake MP says the sale of loans to third parties, not subject to UK banking regulations, should be banned.

CHAPTER 12

Everything Must Change

'For unto everyone that hath shall be given, and he shall have an abundance; but from him that hath not shall be taken even that which he hath.'

The Parable of the Talents, *Matthew* 25:29

'If we want everything to stay the same, everything must change.'

Giuseppe Tomasi di Lampedusa,
Il Gattopardo (The Leopard)

This chapter aims to offer a critique of the structure of the British economy and what reforms are needed to create a more equal society. That aspiration is a moral one – the current structures allow the rich to take much more than they are due for their economic efforts and result in lives of abject poverty for those in the bottom 10% of income groups. However, the argument is made that the immorality of such a wealth gap is not the critical issue. The critical issue is that the economic imperatives that have created such division need to be reformed. The maximising of shareholder value model, where the delivery of profits is the all-encompassing aim of economic enterprise, combined with financialisation, has led to a Britain in ransom to rentier capitalism, where the extraction of wealth by its most powerful classes, and not its creation, has become paramount. That model needs to be challenged, not least because the shattering of the social contract between the classes, which it has delivered, brings with it distrust felt by those outside the 1% class of the richest oligarchs. In turn this raises the prospect of challenges from the left and right to the stability of the entire system, based on a perceived lack of legitimacy.

It is no coincidence that in current debates among a section of the strategic thinkers of American capitalism it is suggested that 'capitalism is broken' and there is a mirror image of this in the editorials of the *Financial Times* in the UK that offer panaceas for 'the reform of today's rigged capitalism'. However, the starting point of this discussion has to be how and why we got to where we are now. That analysis could begin with the Sarbanes–Oxley Act, passed in 2002, in the USA, as one of the final pieces of legislation inaugurated during the Bill Clinton presidency.

Sarbanes–Oxley introduced much more punitive rules for American banking in the aftermath of the Enron and WordCom scandals. It forced businesses to make more detailed disclosures of their operations and assets, and introduced severe penalties for misleading regulators and the public. This included the definition of certain company law breaches which carried with them possible jail sentences. Ian Fraser, author of *Shredded*, told me that the American act could be considered as pivotal for the development of the UK economy in the direction of deregulated financialisation, because the Labour government of Blair and Brown 'saw this as an opportunity for the City to exploit the new American regulations by transforming London and the City into the alternative world's banker'.[1]

He says that explains why Brown became the chancellor who cut corporate regulation in the UK to the bone. In the Labour Government's first term, Brown also slashed capital gains tax on assets from 40% to 10% – another indication of where fiscal priorities seemed to lie. 'International money flowed in, including billions of dirty Russian money which had long been looking for a safe home,' says Fraser.[2] He charts this free-for-all as the starter for ten which ended in the catastrophe which engulfed British banking in 2008. He points out that from Brown initially shaping up as a chancellor ready to challenge the greed of Britain's monopoly bankers, he became one who approved the creation of the monsters that, in 2008, became 'too big to fail'. After all, Fraser argues, Brown was the chancellor who approved RBS's £21 billion takeover of NatWest in 2000, RBS's €71 billion takeover of ABN AMRO in 2007 and Lloyds TSB's £20 billion takeover of HBOS in the aftermath of the Crash.

Of course, there is a very simple explanation for the love affair between Blair, Brown and the banks. In part, bankers' taxes were funding the Third Way, New Labour's programme which was going to put an end to the boom and bust of historic capitalism. It was based on what Blairite insiders called 'Tax and Transfer Socialism'. Let the market rip and the taxes drawn from that would pay for spending to create structural social reforms. For example, in 2007, the banking industry paid £68 billion in tax to the UK Exchequer. That was almost 14% of the total tax take that year.[3] It was also double the cost of delivering Labour's tax credit programme for those suffering in-work poverty; that reduced the number of children in the UK living in poverty by two million. Those figures exemplify the economics which were the foundation of New Labour. When the Crash came, the Tax and Transfer Socialism of New Labour went bust along with the banks. What followed was Tory austerity.

In June 2010, in his first post-election Budget statement, George Osborne, the Chancellor of the Exchequer in the victorious Tory-led coalition government, opened with a declaration about debt: 'This emergency budget deals decisively with our country's record debts ... The coalition Government have inherited from their predecessors the largest budget deficit of any economy in Europe, with the single exception of Ireland. One pound in every four that we spend is being borrowed. Questions that were asked about the liquidity and solvency of banking systems are now being asked about the liquidity and solvency of some of the Governments who stand behind those banks.'[4]

This prominent implication that the Crash is the consequence of excessive government spending turned out to be enormously significant. Osborne was about to turn back the clock and use the banking crisis as cover to carry out a ten-year dismantling and looting of the British state. That programme would put special emphasis on the relentless break-up of the welfare state but would also include a massive acceleration of the transfer of the state's industrial assets to private capital through privatisation and outsourcing. The answer to a crisis of private capital was to be a programme to massively increase its share of the spoils. Of course Osborne never stated those intentions openly. Instead he became a sultan of spin. In the same June speech he said: 'In this Budget, everyone will be asked to contribute. But, in return . . . everyone will share in the rewards when we succeed. When we say that we are all in this together, we mean it.'[5] That turned out to be another whopper.

The *Guardian* economics editor, Larry Elliot, describes Osborne's post-Crash analysis as 'completely and utterly bogus'. He argues trenchantly that the crisis was 'not a failure of the public sector, rather it was a failure of the private sector and, in particular, the economic model which had been in place for previous three decades – the whole liberalised, financialised economy'. Elliot says: 'The Conservatives were amazingly good at pinning the blame on the Labour government but it was entirely unjustified.'[6] A more exacting analysis would have to embrace the politics of ideology – the return to the class war of Thatcherism. Osborne saw his chance for a retying of the knot of history with the politics of the breaking up of the state, first established by the government of Margaret Thatcher. Osborne was about to embark on a Thatcherite programme, but with public sector cuts and privatisation programmes whose ferocity would be way beyond those of the Thatcher years. Ideology will out – those who had nothing to do with the crisis were the ones who would pay for it. On that June afternoon in 2010, when Osborne stood at the Dispatch Box, this may not have been transparently evident.

However, Osborne gave due warning. He announced spending cutbacks that would reach £30 billion a year by 2014–15. He pledged that the programmes of the previous Labour government for the NHS and international aid would be maintained, but every other government department would face cuts that would amount to a total spending reduction of 25% by the end of his government's four years in office. Thus, the airbrushing of the banking catastrophe out of history and its replacement with cuts to government spending and 'balancing the books' metamorphoses into a justification of 'austerity'. According to Garry Lemon, the Trussell Trust's director of policy and research, in the year to March 2019 the trust gave out 1.6 million emergency food parcels. Some 580,000 of these emergency supplies went to children. An emergency food parcel amounts to three days' food for one person.

These 2019 figures are yet another Trust record. They are up on the previous year by almost 20%. In the five years from 2014, the number of food parcels distributed by the trust increased by 75%. All these statistics speak about poverty on the march as a direct consequence of the programme of austerity. In November 2019 the Trussell Trust published a devastating three-year report. At the start of 2010 the trust ran 57 food banks, now it's 424, which is the backbone of a food-bank system that runs to over 1,000. In the last three years, one family in fifty in Britain has used a food bank and nine out of ten of them are destitute in the sense that they can't afford to eat regularly, don't have enough money to buy clothes and struggle to keep themselves decent. The most shocking feature of this trend is that in today's Britain, this is somehow accepted as a part of everyday life.

The politics of making the poor pay can be evidenced by the advent of Universal Credit within the British benefits system. Initially those on Universal Credit pilot programmes had to endure six weeks with no payments in the transition from current claims to the Universal Credit system. That was reduced to a five-week interregnum as a concession. Imagine your manager arrives at your work and says to you and the rest of the staff, 'Right, we are introducing a new system for paying salaries. So there is going to be a block on salary payments to everyone for the next five weeks. If that is a problem then we can give you a loan to tide you over if you need it. Of course there will be interest charges on the loans. That's only right, OK?' The Trussell Trust's Garry Lemon says, 'In areas where Universal Credit has been introduced, increased use of food banks averages out at 52%. Now Universal Credit is not responsible for all those going to food banks, but there is a link there even if government ministers deny it.' Warrington was one of the government pilot projects for the roll out of Universal Credit. That was completed in 2017. Use of the Trussell Trust food bank has doubled since then.[7]

Philip Alston, the UN's rapporteur on poverty and human rights, conducted a two-week research mission in the UK in the autumn of 2018. He noted in his report that it seems 'patently unjust and contrary to British values that so many people are living in poverty. This is obvious to anyone who opens their eyes to see the immense growth in food banks and the queues waiting outside them, the people sleeping rough in the streets, the growth of homelessness, the sense of deep despair . . .'[8]

Alston determined that a fifth of the British population, 14 million people, now live in poverty. Four million are more than 50% below the poverty line, and 1.5 million are destitute, in the sense that they are unable to afford basic essentials. It is perhaps useful to note here that more than 8 million of the 14 million are in in-work poverty, that is either in full-time or part-time work, according to a poverty investigation published in *The Times* in late 2018. Alston notes that child poverty rates could reach 40% in 2020.[9] He describes this possibility for almost one in two British children to grow up in poverty as 'not just a disgrace but a social calamity and an economic disaster, all rolled into one'. Alston's analysis concludes that this scale of impoverishment of a huge section of the population is a political choice: 'Austerity could easily have spared the poor, if the political will had existed to do so. Resources were available to the Treasury at the last budget that could have transformed the situation of millions of people living in poverty, but the political choice was made to fund tax cuts for the wealthy instead.'[10] When Jeremy Hunt, then a minister in the Tory government, was asked about the Alston Report, he simply said, 'The UN report is not true.'

Justin Bowden, who led the GMB's blacklisting campaign detailed in an earlier chapter, is a 'basic principles' trade union leader. For him, the core of the union is the workplace and the battle for members, wages and a better deal. He told me that the unions scarcely joined the battle of ideas that should have been fought over Tory austerity. He added: 'Austerity ended with more

than 300,000 statutorily homeless and thousands actually homeless on the street. People couldn't feed the kids and keep a roof over
their head. It seemed we lost the ability to demonstrate anger and
argue for another way. Never mind going into battle. We didn't
even fire a single shot.' The belief is clear – 'Never again.' Whilst
the cuts in the public realm and outsourcing were never-ending,
those at the top of the business class were looting the state and
wallowing in self-enrichment as never before. Jeff Fairburn's story
provides all the evidence needed for that contention.

Fairburn is the former chief executive of Persimmon, the UK's
second biggest housebuilder. Austerity meant nothing to him. He
gamed the system and looted the state. The story starts in 2012,
the year that Persimmon shareholders approved a new long term
incentive plan (LTIP) for its senior managers – 133 of them. The
new share bonuses were to be matched to company performance
over a ten-year period. Crucially, these proposals were not set
according to board or shareholder discretion, but became part
of a legally binding employment contract for the top three directors and senior managers, which had no cap on the size of the
payments due. A greater incentive for these directors to maximise
share prices would be difficult to configure. Thus, the Persimmon
directors' proposals created a system where adhering to the standing imperatives of 'maximising shareholder value' could produce
potentially jaw-dropping personal gains.

Then, perhaps not by coincidence, a year after the new shares
plan was approved the game-changer arrived – the introduction
of the Tory government's generous 'Help to Buy' scheme for first-
time house buyers. By early 2013, the Tory government was in
trouble; the economy was languishing in an historic low growth
and low productivity doldrum. The chancellor, George Osborne,
decided that rebooting the housing market was the answer to this,
whereby new housebuilding would create a multiplier effect of
growth in the economy. 'Help to Buy' was introduced in April
2013. It worked by giving homeowners an interest-free government loan worth up to 20% of a property's value – if the buyer
opted for a new-build house. At the beginning, the programme
was relatively modest, with the whole scheme costed at £3 billion.

A 2019 National Audit Office report now notes that by 2023 the total spend will eclipse £29 billion.[11]

Enter the chief Persimmon directors Jeff Fairburn, Mike Killoran and David Jenkinson. When the 'Help to Buy' scheme was inaugurated, Persimmon shares were trading at £6.20. The shares had soared to £27.38 by the time the first share bonuses under the new system became due in March 2017. Over 2017 and 2018, Fairburn's return on his share options, set by the legal terms of his LTIP contract, was £110 million. When the furore about this became a focus of the national media, he agreed to take a cut of 50% in the shares he could cash in. If he had taken a simple across-the-board cut, that would have left him with a £60 million windfall over the two years. Instead he returned the 50% based on surrendering the shares which had the lowest value. That left his shares pay-out at £75 million for 2017 and 2018. Under the last tranche of his Persimmon LTIP share options Fairburn will lift another £7.8 million in 2022. He left the company in December 2018.

According to the Persimmon annual report for 2017, Fairburn's pay cheque totalled £47 million. That included share options of £45 million. His total pay the previous year had been just over £2 million. Fairburn's share options for 2017 are almost one and half times what Shelter raised in donations that year. The finance director, Mike Killoran, who would have signed off the entire scheme, collected £36.7 million, including share options of £35 million. That was up from the previous year's earnings of £1.4 million. David Jenkinson lifted £20.4 million, including his share options worth £19 million. His previous year's earnings were also £1.4 million. The accumulated totals of this extravaganza are mind-boggling. In 2017 and 2018 the top three were paid £193 million in salary and share options. The share options element within that is £186 million. This along with the share options paid out to the rest of the 133 senior managers totals £438 million. They would probably argue that this was only their just reward for 'maximising shareholder value', because in the period 2012 to 2017 the shareholders' dividends reached £1.5 billion.[12]

In reality, this is a brazen looting of the public purse or a looting of the state, to give it its proper designation. It was the state, in the form of the 'Help to Buy' programme, which created the enormous bonanza of new buyers for the housing companies and the associated booming profits that followed. By 2018, the top five housebuilders in Britain doubled their profits per house built compared to 2007, the year before the Crash. In 2018 the House of Commons Business Energy and Industrial Strategy (BEIS) Committee held an inquiry on chief executive pay. It began on 6 June. Marion Sears joined the Persimmon board in January 2013, so she was not on the board when the new LTIP programme for senior executives was approved in 2012. Nonetheless, she was a board member leading up to the share options pay-outs and, as the new chair of the Remuneration Committee, had to deal with the aftermath. In 2018 Marion Sears was paid £75,000 a year as a non-executive director and chair of the Persimmon RemCo.

The redoubtable Rachel Reeves MP chaired the BEIS inquiry. She asks Sears what the chief executive of Persimmon was paid in 2017. Sears gives her the salary figure of £675,000. Sears adds 'it was a 2% increase in line with the workforce on the year before'. Reeves presses on and asks Sears, 'What about total pay?' Sears gets nearer the mark – 'The total pay was about £45 million,' she replies.[13] That actually represents a 2217% increase on the previous year. Reeves then asks Sears what the average worker at Persimmon is paid. She doesn't know. Sears replies, 'I do not have that figure at my fingertips.' She doesn't have the figures for the lowest-paid worker at her fingertips either. This is a give-away about where priorities lie. Eventually the Persimmon company secretary, Tracy Davison, submits the figures to the Reeves Committee in a written report. In 2017, when the top three Persimmon directors were lifting tens of millions of pounds as a result of what turned out to be their 'Help to Buy' scam, the average wage of a Persimmon worker was £35,665. That made the Persimmon pay ratio for the highest paid employee – Jeff Fairburn – to the average worker 1,320:1. The same pay ratio to the lowest paid worker at Persimmon for that year was 3,195:1.

Deborah Hargreaves, a former business editor at the *Guardian*, founded the High Pay Centre. She is the author of a a recent study of chief executive pay – *Are Chief Executives Overpaid?* She says that LTIPs and bonus pay-outs are unquestionably the major factors in the skewing of pay ratios. Her book establishes that the ratio between average chief executive pay and employee pay was 48:1 in 1998, and by 2016 had risen to 129:1. That reflects the average chief executive pay rising exponentially from £1 million in 1998 to over £5 million in 2015.[14] These facts are highly significant because this huge gulf between chief executive pay and the pay of an average worker is a cornerstone of social inequality in Britain. As stated earlier, that has rendered the idea of British society being governed by a social contract where we are all genuinely in this together utterly redundant. And the results of that are already all too evident in the divisions existing today in Britain. There can be no binding social contract between the have-nots and the haves in these circumstances where currently it would take an average worker 117 years to earn the average annual pay of a chief executive. That gulf undermines the stability of the current economic system. This is not a denial of the importance of reasonable rewards for those who are leaders in industry and whose achievements merit reward. However, the current salaries and share bonuses paid to chief executives are now out of control and are now seldom an accurate reflection of performance. The TUC argues that a maximum of 10% of chief executive remuneration should be paid in pay incentives. And pay ratios between the CEO and the average workers' wage should aim to be no more than 20:1. Deborah Hargreaves told me: 'Put simply, many top bosses pay themselves millions just because they can.'

The collapse of the facilities management company Interserve provides further evidence of the lack of accountability of directors under the current corporate governance codes and, in addition, demonstrates what appears to be the immunity of directors from prosecution, even when flagrant breaches of directors' duties under the Companies Act are identified. Step up Debbie White and Mark Whiteling. In March 2019 they were the chief executive and finance director respectively of Interserve. On 8 March 2019 – a year after the Carillion collapse – White assured shareholders and investors in the Interserve 2018 annual report that, although

in 2018 and 2019 the company had faced 'unprecedented challenges', considerable progress had been made and 'The Group has
a future workload of £7.1bn, as of 31 December 2018, and ...
The Board remains focused on positioning the Group for long-
term, sustainable, success.'[15] Does that sound familiar? It should,
because it is Carillion Mark II.

A week later, on 15 March 2019, Interserve was in administration, in the hands of its creditors, on the verge of going bust.
It had racked up £735 million net debt, had run out of money,
and could not pay suppliers or employees. The other features of a
government outsourcer going down were also there for all to see.
The operating profit was £92.7 million, but there were £98.6 million of 'exceptional items' not included in the calculation of that
figure. The balance sheet had £342 million of goodwill recorded
against net current assets of £98.7 million. Going into administration wiped out what was left of share values. The auditors, Grant
Thornton, are under investigation for signing off on the last four
years' returns.

But wait. Despite this cataclysm the Interserve 2018 annual
report, published one week before the collapse, shows that in that
year, White and Whiteling took bonuses totalling £656,000 out
of the company. Debbie White was paid £1.26 million for 2018,
which included a bonus of £404,000, as the company was going
down. Mark Whiteling's figures are total pay £736,000, which
included £252,000 in bonuses. In the aftermath of the Interserve
collapse none of these payments have been subject to clawback,
which is testimony to the lack of accountability in the system. That
needs to change; for every company with more than 250 workers
there need to be clawback provisions that stick. And that should
be the law – as real as any regulation enforcing the payment of
the National Minimum Wage. In addition, this debacle raises
the question of why breaking the law – in this case the apparent dereliction of the duty of directors to their shareholders and
stakeholders, within the Companies Act – scarcely ever produces
punitive prosecution.

GMB Scotland's regional secretary, Gary Smith, puts it more
anecdotally: 'If a young man is up in court for a third time for

stealing a hundredweight of lead off a roof, he's looking at time in a young offenders institution. The executive at the top of a company which goes down with a hundred million at stake can be confident he can say sorry and then walk away.' Smith believes it is time the voice of the trades unions was listened to about the self-justification for greed served up by the PR spin-doctors of big companies when the latest bonuses paid out to their chief executives come under fire. He says he's also fed up with the proclamations of achievement from chief executives about the decisiveness of their personal contribution to profits. 'Did they make the profits all on their own?' he asks. However, he believes that there is a strange lack of indignation about the scale of exec-utive rewards. 'It's almost as if people are inured to it all. They hear about the latest financial outrage, say "Greedy bastards" and shrug their shoulders. That's why there's a case for more union crusading about all this.'

He was talking some time before the Thomas Cook collapse. It turns out that although the Thomas Cook headlines were about tens of thousands of holidaymakers stranded in the sun, the real story was about the unaccountable, untouchable plundering of the company by a trio of the company's chief executives. A total of £33 million in fees were taken out of the travel business over 15 years by the last three chief executives of Thomas Cook. Take Harriet Green, who was the chief executive through 2013 and 2014. She took a total of £10 million in pay in these two years. The *Financial Times* noted that 'Ms Green relied heavily on advis-ers, leading to £180 million paid in consultancy fees in the 2013 and 2014 accounts'.[16] The looting is ubiquitous, systematic and seemingly never-ending.

Why is this so important? Wealth is a zero-sum game. What is taken out of the pot, in the form of executive rewards, cannot be spent twice. Take the Persimmon shares scandal. One hundred and thirty-three senior managers shared 'Help to Buy' bonuses amounting to £438 million. If instead the managers' bonuses had been restricted to a 20:1 ratio, based on average pay at Persimmon, the total share bonuses would have been £95 million. That would have meant that instead of the state being looted for £438 million there would have been an extra £343 million available for use by the state to tackle homelessness, for example. It seems self-evident that applying the 20:1 ratio in the Persimmon case – it still allows for the average share bonus for each of the 133 managers to reach £713,000 – seems a far more rational way of distributing the resources available to address the worst of Britain's social ills. Of course, the real world is not quite as simple as this, but the Persimmon example allows the raising of the issue.

In the introduction to this chapter the argument was put in outline for what might be termed the moral imperative of a more equal society and the consequent need to reduce the share that the rich are currently taking as their rewards. However, as referenced, there is a far more important imperative beyond all these considerations. The gross social inequality perpetuated by the current scale of chief executive rewards is a serious social issue, but the morality of it is not the most important consideration. Financialisation, combined with the continued hegemony of the maximisation of shareholder value (MSV) model in business, has resulted in the evolution of what is defined as 'rentier capitalism' in Britain. Rentier capitalism is a feature of the late development of capital, where extraction of wealth in the economy supersedes the actual creation of wealth. It is counterproductive to delivering investment in the creation of real wealth and so jeopardises the long-term future of the economy. That, in the long run, is a death knell for that system unless things are changed. Martin Wolf of the *Financial Times* has a working definition: 'In this case "rent" means rewards over and above those required to induce the desired supply of goods, services, land of labour. "Rentier capitalism" means an economy in which market and political power allows privileged individuals and businesses to extract a great deal of such rent from everybody else.'[17]

In the service of the maximisation of shareholder value (MSV) the pay of a chief executive is linked to the company share price. This relationship guarantees that there is a huge incentive for the chief executives to do everything to raise that share price, since that, in due course, determines their own pay. So, for example, the stage is reached where chief executives in the USA are investing

$1 trillion in share buybacks every year. That is solely because share buybacks increase the value of shares and the share price. Instead of that money being invested in genuine investment to drive the company forward, it is spent to increase the extraction of wealth for the already wealthy. In this process, it is more than possible for profits to be static but for share prices to rise.

Here's how the average buyback works. Let's say a fictional company, Divine Investments Ltd, has 100 shares. In 2018 it makes £100 in profit. If we divide the profit by the number of shares we see Divine Investment Ltd's earnings per share will be £1. Then in 2019, let's say the company makes another £100 pound in profits. However, it also buys back 20 shares, leaving only 80 shares on the market. This means that the company's earnings per share will be determined on the £100 profit, divided by 80 – the number of shares. So the earnings per share become £1.25, despite the company's profits remaining stationary. So through the share buyback the earnings per share have gone up by 25% despite static profits. In September 2018 Rio Tinto published plans for a £2.5 billion buyback, depending on the state of the stock markets in 2018–19. Right on cue, the chief executive of Rio Tinto, J. S. Jacques explained: 'Returning $3.2 billion of coal disposal proceeds demonstrates our commitment to capital discipline and providing sector-leading shareholder returns. We continue to focus our portfolio on those assets which provide the highest returns and growth, which will ensure that we continue to deliver superior value to our shareholders in the short, medium and long term.'

That is a classic example of the link between share price, dividend and chief executive rewards. It is a feature that makes buybacks, and indeed, the explosion of chief executive and corporate pay, classic examples of the extraction of wealth, classic examples of rent extraction, within the MSV model of rentier capitalism. In effect the chief executives of the great conglomerates are appropriating more and more of society's wealth for the benefit of their own families.

When personal financial motivations dominate corporate decision-making we are heading for a world of trouble, where the bonus culture predominates and undermines greater corporate

imperatives like the need for investment and consequent productivity growth. Some economists, like the *Financial Times*'
Martin Wolf, recognise the danger of what is going on: 'We need a
dynamic capitalist economy that gives everybody a justified belief
that they can share in the benefits. What we seem to have instead is
an unstable rentier capitalism, weakened competition, feeble productivity growth, and not coincidentally an increasingly degraded
democracy.'[18]

The MSV system was directly responsible for the Carillion
and Persimmon scandals. The Carillion accounts for 2016 show
that the chief executive, Richard Howson, was paid a salary of
£660,000, an annual bonus of £245,000, long-term share options
amounting to £346,000 and pension payments of £231,000. Thus,
the incentive parts of Howson's salary account for 55% of his
pay. We already know that these figures explain why the Carillion
directors ran the Ponzi scheme of borrowing more and more to
pay dividends and in turn to hoist their own pay. Even if it couldn't
last forever. What is needed is a change in the system from the
short-termism of the MSV model to a much more long-term investment model, based on the more balanced system of stakeholder
values and rights. To argue for change now is to argue for new
rules, supported by new laws, which would involve the democrati-
sation of business in Britain. A reform agenda is urgently needed.

The loading of share options onto chief executive accounts in
the form of Long-Term Incentive Plans (LTIPs) should go. LTIPs
and the cult of executive bonuses were banned in Ireland in the
aftermath of the Irish banking crash. That lasted for years, and
there are still government restrictions on chief executive pay now.
At the time the ban was introduced, an exodus of bankers was predicted. The word was that the giants of the banking industry would
not abide bonus bans and would seek more lucrative posts across
the globe. It never happened. In her book *Are Chief Executives
Overpaid?* Deborah Hargreaves writes about a Fortune 500 study
of the appointments of 489 global chief executives which showed
that only four were recruits from outside the country where the
appointment was on offer. The overwhelming number of new
appointments to senior positions in global companies are actually

from within company ranks. LTIPs have been banned in the past. Switzerland also bans the practice of paying out ridiculous 'golden hellos and goodbyes'. So should the UK. This would require building more substantial pay in ordinary salaries for chief executives and, provided that meets the 20:1 ratio of CEO pay to average pay, that should be acceptable.

It is also worth commenting on the role of today's Remuneration Committees (RemCos), especially the chairs of such committees. As we have seen, these are the internal committees in most big companies which provide a cover of so-called objectivity in the setting of company executive pay. Originally they were set up with the aim of controlling executive rewards and obviating the practice hitherto of executives setting their own pay. It did not work out that way. Take Alison Horner, the one-time chair of Carillion's RemCo, which implemented a payments by results strategy in reverse – growing salaries and bonuses were awarded to Carillion executives as the company and its performance faltered and its debt mountain grew. Horner blithely told the Carillion inquiry that all the awards were justified by industry averages. Her committee actually presided over changes to Carillion's policy on the clawback of executives' bonuses in the event of company failures which made it more difficult to achieve clawback. In December 2016, Horner proposed a scheme that would increase Carillion executive bonuses to 150% of salary, up from 100% only months before the £845 million hole in the accounts was discovered. Horner's CV is fairly typical of that of the chair of the RemCo of a mega-concern. Far from challenging excess, today's RemCos seem to exist to justify it. That should end. After the Carillion collapse, Horner took up a post as the CEO of Tesco Asia, with a £1.1 million 'golden hello' shares bonus.

If there is to be reform of corporate pay structures, it could also start with a number of union or worker representatives being legally guaranteed a place on company RemCos. Professor Prem Sikka argues additionally that corporate pay proposals should be put to a binding vote of the entire company workforce. Beyond the role of the RemCo there is an ongoing demand for workers to be on the board – both as a brake on the more egregious demands for chief executive rewards and also as a source of information, from the union or workers' point of view, for the entire workforce, The TUC argues that one third of the positions on company boards should be given over to union or worker representatives. These recommendations have been met with howls of anguish from the CBI. The German experience is that the law there legitimises two boards for big companies – a supervisory board oversees the decisions and operations of the company board. Both boards have worker or union representation on them. The CBI needs to consider if these structures significantly contribute to the strength of the German economy compared to its hidebound, conservative and failing British counterpart.

The Maximising Shareholder Value model, and the consequent levels of chief executive pay, have been considered in detail here because MSV and CEO pay are the base on which much else that is wrong about Britain's corporate superstructures has been built. That includes the crisis in the scandal-ridden audit industry, the UK's feeble, compromised regulators, and the failing system of outsourcing and privatisation. Richard Brooks, who wrote *Bean Counters: The Triumph of the Accountants and How They Broke Capitalism* about the audit industry, notes that for too long the auditors have been guilty of signing off balance sheets that were full of dross 'as if they were gold'.[19] And, as this went on and on, the regulators took on the $150 billion-a-year rewards of the Big Four – Deloitte, PwC, EY and KPMG – by fining them pennies in comparison to their huge earnings.

The House of Commons Carillion Inquiry, and its findings on audit and regulation, are a suitable reference point. The indictment of the auditors in the report is excoriating. It starts with KPMG, whose worldwide annual earnings at $29 billion make them the smallest of the Big Four. The House of Commons Carillion Report uses the standing international definition of what is supposed to happen in the real world of audit: 'It is the responsibility of the board of directors to prepare and approve the company's financial accounts. The role of the auditor is to obtain reasonable assurance about whether the financial statements as a whole are free from material mis-statement. If they are unable to obtain sufficient appropriate audit evidence to support that assessment they should issue a modified opinion on the accounts.'[20]

KPMG audited Carillion accounts over its entire existence. In those 19 years the auditors never once found cause to offer a qualified opinion on the accounts. When the head of audit at KPMG, Michelle Hinchliffe, was asked in the Carillion inquiry if the 19-year audit had compromised the auditor's impartiality and independence she replied: 'For myself and all my fellow partners, independence and integrity are absolutely critical to our profession . . . as opposed to the length of time.'[21] This is typical of the stone-walling tactics that the auditors utilised throughout the inquiry. In the evidence exchanges, Rachel Reeves MP, the chair of the Carillion Inquiry, notes that when Ernst and Young (EY) auditors were called in to create a recovery plan for Carillion, their first report to the Carillion audit committee concluded there was 'a lack of accountability and a culture of making the numbers up'. When Rachel Reeves asked Peter Meehan, who was the KPMG head of audit for Carillion, about this, he told Reeves, 'I cannot remember EY going to an audit committee.'[22]

In a 2017 review, the Financial Reporting Council (FRC), the so-called watchdog for the audit industry, reported that in KPMG's testing of the impairments of goodwill in the Carillion accounts there was sometimes 'insufficient challenge of management's assumptions'. That is regulator-speak for, 'perhaps the auditors turned a blind eye to the goings-on'. The Carillion 2016 accounts recorded total goodwill of £1.6 billion. That was more than double the net assets of £730 million. No alarm-bells were ever rung by KPMG, the external auditor, or Deloitte, the internal risk auditor, about that state of affairs. After the 2011 Eaga takeover, the goodwill added to the Carillion balance sheet was £330 million. It stayed that way for evermore in audit, despite the fact that Eaga (renamed Carillion Energy Services) went bust. The Carillion House of Commons hearings revealed that Carillion was compromised by accounting scandals; these included 'cover-up' auditing, conflicts of interest prejudicing its auditors and exorbitant fees charged by the Big Four – Deloitte, PwC, EY and KPMG – as a result of their auditing cartel.

KPMG were Carillion's external auditors, Deloitte the internal auditors, and EY were in charge of the Carillion rescue plan. PwC were Carillion's pension advisers, but come the collapse they were the least financially compromised of the Big Four. So PwC got the liquidation contract for special managers to assist the Liquidator. By the first anniversary of Carillion's crash, PwC had made more than £44 million from that contractual obligation.[23] Deloitte as Carillion's internal auditor charged £775,000 a year for risk management. The official definition of internal audit is to 'provide independent assurance that an organisation's risk management, governance and internal control processes are operating effectively.'[24] The House of Commons Carillion Report shows Deloitte did not make the grade there. Carillion tanked to oblivion whilst the Deloitte auditors collected their cash. Between 2015 and 2016, for example, Deloitte filed 61 internal reports – only one raised concern about inadequate risk controls, in one section of the business. Deloitte advised Carillion on debt recovery. It should be recalled that they did not know about the life and death struggle between Carillion and the Msheireb Qatari development company over a £200 million disputed debt.

All these audit failings for Carillion are symptomatic of the industry. Late in October 2019, the executives of EY and PwC appeared before the House of Commons BEIS Committee to defend their audit practices at Thomas Cook, the travel firm that collapsed late in September 2019. PwC were Thomas Cook's auditors between 2007 and 2016, and EY took over after them until the collapse late in September 2019. The BEIS hearing found that both auditors repeatedly signed off accounts with a clean bill of health, despite having misgivings about the financial stability and accounting practices at the travel firm. In the evidence heard at the BEIS committee, it emerged that over a period of eight years the executives at the company had stripped out 'exceptional items' from the accounts amounting to £1.8 billion. This flattered the company's financial results which were then utilised to justify executive bonuses. A spokesman for the former directors told the *Financial Times* that these accounting practices only affected 'at best 14%' of their bonuses which 'exploded the myth' that they had exploited accounting practices to deliver bigger bonuses for themselves.[25] The auditors signed off on the practice for years. The Thomas Cook auditing failings also included lack of concern about goodwill. £1.1 billion of goodwill stayed on the books without impairment for ten years, following the takeover of MyTravel. The facts that emerged at the BEIS hearing confirm that the accounting scandal which enveloped Carillion's audit seems to be replicated in almost every company collapse that has followed since, or occurred before. In order for the ubiquitous practice of chief executives looting their own companies and the state to succeed, the practice of covering that up in false audits has to be ubiquitous.

The Big Four now have a worldwide income approaching £150 billion. In 2018 they employed more than a million employees throughout the world. Deloitte is the biggest of the Big Four with annual global revenues of $43 billion. In 2018, the Big Four made $56 billion out of their audit function worldwide. However, by 2018, the earnings from the consultancy/advisor function, including tax avoidance advice, reached £85 billion.[26] How can an auditor fail a client's audit when it will jeopardise fees, in the millions, for the consultancy end of the business? Then there's what has already been referred to as the Big Four cartel. In 2016, the Big Four audited 99% of the FTSE 100 companies and 97% of the FTSE 250. They also audited 75% of the listed firms outside the FTSE 250 for the first time since 2006.[27] The House of Commons Carillion Report recommends that the Big Four should be divided up into more audit firms, and that there should be a complete split between audit and consultancy services. Professor Prem Sikka's analysis on audit goes much further than the House of Commons Carillion Report. He makes the point that in 2007–8 every major bank crash in the UK was preceded by an audit with a triple-A 'going concern' audit approval. He argues for much more far-reaching change – a national state agency for major company audits; the permanent division between audit and adviser, so by law no company can complete audits and also be an adviser for the same firm; and that there should be another national state agency to appoint auditors to major companies.[28]

Carillion went down in January 2018. You could expect that the Big Four would pay a price for their culpability, especially since the House of Commons Carillion report accused them of being complicit in Carillion's downfall. The opposite actually took place. The Deloitte UK returns to the end of May 2019 delivered the biggest pay-day for its partners in a decade. Revenue rose 10% to almost £4 billion, and profits to £617 million.[29] That made the average pay-out for the 700 equity partners in the firm £822,000 – up £50,000 on the bad old Carillion year. For the record, it should be mentioned, in the context of current debates, that the UK takings were divided into £582 million for audit and £1.81 billion for consulting and tax services. That makes for a UK total of £2.4 billion. This is an enormous sum by any measure. The reason is the Big Four cartel, which is an oligopoly with the power to set its own prices. There are around 34,000 GPs in the UK. There are 360,000 accountants. Something has gone wrong somewhere. A matter of weeks after the Deloitte declaration, on 16 September 2019, PwC UK also announced its best-ever results since 2009. Every one of its 900 equity partners was in line for a personal pay-out of £765,000. Anyone who thinks that the auditors, as a whole, will not fight tooth and nail to defend these revenues and these personal profits, in the face of calls for redistributive reform, is underestimating their power. Sacha Romanovitch's story stands as a warning.

Sacha Romanovitch – her father was a Russian emigré – joined Grant Thornton in 1990. In 2001 she was made a partner and became chief executive of Grant Thornton's UK business in 2015. She was bold. She developed a John Lewis-style profit-sharing scheme for all the Grant Thornton staff and introduced a 20–1 cap on her salary against the firm's average pay. In March 2018, she announced that Grant Thornton would no longer compete for FTSE 350 contracts. Her implied message was essentially, 'Why bother when the Big Four have rigged the market?' Then Grant Thornton announced that they supported a ban on audit firms accepting advisory work for major audit clients they were working with. Grant Thornton followed that by going public on its support for a public agency to control audit appointments to replace the current system where companies choose their own favourite auditor. Quite a list. At that time, in 2018, I pitched for an interview with Romanovitch in her office. Two weeks later there was a boardroom coup against her. Romanovitch had allegedly 'misdirected' the firm and had ignored falling profits. Anonymous leaks to the media announced that the board had had enough of her 'socialist agenda'. Then she was gone.

The House of Commons Carillion Report is equally damning about the UK's regulators. So is Prem Sikka. 'Where were the regulators when Carillion was going bust?' He asked me suddenly in the middle of one of our conversations. 'Where were they when the directors were maxing out on dividends and refusing to do anything about the staff pension deficit? Here we are nearly two years after the Carillion collapse and no report from the Financial Reporting Council on audit and accounting, no report from the Insolvency Service about what it's going to do about the directors. We've seen no report from The Pensions Regulator and we've seen no report from the Financial Conduct Authority. You might think that at least they'd cover their ineptitude by reporting on time.' He dismisses the decision to replace the FRC with a new authority after the Kingman Report on Carillion and after the Competition and Markets Authority (CMA) review. He calls for more regulation to force the Big Four to split their audit and consultancy divisions. He told me: 'This is only rearranging the deck-chairs on the *Titanic*, you actually have to look at the design of the *Titanic* itself – the whole regulatory architecture. Otherwise . . .' his voice tailed off into a shrug of the shoulders. In another conversation, Ian Fraser was more laconic: 'The so-called regulators are not watch-dogs, they're lap-dogs.'

Lesley Titcomb was director of The Pensions Regulator (TPR) during the five years between 2013 and 2018 when the dispute inside Carillion was raging about the yawning staff pension deficit.[30] By law, a company has to fund the pensions of its employees. The fund is administered by a pension trustee who negotiates with the company about payments made to the fund. Every three years there must be an independent review to assess if there is enough in the fund to meet pension liabilities. If there is not, 'the Trustee and sponsor company are required to agree a recovery plan and when the scheme will be returned to full funding, including deficit recovery payments to be made by the sponsor'.[31] That sets the scene for Carillion. In 2011 the trustee calculates that there is a £770 million deficit on the scheme and tries to negotiate a pay-back scheme over 14 years with Richard Adam. The trustee pitches for £65 million a year to square all that up. Carillion offers £33 million a year – take it or leave it.

In 2013, TPR intervenes and tries to get Carillion to do a deal. Now, under section 231 of the Pensions Act, TPR has the powers to impose a schedule of payment on the sponsor company so that they have to pay what the TPR determines. Over two years of negotiation, TPR threatened to use the mandatory powers of Section 231 seven times, but never once actually did so. TPR has never used its Section 231 powers in any dispute with sponsor companies in the last 13 years. Fact. In the end a compromise is reached for Carillion on a sliding scale of payments. That sets the recovery plan at 16 years.

When Carillion went bust the workers lost 10% of their pension entitlement and the Pension Protection Fund, and taxpayers were left with a £2.6 billion liability. Richard Adam's private pension pay-out was not affected. There should be a section added to the Pensions Act that if a company has a deficit on staff pensions it can't pay into directors' pensions until a recovery plan is agreed. That would have done for about half of the £800,000 sloshed into Adam's private pension. He might not have considered work pensions 'a waste of time' then.

Lesley Titcomb's performance at the Carillion Inquiry embodied the total ineffectiveness, not just of The Pension Regulator but all the so-called regulators. At the inquiry she can't explain why the Section 231 powers were never used during her tenure. She can't say how many companies have 16-year recovery plans like Carillion's. She can't say if there is a red-amber-green system to highlight the state of possible problem schemes. She can't tell Rachel Reeves MP how many problem schemes TPR is engaging with at this time. Frank Field, who is in the chair, says to her, 'If Rachel and I bumped into you at a bus stop, we would expect you to be better informed than you are now.' Chris Stephens, the Glasgow MP, remembers thinking, 'We are in chocolate fireguard territory here,' – a memorable metaphor for the entire regulatory system.

The Joint House of Commons BEIS and Work and Pensions Committees produced an erudite, penetrating analysis of Carillion's downfall in four months, with detailed recommendations about the lessons to be learned and for changes to the law. The average regulator report takes years. In the case of the HBOS collapse the FCA took eight years to complete its investigation. Why is that? Further, how is it possible for the FCA to investigate the monstrous persecution of 12,000 businesses by RBS's Global Restructuring Group and conclude there is no case to answer? How can it be explained that after the gigantic worldwide sub-prime fraud perpetrated by the world's bankers leading to the Crash only 47 of them got jail sentences – 25 of them from Iceland, 11 from Spain, 7 from Ireland, and one each from Cyprus, Germany, Italy and the US. No British banker went to jail. The FCA in the UK could find no grounds for any charges. That's why this book's call for a British Royal Commission on the finance industry is such an urgent demand. The Carillions of this world have had their day. They lasted too long. Carillion's downfall is really an historic avalanche. There is no way back. That includes no way back for outsourcing of public services and PPI.

The PFI and PPP revolutions promised a new way to deliver public services to the people but ended up building one hospital for the price of two. 'Public bad, private good' didn't quite work out in the hospitals that Carillion never built. That's the Midland Metropolitan in Birmingham and the Royal University Hospital in Liverpool. These were contracts started in 2013, which seven years later have no guaranteed finishing dates. Carillion was built on the asset-flogging, state-sector looting, privatisation model. In the end it never worked, and we were left to pay. According to the National Audit Office (NAO): 'There are currently over 700 operational PFI and PF2 deals, with a capital value of around £60 billion. Annual charges for these deals amounted to £10.3 billion in 2016–17. Even if no new deals are entered into, future charges, which continue until the 2040s, amount to £199 billion.'[32]

One of those projects is the Strathclyde Police Training Centre in East Kilbride. (It later became Police College Scotland when all the Scottish forces were amalgamated into one single force – Police Scotland). It was opened by Prince Charles in 2002. Nicholas Shaxson, in his penetrating book about the City, *The Finance Curse: How Global Finance Is Making Us All Poorer*, has done the names and the numbers. They are typical of the sort of PFI deals that were done. The structure of all PFI deals is complicated, but the first step is to set up a special purchase vehicle (SPV) as a holding company for the project. This lets the wolves of private equity into the game. They put the money up for the project, so up-front it does not cost the government's balance sheet a penny. The price is paid in HP-style payments long term.

In the Strathclyde Police Training Centre project a company called International Public Partnerships Ltd (INPP), with its £2 billion infrastructure fund listed on the London Stock Exchange, is one of the controlling players. In turn, its investments are managed by Amber Infrastructure Group Holdings Ltd. Half of Amber is owned by Hunt Companies, based in El Paso in Texas, and most of the other half by shareholders in Luxembourg and Jersey.[33] So when new recruits are sweating their way through riot control training at what is now known as Police College Scotland, some unknown face in El Paso, Luxembourg or Jersey is sweating the money. Raising tax out of that corporate miasma could prove to be tricky.

Balfour Beatty were appointed as the main contractors for the centre. It cost £17 million. The annual payments made by the Government to the Strathclyde Special Purchase Vehicle consortium average well over £4 million a year. There's a 25-year contract, which means that between 2001 and 2026 the Treasury estimate the total costs at £112 million. Shaxson estimates that if the government had raised a 25-year bond to pay off the £17 million, that would have cost £37 million in total. That's £75 million south of the estimated total cost that will eventually be paid. Come 2026, down El Paso way, in Luxembourg and Jersey, they'll be celebrating their share of the £75 million difference.

After the Crash, the new Tory government moved on. PFI and

similar privatisation models were replaced by outsourcing – the straightforward contracting of public projects and services to the private sector. Where once the state had been the provider in sectors like education, health, social care and justice services, enter Carillion, Serco, Capita, Interserve, Sodexo, Mitie, Ingeus, Atos, Amey and their outsourcing counterparts. The procurement of external suppliers is the single biggest element of UK government expenditure and it accounts for around one third of all expenditure. That is a massive £300 billion a year spent through the procurement process to contract almost exclusively with private-sector companies. In time, it would become evident that the new model was simply a variation on the ideological obsession of dismantling the state, based on the 'irrefutable' economic doctrine of 'Public bad, private good'.

In 2018, an Institute for Government (IfG) report found that since 2012 there has been huge growth in the market share of the biggest 25 of these private companies, which government calls its 'strategic suppliers'. At that time, these strategic suppliers accounted for at least 20% of the £300 billion spend already referenced. Before it collapsed, Carillion was not only one of the 25 strategic suppliers, but was sitting at number two in the league table of companies that had won the biggest share of government expenditure.[34] Since the time of the IfG research the number of strategic suppliers to government has risen to 34 – organisations that receive £100 million or more annually in revenue for completing government projects. According to a 2019 report by the think-tank Demos, 25 of the 34 have operations in offshore tax havens.[35] Demos found that between 2011 and 2017, 20 of these 25 tax dodgers had contracts for government projects worth more than £40 billion.[36] So while the government is filling the coffers of its private suppliers in billions, they are filing returns from offshore tax havens to make sure they evade tax on their taxpayer funded income. This is tax evasion on an industrial scale. This isn't private enterprise, it's private larceny. It would be relatively easy to stop – British companies contracting for state contracts should have to file their annual returns with HMRC in the UK.

Lesley Titcomb has been revealed as a personification of the weakness and ineptitude of the regulators. In this context, one former Tory minister is without peer as the epitome of the broken model of outsourcing – Chris Grayling MP. He has achieved this rank by his unshakeable vision of privatisation as the unquestionable political force for improving the cost, the efficiency and the delivery of public services, despite the real world contradicting that concept year after year. One of Grayling's last failings as Minister for Justice serves as a typical example of his blunderings. He believed that private enterprise could end the revolving door of recidivism which is the greatest failing of the probation service in England and Wales. Some two-thirds of those who experience prison in the UK finish up back inside within a year of their release. Grayling's big idea at the heart of his justice reforms was to put the National Probation Service in the hands of the private strategic suppliers of government services and pay them to reduce reoffending. Simple. Payment by results – the beating heart of the free market. With a winning bonus for each individual turned away from a life of crime, what could possibly go wrong? Everything, was the answer.

Probation services were outsourced, after contract bidding, to 21 regional community rehabilitation companies (CRCs), 20 of which were led by a private consortium. One contract out of the twenty-one was won by a public sector provider. Its successful bid was based on joining up local probation services with charities and community organisations, working on the rehabilitation of offenders on Teesside. Scarcely three years into Grayling's £2.5 billion 'Transforming Rehabilitation' programme, the government cancelled all the contracts with the private providers. Instead of lasting until 2022, they were terminated from 2020. That cost £170 million for starters. Only the public sector Teesside project was successful. Probation is to be renationalised with the establishment of similar services to those provided before.

Despite the facts, the Conservatives' ideological obsession with outsourcing continues unabated. In reality, all the political promises of neo-liberalism, that letting the markets rip, deregulating the banks and finance industry and slashing public sector spending would overcome the legacy of the Crash, boost the economy and balance the books, have proved to be monumentally false. According to an IMF Report, which termed the UK's austerity programme 'a fiscal illusion', the UK is £1 trillion pounds worse off after a decade of austerity. It found that Britain's public finances are second bottom of an international league table of 31 countries.[37] Commenting on the report, the *Financial Times* noted that the IMF statistics, which compare the assets available to government with its long-term liabilities, 'show the UK government having £5 trillion of liabilities and less than £3 trillion in assets – a negative net worth of more than £2 trillion'.[38] That's £2 trillion in the red. The IMF report found that since the Crash, Britain's net wealth has plunged by £1,000 billion. By comparison, in the same time period, Norway's net worth rose by 167% of its national income.[39]

The opening paragraphs of this chapter promised a critique of the current structures of the British economy and an analysis of what reforms are necessary to address current failures. However, doesn't the election of the Johnson government, with its stridently right-wing agenda on most issues, rule out the calls for reform made in this chapter? After all, it seems a majority of Johnson's devotees are said to be enthusiasts for Ayn Rand and her idiosyncratic small-state economic philosophy, the musings of which were first published in the 1950s. In fact it could be argued that Rand has become the new guru for the Tory right in the UK and their counterparts in the USA. At one time she advocated that 'Apart from the police, the courts and the armed forces, there should be no role for government: no social security, no public health or education, no public infrastructure or transport, no fire service, no regulations, no income tax'.[40] So surely there is little chance of this Tory government heeding warnings about the dangers of social inequality, the need to do something about chief executive pay, or the call for Britain's regulators to have real powers to act against corporate greed and corruption?

Even supposing that logic holds, it does not invalidate the necessity of reform of the system proposed in these pages, whether the politics of the current government reject that or not. For example, the Queen's Speech of December 2019 contained only a vague commitment to the appointment of a new audit regulator to head the new regulatory watchdog for the industry – the Audit Reporting and Governance Authority. This government prevarication has to be acknowledged for what it signals, but it does not invalidate the need for such an appointment to be made to lead urgently needed change.

It may be that events will determine that the reform of the present UK system of liberal-democratic capitalism cannot be postponed indefinitely. Certainly that is the conclusion that has already been reached by a section of the strategists of American capital concerning the future shape of the American system. Significant voices are being heard there recognising that current inequalities of wealth, power and opportunity have gone too far, and that capitalism has to reform for its own good. The corollary being that current modes of production are bad for business. In August 2019, the Business Round Table conference in Washington D.C. seemed to herald the coming of an historic turning point. The Business Round Table, which represents the chief executives of 181 of the world's largest companies, issued a declaration that the purpose of a company had to embrace much more than the maximisation of profits. The big-ticket declaration stated: 'While each of our individual companies serves its own corporate purpose, we share a fundamental commitment to all our stakeholders.' That was announced under the main headline 'Business Round Table redefines the purpose of a corporation to promote an economy that serves all Americans'. In October 2019, the World Economic Forum (WEF) – which runs the annual Davos event – followed suit. It took out full-page adverts in all the major business papers across the globe to promote the new WEF manifesto calling for business to embrace 'a stakeholder perspective'. Included was a five-point plan about how to achieve that.

This, after four decades of evangelising about the sanctity of the maximisation of shareholder value as the very foundation of the capitalist system. Suddenly, after all these years of eulogising Milton Friedman's theories about profits and dividends as the driving force, the Round Table, and its WEF partner, were declaring that the building of a more egalitarian capitalism, based on embracing stakeholders – customers, employees, suppliers, communities and shareholders – had become paramount. The Round Table signatories included Apple, Amazon, J.P. Morgan and Walmart to name a few. Here was an acknowledgement that something has gone wrong and that the reform of today's capitalism is a necessity. The Business Round Table declaration was only a punctuation mark in a debate about the future of American capitalism. But the debate has suddenly grown apace since the election of Donald Trump demonstrated the dangerous alienation of the white working class in America and its corrosive hatred of America's billion-dollar elites.[41] Forty per cent of wage earners in America earn less than $15 dollars an hour, and have less than $400 in savings.[42] The top 10% of wealth holders in the USA own 90% of all financial assets – the percentages would be even more extreme if the distribution of income was the sole variant. According to the American economist Joseph Stiglitz, just three Americans have as much wealth as the bottom 50% of the US population.[43] The *Economist*'s special report on poverty in America[44] indicated that in one county of South Dakota, life expectancy is lower than in Sudan, whilst in 2019 the investment bank J.P. Morgan made the largest recorded bank profits in history – $36 billion.

Throughout 2019 the calls for radical reform of the current American economy have resounded as never before in the lengthy 'state of the nation' dissertations American chief executives habitually deliver along with their annual reports. Ray Dalio is the founder of the world's biggest hedge fund, Bridgewater Associates. He's worth $17 billion according to Bloomberg. He is on record as saying, 'I'm a capitalist and even I think capitalism is broken.' Dalio says capitalism is now reinforcing inequality to the degree that it was at a juncture where it would have to 'evolve or die', which could be done peacefully or 'in conflict'.[45] Otherwise, Dalio says, 'Some sort of revolution is possible.' The Disney heiress, Abigail Disney, whose grandfather Roy, along with his brother Walt, was the co-founder of the Disney empire, has joined the fray on US executive pay. For most of 2018 and 2019 she's made the earnings of the current Disney CEO, Bob Iger, a target for her scorn. She has described Iger's $65.7 million salary for 2018 as 'insane', when Disney's lowest-paid workers have to claim food stamps to make ends meet. She argues that if the executive bonus pool at the company were cut in half they would never notice it, and Disney's 125,000 lowest paid would get a $2,000 dollar bonus that just might be 'a ticket out of poverty'. In 2018 Iger's total pay was 1,424 times the median salary of a Disney worker. When her outspoken views were getting traction in the US media, Abigail Disney said: 'Jesus Christ himself isn't worth 500 times his median worker's pay.'[46]

Disney is a member of the lobby group called Patriotic Millionaires. For the best part of a decade it has been lobbying for higher taxes on the rich. Patriotic Millionaires have 200-plus members. To join you must have annual earnings of more than a million dollars or an asset base worth more than five million dollars. It employs 17 workers in its full-time office, not far from the White House in Washington. The chair is Morris Pearl, a former Blackrock equity chief. He says it has got to the stage now where the level of the public anger in the US about inequality means America's capitalists need to start thinking about preserving themselves, not just their system. He told the *Financial Times*: 'Given the choice between pitchforks and taxes, I'm choosing taxes.' In this context, the widespread debate among American leaders about change being led by the introduction of a progressive wealth tax on America's mega-millionaires is symptomatic of a realisation that things cannot stay as they are. Something has to be done about what is going on, before it is too late, seem to be the watchwords.

Much has been made by the American commentariat of the findings that 51% of Americans between 18 and 29 favour 'socialism' over 45% who support 'capitalism'. Of course, that support for socialism should be understood as a support for a greater welfare state, government-funded university education and more equality of employment opportunities and the like, rather than a conviction in favour of a Bolshevik revolution. In a recent article in the *Foreign Affairs* journal, Joseph Stiglitz summed it up thus: 'By eating up the state, capitalism eats itself . . . Allowing states to collect their fair share of revenue in the form of taxes will not usher in some dystopian era of oppressive government. Instead, strengthening the state will return capitalism to a better path, toward a future in which markets function in the interests of the societies that produce them, and in which the benefits of economic activity will not be restricted to a vanishingly small elite.' [47]

These American perspectives are symptomatic of a recognition of the crisis haunting Western capitalism, on the one hand, and of a fear of what the future holds on the other. Whether that takes the form of 'pitchforks' or not. The German academic, Wolfgang Streeck, supports the 'crisis' viewpoint in reference to the long-term trends within Western capitalism. He argues that the persistent decline in economic growth rates, an equally persistent rise in indebtedness in most major capitalist economies and the pervasive and exponential growth of inequality both in income and wealth evident in today's capitalism in the West, justify the conclusion that 'capitalism is in crisis'.[48] *Financial Times* commentators agree. However, Streeck adamantly disavows the theories of those who argue that the advent of crisis indicates that the end is nigh for capitalism, which is about to give way to a new historical epoch based on the development of socialism.

In his book *How Will Capitalism End?* Streeck, representative of many others, recognises that capitalism is now in what looks like a final crisis. But he says pointedly that a social order breaks down when its elites are no longer able to maintain it, but can only be removed when new elites are present who are prepared and able to install a new order. According to Streeck, that 'new elite' vanguard is missing in today's struggles within capitalism. This, according to Streeck, suggests that the crisis of capitalism is likely to give way to a crisis of disorder and disintegration, where the only certainty is uncertainty rather than the guaranteed emergence of a new socialist order. Then there is the body of thought that considers that any predictions about the future of capitalism have to factor in the emergence of Chinese state capitalism. In *Crashed: How a Decade of Financial Crises Changed the World*, Adam Tooze concludes that post-2008, the massive spending programme of the Chinese government might have rescued the entire world system. Its $600 billion investment, predominantly in infrastructure and health care, amounted to 12% of Chinese GDP in 2008. In one province, Hubei, over three years, the stimulus was larger than anything put together, at any time, by any American administration.[49] In a similar vein, in the January 2020 edition of *Foreign Affairs*,[50] the economist Branko Milanovic draws conclusions about the potential longevity of capitalism based on a recognition of the new capitalist power in China. Milanovic submits that the evolution of the Chinese economy, as a variant of classical capitalism based on the evolution of a capitalist class which is however still ultimately subservient to the political bureaucracy of Chinese communism, is historically significant. In fact he reasons that this means for the first time in history the capitalist mode of production 'rules the world'. That hegemony, he reasons, could see the crisis of Western capital descend into a state capitalism on the Chinese model, based on the power of the current plutocratic oligarchy. Therefore capitalism, in one variant or another, survives to span the globe. At least in the meantime, you might say.

These conceptions have to be considered in any deliberations about the possible coming of a new world order. To an extent, they informed the narrative of this book and the reform agenda contained in this final chapter. This takes these concluding paragraphs full circle, back to the Russian oligarchs. Their evolution, as considered in the Prologue, was dependent on their looting of the Russian state. That created a Mafia capitalism – a capitalism in a criminal gangster form – because the emerging oligarchs knew their emergence as a new, if deformed, capitalist class was the result of a criminal looting of the Russian state. This looting was carried out through a gigantic fraudulent sell-off of state assets rather than the creation of new assets produced by classical capitalist development. The evolution of the American and British oligarchs is no less a criminal economic injustice, precisely because their emergence is now actually contrary to the long-term interests of the sustainability of the capitalist system. And it is also based on looting the state. The maximisation of shareholder value in the West has produced a Mafia oligarchy here, as real as any Russian oligarchy in the East, even if the scale of the theft is different. That is why these pages are an indictment of the corruption of the high echelons of British capital as well as a call for that to be changed utterly. It is also actually why, to coin a phrase, 'We are all in this together'.

So, from where is the army to be assembled to force that change? Could it be that the leadership of British capitalism will come to realise what needs to be done and fight for reform of their shareholder capitalism? Or will their failure to do so push the ranks of the youth, enraged by the climate emergency to eventually become evangelists for a better, more equal society? Can the present vanquished ranks of the Labour Party be transformed into their opposite, to play a significant part in the battle for a different way forward? Or will the economic programme of Boris Johnson's 'English Nationalist' Conservatives for the building of Britain as a Singapore-on-Thames force a rebirth of the enfeebled trade union movement? That, as a result of the desperate last stand to defend workers' rights they seem likely to face in the future? The GMB's Gary Smith believes the trade union movement is going to be confronted with a life-or-death ultimatum: 'We've got a choice now – we can go to the powers that be, on our knees with a bigger and bigger begging bowl. Or we can build our union relentlessly to make sure we have the power to demand our rights and make things change. The time for Oliver Twist unions is over. It isn't actually a choice.' Brave words.

History awaits. One way or another.

Epilogue

'Once you run out it is a question of being down to Marigolds and bin liners.'

Nadra Ahmed, the National Care Association,
The Guardian, 6 April 2020

Then the coronavirus pandemic arrived and the world was turned upside down. Things could never be the same, they said. A new Britain would emerge from the canyons of horror in our hospitals and care homes after the virus was vanquished. But Nadra Ahmed spoke long before any 'hope springs eternal' new dawn. She is the chair of the National Care Association, which represents small care-home providers in the UK. Early in April 2020 she told *The Guardian*: 'The issue we hear most is "I am desperate for masks. Has anyone got any gloves?". . . Once you run out it is a question of being down to Marigolds and bin liners.'

The failures of British capitalism outlined in this book will still exist when the pandemic eventually ends. The virus will not change the chronic economic crisis of capitalism here, its excoriating inequalities spearheaded by the disgraceful excesses of top pay and the corrosive corruption of its accountancy corporations and their associates among the regulators. No. Long after the last Covid-19 funeral has been held, the last contaminated face mask incinerated, and hospitals and care homes try to resume normal service, these failures will still be blighting Britain. What the coronavirus crisis has done is bring them into sharper focus.

Recall what has already been written here about the decades of the imperative of the maximisation of shareholder value and the wanton greed that transpired with it; about the financialisation of the British economy and the consequent destruction of the country's manufacturing base; and about the results of the 'grim reaper' of austerity hollowing out the nation's public services practically to the point of no return. In concert, they have resulted in a Britain which, when confronted by the worst plague in modern history, could not deliver Personal Protection Equipment (PPE) to the legions of NHS and care workers fighting the virus face-to-face; and which, months after it was known that Covid-19 was coming, could only test around 2,000 of Britain's half a million health workers for the virus. In the same timescale, Germany could seemingly test 500,000 people a month. By mid-June 2020 the UK had the highest excess deaths from Covid-19 of any country in the world – up 49% on January to June 2019 to 65,700. Another word-beating achievement for the Johnson government. In contrast, Germany's total excess deaths was up 6% to 9,200. By mid-June New Zealand was declared virus-free after suffering 22 coronavirus deaths. Something has gone desperately wrong. Part of the answer is the remorseless dismantling of the welfare state over the last ten years in homage to the zealotry of neo-liberalism already considered earlier in this book.

However, the coronavirus has also produced new indictments. For example, it has exposed the private provision of residential care in the UK for what it has become – just another way of making money by looting the state. This looting has followed the economic parameters of what might be described as the 'privatisation pandemic'. Previously unheard-of returns were suddenly paid out to new owners and their executives as, year on year, financial chicanery on a scale never seen before in the care sector became all encompassing, with the scam of the sale of assets and their leaseback probably marking the highest point of this particular Ponzi scheme. And these false profits were delivered universally on the backs of residential carers paid the minimum wage or even less, which is the case for 40% of them currently. When Covid-19 called, it laid bare the appalling reality that this neoliberal market in care has failed us. The promise of financial efficiencies and the better services private care would bring actually ended up with the sector being unable to provide its own workers with PPE when the virus spread to our shores. Meanwhile, offshore, the investors and their executives had millions salted away long before Marigolds and bin liners told us the truth.

Of course, it may be that the coronavirus has forced Chancellor Rishi Sunak to resurrect the power of the state to spectacular levels, crushing once and for all the 'small state' orthodoxies that have mesmerised him and every one of his Cabinet colleagues for decades. It may be that a million people clapping every Thursday in thanks, and in recognition that the key workers in the economy deserve a new deal, is a harbinger of a fairer Britain to come. It may be that the new leader of the Labour Party, Keir Starmer, saying that in post-coronavirus Britain 'the last shall be first' actually means the Labour movement will do something about that. However, the portents of a New Jerusalem emerging from the coronavirus catastrophe are not good. When the markets plunged as a consequence of the first Stock Market panic associated with the emergence of the virus, the short-sellers moved in. According to *The Financial Times*, the biggest killing was made by Ruff Investments – £2.4bn was their return on a series of 'short' trades in a week or so. Tesco took £585 million tax relief on the Government's bail-out scheme and promptly paid out £635 million in dividends – to maximise shareholder value, of course. Throughout the crisis, the Westminster Government maintained its ideological commitment to the private sector, bypassing local government health departments. Instead, without any tendering, 177 major contracts, worth £1.1 billion, went to private firms. That included a £133 million contract for testing services to Randox Laboratories, where Tory MP Owen Paterson is a paid consultant. These examples speak volumes for fears that, despite other claims to the contrary, in post-virus Britain things will return to 'business as usual'– the same chief executives' gorging greed, the same shameful inequalities and the same 'looking the other way' corruption of the accountants. This time founded on an economy ravaged by coronavirus. Perhaps that may not be the case, but what will decide the future will be the answer to the towering question about Britain's £300 billion deficit: 'Who pays?'

Before the arrival of coronavirus, this book ended with the declaration that 'History awaits'. It still does. One way or another.

Bob Wylie
Glasgow, July 2020

Notes

Prologue

1   Chrystia Freeland, *The Sale of the Century*, Crown Publishers (2000). All 'loans for shares' figures are from this source.
2   *Guardian* website, Thursday 19 July 2018
3   *This is Money* website, 30 June 2018.
4   *Construction News*, 22 January 2018.
5   *Financial Times*, 16 January 2018.

Chapter 1

1   Carillion Annual Report and Accounts 2016, 1 March 2017, p. 66.
2   House of Commons Business Energy and Industrial Strategy and Work and Pensions Select Committees Oral Evidence, 6 February 2017, Q468.
3   House of Commons Library Briefing, 'The collapse of Carillion', 14 March 2018.
4   House of Commons Library Briefing, *op. cit.*, 14 March 2016.
5   House of Commons Business Energy and Industrial Strategy and Work and Pensions Select Committees 'Carillion' Second Joint Report, 16 May 2018, p. 22.
6   Wikipedia: 'Associated British Ports'.
7   *The Times*, 20 January 2018.
8   Jonathan Ford, 'Carillion's troubles were shrouded in a fog of goodwill', *Financial Times*, 18 June 2018.
9   *The Economist*, 1 September 2018, p. 56.
10 *Financial Times*, *op. cit.*, 18 June 2018.
11 *Financial Times*, *op. cit.*, 18 June 2018.
12 *Financial Times*, *op. cit.*, 18 June 2018.

13 *Financial Times*, *op. cit.*, 18 June 2018.
14 *Financial Times*, 'The Big Read. Accounting', 19 June 2018.
15 Ali Bongo was a British comedy musician and president of the Magic Circle; he died in 2009.
16 *Financial Times*, *op. cit.*, 19 June 2018.
17 *Financial Times,* The big flaw – auditing in crisis, 1 August 2018.
18 *Financial Times, op. cit.*, 1 August 2018.
19 House of Commons Business Energy and Industrial Strategy and Work and Pensions Select Committees Second Joint Report, 'Carillion' p. 5.
20 Carillion plc, Annual Report and Accounts 2016, 1 March 2017.
21 House of Commons Business Energy and Industrial Strategy Committees, 'Carillion' 16 March 2018, Oral Evidence Q552.
22 Carillion Annual Report and Accounts 2016, page 7.
23 Carillion Annual Report and Accounts 2016, p. 85.
24 House of Commons Joint Select Committee Report 'Carillion', *op. cit.*, p. 46.
25 Richard Adam and Zafar Khan are currently subject to an investigation by the Financial Reporting Council which also includes the board signing off on financial audits carried out by KPMG. The Insolvency Service is also leading a 'fast track' investigation in conjunction with the Financial Conduct Authority and the Pensions Regulator into the conduct of 'all those who were previously directors of the company'.
26 Countrywide plc Annual Report 2017, p. 38.

Chapter 2

1 Carillion Annual Report and Accounts, 1 March 2016, p. 3.
2 Carillion Annual Report and Accounts, 1 March 2016, p. 5.
3 Carillion Annual Report and Accounts, 1 March 2016, p. 45.
4 House of Commons Library Briefing Paper 'The collapse of Carillion', 14 March 2018.
5 Carillion Annual Report and Accounts, 1 March 2016, p. 15.
6 Carillion Annual Report and Accounts, 1 March 2016, p. 62.
7 Carillion Annual Report and Accounts, 1 March 2016, p. 7.
8 *Daily Mail*, City Diary, 16 January 2018.

9   Oral Evidence to the House of Commons Joint Select Committee Carillion Inquiry, 7 February 2018, Q416.

10   Carillion Board Minutes, 26 January 2017, p. 6.

11   Carillion Annual Report and Accounts, 1 March 2016, p. 6.

12   National Audit Office Report 'Investigation into the government's handling of the Carillion collapse', 7 June 2008, pp. 14-16.

13   Emma Mercer, Letter to the chairs of the House of Commons Carillion Inquiry, Rachel Reeves MP and Frank Field MP, 5 March 2018.

14   Richard Howson, Letter to the chairs of the House of Commons Carillion Inquiry, Rachel Reeves MP and Frank Field MP, 10 April 2018.

15   Carillion Board Minutes, 9 May 2018 – see the correspondence section of the House of Commons Joint Inquiry 'Carillion', 16 May 2018.

16   Carillion Board Minutes, 9 May 2018, p. 4.

17   Carillion Annual Report and Accounts 2016.

18   *Financial Times*, 10 October 2018.

19   Carillion Board Minutes, 9 May 2017, p. 4.

20   Carillion Board Minutes, 9 May 2017, p. 4.

21   House of Commons Business Energy and Industrial Strategy and Work and Pensions Committees, 'Carillion – second joint report', 16 May 2018, Oral Evidence Q551-552.

22   Carillion Board Minutes, 9 May 2017, p. 5.

23   House of Commons Business Energy and Industrial Strategy and Work and Pensions Committees, 'Carillion – second joint report', 16 May 2018, p. 45.

24   *Ibid*, p. 45.

25   Carillion Board Minutes, 23 May 2018, p. 3.

26   Andrew Dougal, Letter to the chairs of the House of Commons Carillion Inquiry, Rachel Reeves MP and Frank Field MP.

Chapter 3

1   Weir Group plc 2016 Annual Report and Accounts, p. 103.

2   Kevin Scott, *The Herald*, 20 March 2018.

3   High Pay Centre, *www.highpaycentre.org,* 'Fat Cat Tuesday 2016', 4 January 2016.

4   Carillion Board Minutes, 7 June 2018 – see correspondence section of the House of Commons Joint Inquiry, 'Carillion', 16 May 2018.

5   House of Commons Joint Inquiry, 'Carillion', 16 May 2018, p. 21.

6   *Ibid*. p. 18.

7   *The Guardian*, 3 June 2011.

8   *The Economist*, 22 December 2018, 'The elite that failed', p. 48.

9   Simon Smith, Morgan Stanley letter to the chairs of the Joint Parliamentary Committee, 21 February 2018.

10   Carillion Board Minutes, 5 July 2018, p. 4 – House of Commons Joint Inquiry, 'Carillion', 16 May 2018.

11   *Ibid*. p. 5.

12   Keith Cochrane letter to Rachel Reeves MP and Frank Field MP, 20 February 2018, from correspondence to House of Commons Joint Inquiry, 'Carillion', 16 May 2018.

13   House of Commons Joint Inquiry, 'Carillion', 16 May 2018, Oral Evidence Q240.

14   Carillion Board Minutes, 5 July 2018, p. 5 – House of Commons Joint Inquiry, 'Carillion', 16 May 2018.

15   Alistair Osborne, 'The more you have got the more you should give away', *Daily Telegraph*, 28 May 2005.

16   *Sunday Times South Africa*, 21 January 2018.

17   United Utilities plc, Annual Report 2007, 'CEO statement'.

18   United Utilities plc, Annual Report 2008, 'CEO statement'.

19   United Utilities plc Annual Reports 2007, 2008, 2009, 2010, 2011.

20   Patrick Hoskins, *The Times*, 27 May 2014.

Chapter 4

1   House of Commons Joint Committee Report, 'Carillion', 16 May 2018, p. 29.

2   *Ibid*., p. 34.

3   *Ibid*., p. 35.

4   Alison Horner, letter to Blackrock Investment Services, 12 December 2016 – House of Commons Joint Report, 'Carillion', 16 May 2018.

5   *The Times*, 20 January 2018.
6   Carillion RemCo Minutes, 9 July 2017 – see House of Commons Joint Report, 'Carillion'.
7   Carillion RemCo Minutes 9 July 2017 – *ibid.*
8   Carillion RemCo Minutes, 7 September 2017 – see House of Commons Joint Report, 'Carillion'.

Chapter 5

1   Investopedia.com provides a general description of the parameters of shorting: 'Imagine a trader who believes that a stock, which is trading at \$50, will decline in price. [Under current Stock Exchange protocols] she borrows 100 shares and sells them. The trader is now "short" 100 shares, since she sold something that she did not own in the first place. The short sale was only made possible by borrowing the shares . . . A week later, the company whose shares were shorted reports dismal financial results for the quarter, and the stock falls to \$45. The trader decides to close the short position and buys 100 shares for \$45 on the open market to replace the borrowed shares. The trader's profit on the short sale, excluding commissions and interest on the margin account, is \$500: (\$50-\$45) X 100 Shares = \$500.' *Investopedia.com* / 'Short selling'.
2   Investegate – Carillion 2017 first-half trading update, 10 July 2017, Investegate.co.uk/index.
3   See National Audit Office, 'Investigation into the government's handling of the collapse of Carillion', 7 June 2018, p. 25.
4   House of Commons Joint Inquiry, BEIS and World and Pensions Committees, HC 769, Oral Evidence Q1127.
5   *Ibid.* Murdo Murchison, Q1125.
6   *Building*, 'Carillion by numbers', 12 July 2018.
7   Public Accounts Committee House of Commons, 'Service Family Accommodation', 8 June 2016, Q10-11.
8   *Ibid.*, 13 July 2016, p 10.
9   *Ibid.*, 13 July 2016.
10 House of Commons Joint Committee Report, 'Carillion', 16 May 2018, p. 4.
11 Bill Michael of KPMG, letter to Rachel Reeves and Frank

Field, 2 February 2018, from House of Commons 'Carillion' / Work and Pensions Committee website / Correspondence.

12   House of Commons Joint Parliamentary Inquiry, 'Carillion', Oral Evidence 22 February 2018, Q933.

13   *Ibid.*, Q982.

14   *PR Weekly*, 3 October 2016.

15   'Jacob Zuma, the Guptas and the selling of South Africa', David Pilling and Joseph Cotterill, *Financial Times*, 30 December 2017.

16   *Guardian*, 5 October 2017.

17   In conversation with the author on 13 September 2018.

18   House of Commons Library Briefing Paper, 'The collapse of Carillion', 14 March 2018.

19   Frances Coppola, 'Coppola Comment', 29 January 2018.

20   National Audit Office, 'Investigation into the government's handling of the collapse of Carillion', 7 June 2018, p. 21, 22.

21   Keith Skeoch and Martin Gilbert of Standard Life Aberdeen, letter from House of Commons 'Carillion'/Work and Pensions Committee website/Correspondence.

Chapter 6

1   National Audit Office, 'Investigation into the government's handling of the collapse of Carillion', 7 June 2018.

2   *Guardian*, 2 October 2014, 'Government accused of big business love-in over Manzoni Whitehall job'.

3   Cabinet Office letter to Meg Hillier MP, Public Accounts Committee, from Rhys Williams Cabinet Office, 14 February 2017.

4   Figures drawn from National Audit Office, 'Investigation into the government's handling of the collapse of Carillion', 7 June 2018, pp. 14, 15, 27, 30.

5   House of Commons BEIS and Work and Pensions Committee, 'Carillion', HC769, 16 May 2018, p. 62.

6   National Audit Office, 'Investigation into the government's handling of the collapse of Carillion', 7 June 2018, p. 26.

7   BEIS and Work and Pensions Joint Committee Media Release, 'Chairs write to the Secretary of State for Transport', 21 May 2018, including Grayling 12 March 2018 letter.

8   House of Commons Public Administration and Constitutional Affairs Committee, 13 March 2018, Q306/307.

9   House of Commons Liaison Committee, Oral Evidence, Response to the collapse of Carillion, 7 February 2018, p. 38.

10 Fees report from EY submitted to House of Commons Joint Inquiry BEIS and Work and Pensions Joint Committees, 'Carillion', 16 May 2018.

11 *Ibid.*, Correspondence of Chris Grayling to the Chairs.

12 *Ibid.*

13 *www.building.com*, 22 February 2018, 'Carillion exploited awards to calm supplier nerves, documents show'.

Chapter 7

1   Investegate: Carillion PLC 'Half year report', 29 September 2017.

2   Murdo Murchison, letter to Rachel Reeves MP and Frank Field MP, House of Commons 'Carillion Inquiry', Correspondence 2 February 2018.

3   These estimates are taken from RemCo minutes published by the Reeves-Field House of Commons Inquiry, 'Carillion', 16 May 2018.

4   Carillion Annual Report and Accounts 2016, p. 70.

5   House of Commons Joint Committee Inquiry, 'Carillion', oral evidence, Qs 381, 388.

6   Carillion Annual Report and Accounts 2012, 2013, 2014, 2015, 2016.

7   Philip Green, former chair of Carillion, letter to Rachel Reeves MP and Frank Field MP, House of Commons Joint Committee Inquiry, 'Carillion', 11 June 2018.

8   National Audit Office, 'Investigation into the government's handling of the collapse of Carillion', 7 June 2018, pp. 36, 37.

9   *Ibid.*, p. 38.

10 Philip Green, 13 January 2018 letter to John Manzoni, Permanent Secretary for the Cabinet Office, from House of Commons BEIS and Work and Pensions Committee, 'Carillion', 16 May 2018, Correspondence.

11 Philip Green, *ibid.*

12 National Audit Office, 'Investigation into the government's handling of the collapse of Carillion', 7 June 2018, p. 44.

13 At the time both banks said that they could not continue to

take hits indefinitely due to Carillion's cash crisis. RBS lost a minimum of £150 million and Santander £200 million when Carillion crashed.

14 House of Commons BEIS and Work and Pensions Committee, 'Carillion', 16 May 2018, p. 65.

15 The Insolvency Service, 10 May 2019.

16 *The Times*, 7 February 2019.

Chapter 8

1 Dave Smith and Phil Chamberlain, *Blacklisted: The Secret War between Big Business and Union Activists*, New Internationalist Publications, 2016; High Court papers, Appendix 5, p. 398.

2 GMB Report, 'Blacklisting – illegal corporate bullying: endemic, systemic and deep-rooted in Carillion and other companies', September 2014 (the actual figure is £32,393 + VAT).

3 Much of the detail of the blacklisting struggle here is drawn from the bible of blacklisting cited in the previous footnote, Smith and Chamberlain's *Blacklisted*.

4 *The Guardian*, 'Construction firm accepts engineer was blacklisted over union membership', 17 January 2012.

5 Carillion, Half-year financial report for six months ended 30 June 2016, p. 27.

6 Smith and Chamberlain, *op. cit.*, p. 43.

7 Smith and Chamberlain, *op. cit.*, p. 31.

8 These figures are drawn from Carillion's Annual Report and Accounts 2007; it is accepted that the figures, especially as they include totals from the Middle East, may not be totally accurate; however they serve as an indication of significant trends.

9 www.building.co.uk, 18 January 2018.

10 HM Treasury PFI and PF2 Summary data, 2016.

11 Statistics here are drawn from NAO 'Investigating the government's handling of the Carillion collapse', 7 June 2018; House of Commons Library Briefing Paper, 'The collapse of Carillion',14 March 2018, pp. 32-35.

12 www.building.co.uk, 'Carillion did not buy a pup. It was a monster', Angela Monaghan, 20 April 2007.

13 Carillion plc Annual Report and Accounts 2011, p. 26.

14 *Financial Times*, Jonathan Ford, 'The Fog of Goodwill', 18 June 2018.
15 CES Annual Accounts 2011–2016.
16 House of Commons PACAC Inquiry Report, 'After Carillion – Public Sector outsourcing and contracting', 9 July 2018, p. 25.

Chapter 9

1 Robin Varghese, 'What did you expect from capitalism?' *Foreign Affairs*, July-August 2018.
2 Robin Varghese, *ibid.*
3 Mariana Mazzucato, *The Value of Everything*, Allen Lane, 2018, p. 179.
4 Grace Blakeley, 'On Borrowed Time', IPPR Commission on Social Justice Discussion Paper, June 2018.
5 Nicholas Shaxson, *The Financial Curse: How Global Finance Is Making Us All Poorer*, The Bodley Head, London 2018, p. 135. This book has been a significant source for my analysis of financialisation.
6 US dollars are the currency of equivalence here.
7 Fintan O'Toole, *Ship of Fools: How Stupidity and Corruption Sank the Celtic Tiger*, Faber and Faber, 2010, p.127. This book has also been a significant source on these issues.
8 *Irish Times*, Professor Jim Stewart, 'How the IFSC "HQ" became a shadow of its intended self', 6 September 2010.
9 *Financial Times*, 16 September 2019.
10 Shaxson, *The Financial Curse op. cit.*, p. 134.
11 Fintan O'Toole, *Ship of Fools op. cit.*, p. 46.
12 Fintan O'Toole, *Ship of Fools op. cit.*, p. 102.
13 Shaxson, *The Financial Curse op. cit.*, p. 135; other estimates put the costs of the Irish bail-out as high as 319% of Ireland's GDP.
14 Fintan O'Toole, *Ship of Fools op. cit.*, p. 207.
15 Ian Blackford in conversation with the author on 22 October 2018.
16 Adam Tooze, 'The Forgotten History of the Financial Crisis', *Foreign Affairs*, September/October 2018.
17 *London Review of Books*, Simon Wren-Lewis, 'Bait and Switch', 25 October 2018.

18 Gillian Tett, *Fool's Gold: How Unrestrained Greed Corrupted a Dream, Shattered Global Markets and Unleashed a Catastrophe*, Abacus, 2010.

19 Bethany McLean and Joe Nocera, *All the Devils Are Here: The History of the Financial Crisis*, Portfolio, 2010, p. 8.

20 Gillian Tett, *Fool's Gold, op. cit.*

21 *Ibid.*

22 Gillian Tett, *Fool's Gold, op. cit.*

23 John Lanchester, *Whoops: Why Everyone Owes Everyone and No-one Can Pay*, Penguin, 2010.

24 Gillian Tett, *Fool's Gold, op. cit.*

25 Adam Tooze, 'The Forgotten History of the Financial Crisis', *Foreign Affairs*, September/October 2018.

26 The detail here is drawn from the excellent 'The story of a house', *Financial Times*, 5 September 2018.

27 *Financial Times, ibid.*

28 John Lanchester, *Whoops, op. cit.*, p. 62.

Chapter 10

1 Parliamentary Commission on Banking Standards, 'An accident waiting to happen – the failure of HBOS', House of Lords/ House of Commons, 4 April 2013, p. 34.

2 *Ibid.* p. 40.

3 This account draws on Ian Fraser's *Shredded: Inside RBS, the Bank that Broke Britain*, Birlinn, second edition 2019.

4 Ian Fraser in conversation with the author, 21 November 2018.

5 Ian Fraser, *op. cit.*, p. 296.

6 National Audit Office, 'Taxpayer support for UK Banks, FAQs', August 2018.

7 *Hansard* Volume 656, 'Clydesdale Bank and SMEs', 19 March 2019.

8 Treasury Committee Oral Evidence, 'SME Lending', 17 June 2014.

9 Treasury Committee, 'Conduct and Competition in SME Lending', HC 204, 10 March 2015, p. 53.

10 Dr Fiona Sheriff, Director of Communications, APPG Fair Business Banking, Summary of the case of John Guidi, March 2019.

11 Professor Michael Dempster, 'Tailored Business Loan contracts with Clydesdale /NAB', Cambridge Systems Associates Ltd, 15 May 2018 (not published).

12 John Gatt, letter to John Glare, NAB support group, 23 March 2016.

13 Treasury Committee, 'Conduct and Competition in SME Lending', HC 204, 10 March 2015, p. 59.

14 Drawn from the contents of the Dempster Report and conversation with Ian Lightbody of CYBG Remediation Group on 7 June 2019.

15 Ian Fraser, *Shredded: Inside RBS, the Bank that Broke Britain*, Birlinn, second edition 2019, p. 430.

16 'RBS Group's treatment of customers referred to the Global Restructuring Group', a report prepared by Promontory Financial Group for the Financial Conduct Authority, September 2016.

17 Figures from Ian Fraser, *Shredded*, p. 476.

18 Lawrence Tomlinson, 'Banks' Lending Practices', BIS, November 2013, p. 2.

19 'RBS Group's treatment of customers referred to the Global Restructuring Group', a report prepared by Promontory Financial Group for the FCA, September 2016.

20 *Guardian*, 20 February 2018.

21 *Guardian*, ibid.

22 *Financial Times*, 'Ross McEwan to step down as RBS chief executive', 25 April 2019.

23 *Financial Times*, 'More than a third of bank branches axed in past four years', 27 September 2019.

24 *Guardian*, 23 October 2017.

25 *Financial Times*, 'Report into disgraced RBS unit branded a "whitewash"', 13 June 2019.

26 *Guardian*, 'FCA proves to be a paper tiger in case of RBS mistreatment', 31 July 2018.

Chapter 11

1 Interview with, and briefing notes sent to the author by Anthony Stansfeld, on 10 June 2019.

2 *Ibid.*

3   Halifax/Bank of Scotland (HBOS) had been taken over by Lloyds Bank post Crash.
4   No relation or connection to Lord Turnbull, the former Cabinet Secretary.
5   *Financial Times*, 30 January 2017.
6   *The Times*, 20 June 2018.
7   Jonathan Ford, 'Lloyds was repeatedly warned of criminality at HBOS', *Financial Times*, 4 July 2017.
8   *Ibid.*
9   FCA: Financial Conduct Authority; FRC: Financial Reporting Council; CMA: Competition and Markets Authority; PRA: Prudential Regulatory Authority.
10   In conversation with Anthony Stansfeld, 10 June 2019.
11   'Commonwealth Bank response to Four Corners and Fairfax investigation', *Illawara Mercury*, Australia, 6 May 2014, www.illawaramercury.co.au.
12   *Financial Times*, 7 February 2019,
13   See Prem Sikka, 'British Steel crisis shows dangers of private equity', 23 May 2019, http://left foot forward.org/prem-sikka.
14   *Guardian*, 15 May 2019.
15   Society of Motor Manufactures and Traders figures from *Financial Times*, 8 June 2019.
16   *PropertyEU* magazine, February 2019, no 1, www.propertyeu.info.
17   The fund which pursued John Guidi was entitled Cerberus Promontoria (Chestnut).
18   'Cerberus Capital Management: purchase of distressed assets', Westminster Hall, House of Commons, 22 Feb 2017.

Chapter 12

1   In conversation with Ian Fraser, 22 November 2018.
2   *Ibid.*
3   Ian Fraser, *Shredded: Inside RBS, the Bank that Broke Britain*, Birlinn, second edition 2019, p. 490.
4   *Hansard*, House of Commons Debates, 22 June 2010, col. 166, Financial Statement.
5   *Ibid.*
6   BBC Politics Weekly Podcast, 20 September 2018.

7   *New Statesman*, 'Inside the pilot Universal Credit then doubling the size of its food bank', 19 September 2019.

8   The United Nations Office of the High Commissioner for Human Rights, Statement on visit to the UK by Professor Philip Alston, 16 November 2018.

9   *Ibid.* p. 1.

10   *Ibid.* p. 22.

11   NAO, 'Help to Buy – Equity Loan Scheme progress review', 13 June 2019.

12   Persimmon Annual Report to December 2017, p. 64.

13   Fairburn's actual pay as identified in the Persimmon accounts was £47 million.

14   Deborah Hargreaves, *Are Chief Executives Overpaid?*, Polity Books, 2018.

15   Interserve Annual Report and Accounts 2018, p. 9.

16   *Financial Times*, 27 September 2019.

17   Martin Wolf, 'Why rigged capitalism is damaging liberal democracy', *Financial Times*, 18 September 2019; this section draws considerably on the definitions and analysis of his article.

18   Martin Wolf, 'How to reform today's rigged capitalism', *Financial Times*, 3 December 2019.

19   Richard Brooks, 'The financial scandal no-one is talking about', *Guardian*, 29 May 2018.

20   House of Commons Joint Report, 'Carillion', HC 769, 16 May 2018, p. 51.

21   *Ibid.*, Oral Evidence, 22 February 2018, para 945.

22   *Ibid.*, Oral Evidence, 22 February 2018, para 978.

23   See Chapter 7, Downfall.

24   House of Commons Joint Report, 'Carillion', HC 769, 16 May 2018, p. 54.

25   *Financial Times*, 20 October 2019.

26   www.statista.com, 'Revenue of the Big Four by function in 2018'.

27   For the record they also audit 97% of all US public companies and 80% of all Japanese companies.

28   See Prem Sikka *et al.*, 'Reforming the Auditing Industry, Occasional Research Paper', December 2018. See LabourPolicymaking-AuditingReformsDec2018.pdf.

29 These figures include income and expenditure from the company's operations in Switzerland.
30 See Chapter 1, 'The Paul Daniels of Profit'.
31 Pensions Act 2006, section 226.
32 National Audit Office, 'PFI 1 and PFI 2', Treasury Office, 18 January 2018.
33 Nicholas Shaxson, *The Finance Curse: How Global Finance Is Making Us All Poorer*, Bodley Head, 2018, p. 222.
34 Institute for Government, 'Government Procurement: The Scale and Nature of Contracting in the UK', December 2018.
35 Demos, 'Value Added – how better government procurement can build a fairer Britain', October 2019.
36 *Ibid.*
37 IMF, 'An assessment of the financial health of 31 countries', 9 October 2018.
38 *Financial Times*, 10 October 2018.
39 *Ibid.*
40 George Monbiot, 'How Ayn Rand became the new right's version of Marx', *Guardian*, 5 March 2012.
41 See *Financial Times*, 'Why American CEOs are worried about capitalism', 22 April 2019.
42 *New Yorker*, 'The ultra-wealthy who argue they should be paying higher taxes', 6 January 2020.
43 Joseph Stiglitz, 'The American economy is rigged', *Scientific American*, 1 November 2018.
44 *Economist*, 28 September 2019.
45 *Financial Times*, 'Why American CEOs are worried about capitalism', 22 April 2019.
46 See *Financial Times*, 24 April 2019 and 5 July 2019.
47 Joseph Stiglitz *et al.*, 'Why Capitalism's salvation depends on taxation', *Foreign Affairs*, January/February 2020.
48 See Wolfgang Streeck, *How Will Capitalism End: Essays on a Failing System*, Verso, 2016.
49 Adam Tooze, *Crashed: How a Decade of Financial Crises Changed the World*, Allen Lane, 2018, pp. 241-254.
50 Branko Milanovic, 'The clash of capitalisms – the real fight for the global economy's future', *Foreign Affairs*, January/February 2020.

Appendix

Carillion Major Projects

(from lists created in Wikipedia/Carillion 2019)

Major projects involving Carillion, with completion date, have included:

New facilities for the Royal Opera House – 2000

The Tate Modern – 2000

Darent Valley Hospital, Kent – 2000

Star City in Birmingham – 2000

The Grand Mosque in Oman – 2001

Harplands Hospital, Stoke-on-Trent – 2001

The Copenhagen Metro – 2002

The Great Western Hospital, Swindon – 2002

The de Havilland campus, University of Hertfordshire – 2002

The M6 Toll – 2003

GCHQ – 2003

Northern Express Transit Phase 1 – 2004

Marina Towers, Dubai – 2004

The Sheppey Crossing – 2006

Redevelopment of the John Radcliffe Hospital, Oxford – 2006

Beetham Tower, Manchester – 2006

Royal Ottawa Hospital, Canada – 2006

High Speed 1 – 2007

The Riverside Building, Lewisham – 2007

Brampton Civic Hospital, Canada – 2007

The Great Northern Tower, Manchester – 2007

Dubai Festival City Shopping Centre and Intercontinental Hotel – 2008

Aylesbury Vale Parkway – 2008

Redevelopment of the Queen Alexandra Hospital, Portsmouth – 2009

The Yas Hotel, Abu Dhabi – 2009

The New York University, Abu Dhabi – 2010

Sault Area Hospital, Sault St Marie, Canada – 2010

Northwood HQ, MOD, Hertfordshire – 2010

The Royal Opera House, Muscat – 2011

The Rolls Building, London – 2011

London Heathrow Terminal 5C – 2011

London Olympics Media Centre, – 2011

The Ontario Centre for Forensic Science – 2012

Al Bahr Towers, Abu Dhabi – 2012

The Majlis Trade Centre, Dubai – 2013

The Birmingham Library – 2013

Cairo Festival City, Egypt – 2013

Southmead Hospital Bristol – 2014

Union Station, Toronto, Canada – 2014

Redevelopment of the military garrisons at Aldershot and Salisbury Plain – 2014

Oakville-Trafalgar Memorial Hospital, Oakville, Canada – 2015

Queen Elizabeth University Hospital, Glasgow – 2015

Al Jalila Children's Hospital, Dubai – 2016

The Oman Convention and Conference Centre, Muscat, Oman – 2016

Liverpool FC stadium redevelopment – 2016

One Chamberlain Square, Birmingham – 2017

HM Passport Offices, Durham – 2017

Battersea Power Station redevelopment Phase 1 – 2017

Msheireb Downtown Doha phase 1B, Qatar – 2017

Sunderland Brewery Site Redevelopment – project taken over by Tolent Construction in July 2018

Aberdeen West Peripheral Route – completed by Carillion partners, 2019

Royal Liverpool University Hospital redevelopment – no completion date finalised

Midland Metropolitan Hospital, Birmingham – no completion date finalised

High Speed 2 lots C2 and C3 – no completion date finalised

Angel Gardens Manchester – project taken over by Caddick Construction in 2018

Airport City Manchester – project taken over by lead partner Beijing Construction Engineering Group (BCEG) in 2018

Bibliography

Books

Grace Blakeley, *Stolen: How to Save the World from Financialisation*, Repeater Books, 2019.

James Bloodworth, *Hired: Six Months Undercover in Low-wage Britain*, Atlantic Books 2018.

Richard Brooks, *Bean Counters: The Triumph of the Accountants and How They Broke Capitalism*, Atlantic Books, 2018.

Ken Clarke, *Kind of Blue: A Political Memoir*, Pan Books, 2017.

Paul Collier, *The Future of Capitalism*, Allen Lane, 2018.

Ian Fraser, *Shredded: Inside RBS, the Bank that Broke Britain*, Birlinn, 2014, second edition 2019.

Danny Dorling, *The Equality Effect*, New Internationalist, 2017.

Chrystia Freeland, *Sale of the Century: Russia's Wild Ride from Communism to Capitalism*, Crown Business, 2000.

Anand Giridharadas, *Winners Take All: The Elite Charade of Changing the World*, Allen Lane, 2019.

Deborah Hargreaves, *Are Chief Executives Overpaid?*, Polity Books, 2019.

John Lanchester, *Whoops: Why Everyone Owes Everyone and No-One Can Pay*, Penguin, 2010.

Owen Jones, *The Establishment: and How They Get Away with It*, Penguin, 2015.

V. I. Lenin, *Imperialism: The Highest Stage of Capitalism*, Penguin Books, 2010.

Karl Marx, *The Revolutions of 1848*, Penguin, 1973.

Mariana Mazzucato, *The Value of Everything: Making and Taking in the Global Economy*, Allen Lane, 2018.

Mariana Mazzucato, *The Entrepreneurial State: Debunking Public v Private Myths*, Penguin, second edition 2018.

Paul Mason, *Post Capitalism: A Guide to our Future*, Allen Lane, 2015.

Bethany McLean and Peter Elkind, *The Smartest Guys in the Room: The Amazing Rise and Scandalous Fall of Enron*, Penguin, 2004.

Fintan O'Toole *Ship of Fools: How Stupidity and Corruption Sank the Celtic Tiger*, Faber and Faber, 2010.

Thomas Piketty, *Capital in the Twenty-First Century*, Harvard University Press, 2014.

Oliver Shah, *Damaged Goods: The Inside Story of Sir Phillip Green, the Collapse of BHS and the Death of the High Street*, Portfolio Penguin, 2018.

Nicholas Shaxson, *The Financial Curse: How Global Finance Is Making Us All Poorer*, Bodley Head, 2018.

Dave Smith and Phil Chamberlain, *Blacklisted: The Secret War between Big Business and Union Activists*, New Internationalist Publications, 2016.

Joseph Stiglitz, *The Price of Inequality*, Penguin, 2012.

Gillian Tett, *Fool's Gold: How Unrestrained Greed Corrupted Our Dreams*, Abacus, 2010.

Adam Tooze, *Crashed: How a Decade of Financial Crises Changed the World*, Allen Lane, 2018.

Yanis Varoufakis, *Adults in the Room: My Battle with Europe's Deep Establishment*, Bodley Head, 2017.

Yanis Varoufakis, *Talking to My Daughter about the Economy*, Bodley Head, 2017.

Francis Wheen, *Karl Marx*, Fourth Estate, 1999.

Richard Wilkinson and Kate Pickett, *The Inner Level: How More Equal Societies Reduce Stress, Restore Sanity and Improve Everyone's Well-being*, Allen Lane, 2018.

House of Commons Reports

Business Energy and Industrial Strategy (BEIS) and Work and Pensions Committees, *Carillion*, HC769, 16 May 2018.

BEIS, *Carillion: Responses from Interested Parties*, HC1932, 12 July 2018.

BEIS, *Corporate Governance*, HC702, 5 April 2017.

BEIS, *Executive Pay Rewards*, HC2018, 26 March 2019.

Committee of Public Accounts, *Service Family Accommodation*, HC77, 13 July 2017.

House of Commons Library, *The Collapse of Carillion*, Briefing Paper 8206, 4 March 2018.

House of Commons Library, *Armed Forces Housing*, Briefing Paper 07985, 16 June 2017.

Liaison Committee, *Oral Evidence: Cross-government response to the collapse of Carillion*, HC770, 7 February 2018.

National Audit Office (NAO), *Transforming Rehabilitation: Progress review*, HC1986, 1 March 2019.

NAO, *Investigation of the government's handling of the collapse of Carillion*, HC1002, 7 June 2018.

NAO, *PF1 and PF2*, HC718, 18 June 2018.

NAO, *The Help to Buy equity loan scheme*, HC1099, 6 March 2014.

Parliamentary Commission on Banking Standards, *An accident waiting to happen: The failure of HBOS*, HC705, 4 April 2013.

Parliamentary Commission on Banking Standards, *Changing banking for good*, HC175, June 2013.

Public Affairs and Constitutional Affairs Committee (PACAC), *After Carillion: Public Sector outsourcing and contracting*, HC748, 9 July 2018.

Scottish Affairs Committee, *Blacklisting in employment*, HC 1071, 16 April 2013.

Treasury Committee, *Conduct and Competition in SME Lending*, HC704, 10 March 2015.

Treasury Committee, *Economic Crime – anti-money laundering supervision and sanctions implementation*, HC2010, 8 March 2019.

Other Reports

Cambridge Systems Associates Ltd, *Report to Scott Simpson on contracts with Clydesdale Bank and National Australia* Bank, 15 May 2018 (unpublished).

Competition and Markets Authority, *Statutory audit services market study*, 18 December 2018.

Demos, *Value Added: How better government procurement can build a better Britain*, October 2018.

GMB, *Blacklisting*, September 2014.

High Pay Centre/CIPD, *Executive Pay – Review of the FTSE 100 executive pay*, August 2018.

IPPR Commission on Economic Justice, *Prosperity and Justice – a Plan for the New Economy*, Final Report, 2018.

IPPR Commission on Economic Justice, *On Borrowed Time*, Discussion Paper by Grace Blakely, June 2018.

John Kingman, *Independent Review of the Financial Reporting Council*, December 2018.

HMP Inspector of Prisons, *HMP Birmingham inspection visit*, 6-17 February 2017.

Promontory Consultants, *RBS Group's treatment of SME customers referred to the GRG*, (Report prepared for FCA), September 2016.

Prudential Regulation Authority *Report of the FSA's enforcement actions following failure of HBOS* November 2015.

Prem Sikka, *Regulatory Architecture to Enhance Democracy and Business Accountability*, January 2019.

——, *A Better future for Corporate Governance: Democratising Corporations for Their Long-term Success*, September 2018.

——, *Reforming the Audit Industry*, December 2018.

——, *Controlling Executive Remuneration: Securing a Fairer Distribution of Income*, November 2018.

TUC, *What lessons can be learned from Carillion?* (undated).

United Nations Office of the High Commissioner for Human Rights, *Statement on visit to the UK by Professor Philip Alston*, 16 November 2018.

Index

Note: Entries with the suffix 'n' refer to the endnotes.